HISTORY OF THE IMPEACHMENT OF ANDREW JOHNSON PRESIDENT OF THE UNITED STATES

By

EDMUND G. ROSS

History Of The Impeachment Of Andrew Johnson President Of The United States

by **Edmund G. Ross**

ISBN: 978-93-58595-53-6

Published by

DOUBLE 9 BOOKS

2/13-B, Ansari Road, Daryaganj
New Delhi – 110002
info@double9books.com
www.double9books.com
Tel. 011-40042856

ABOUT THE AUTHOR

Edmund G. Ross (1826-1907) was an American politician who represented Kansas and later served as governor of the New Mexico Territory. He is best known for his pivotal role in the impeachment trial of President Andrew Johnson. Ross's vote against convicting Johnson, by a margin of one vote, allowed the president to remain in office. Ross had a varied career, starting as a printer and journalist before becoming involved in the antislavery movement and serving in the Union Army during the Civil War. He was appointed to the U.S. Senate in 1866 and served until 1871. Ross cast his historic vote in the impeachment trial in 1868, defying his party and facing political backlash. After leaving the Senate, he continued his newspaper career, served as governor of the New Mexico Territory, and authored a book on the Johnson impeachment. Ross's decision in the trial remains a subject of debate and speculation. He passed away in 1907 in Albuquerque, New Mexico.

CONTENTS

PREFACE 7

CHAPTER I — THE PROBLEM OF RECONSTRUCTION. 9

CHAPTER II — THE BALTIMORE CONVENTION. 28

CHAPTER III — MR. JOHNSON'S ACCESSION TO THE PRESIDENCY. 35

CHAPTER IV — FIRST ATTEMPT TO IMPEACH THE PRESIDENT. 54

CHAPTER V — THE TENURE-OF-OFFICE ACT. 67

CHAPTER VI — IMPEACHMENT AGREED TO BY THE HOUSE 78

CHAPTER VII — IMPEACHMENT REPORTED TO THE SENATE. 92

CHAPTER VIII — ORGANIZATION OF THE COURT ARGUMENT
OF COUNSEL 114

CHAPTER IX — EXAMINATION OF WITNESSES AND THEIR
TESTIMONY. 131

CHAPTER X — A CONFERENCE HELD AND THE FIRST VOTE TAKEN. 162

CHAPTER XI — THE IMPEACHERS IN A MAZE. A RECESS ORDERED. . 172

CHAPTER XII — WAS IT A PARTISAN PROSECUTION? 185

CHAPTER XIII — THE CONSTITUTIONAL POWER OF IMPEACHMENT. 194

PREFACE

Little is now known to the general public of the history of the attempt to remove President Andrew Johnson in 1868, on his impeachment by the House of Representatives and trial by the Senate for alleged high crimes and misdemeanors in office, or of the causes that led to it. Yet it was one of the most important and critical events, involving possibly the gravest consequences, in the entire history of the country.

The constitutional power to impeach and remove the President had lain dormant since the organization of the Government, and apparently had never been thought of as a means for the satisfaction of political enmities or for the punishment of alleged executive misdemeanors, even in the many heated controversies between the President and Congress that had theretofore arisen. Nor would any attempt at impeachment have been made at that time but for the great numerical disparity then existing between the respective representatives in Congress of the two political parties of the country.

One-half the members of that Congress, both House and Senate, are now dead, and with them have also gone substantially the same proportion of the people at large, but many of the actors therein who have passed away, lived long enough to see, and were candid enough to admit, that the failure of the impeachment had brought no harm to the country, while the general judgment practically of all has come to be that a grave and threatening danger was thereby averted.

A new generation is now in control of public affairs and the destinies of the Nation have fallen to new hands. New issues have developed and will continue to develop from time to time; and new dangers will arise, with increasing numbers and changing conditions, demanding in their turn the same careful scrutiny, wisdom and patriotism in adjustment. But the principles that underlie and constitute the basis of our political organism, are and will remain the same; and will never cease to demand constant vigilance for their perpetuation as the rock of safety upon which our federative system is founded.

To those who in the study of the country's past seek a broader and higher conception of the duties of American citizenship, the facts pertaining to the controversy between the Executive and Congress as to the restoration and preservation of the Union, set out in the following pages, will be interesting and instructive. No one is better fitted than the author of this volume to discuss the period of reconstruction in which, as a member of the Federal senate, he played so potent and patriotic a part, and it is a pleasure to find that he has discharged his task with so much ability and care. But it is profoundly hoped that no coming generation will be called upon to utilize the experiences of the past in facing in their day, in field or forum, the dangers of disruption and anarchy, mortal strife and desolation, between those of one race, and blood, and nationality, that marked the history of America thirty years ago.

DAVID B. HILL.

CHAPTER I — THE PROBLEM OF RECONSTRUCTION.

MR. LINCOLN'S PLAN

The close of the War of the Rebellion, in 1865, found the country confronted by a civil problem quite as grave as the contest of arms that had been composed. It was that of reconstruction, or the restoration of the States lately in revolt, to their constitutional relations to the Union.

The country had just emerged from a gigantic struggle of physical force of four years duration between the two great Northern and Southern sections. That struggle had been from its inception to its close, a continuing exhibition, on both sides, of stubborn devotion to a cause, and its annals had been crowned with illustrations of the grandest race and personal courage the history of the world records. Out of a population of thirty million people, four million men were under arms, from first to last, and sums of money quite beyond the limit of ordinary comprehension, were expended in its prosecution. There was bloodshed without stint. Both sides to the conflict fought for an idea — on the one side for so-called State Rights and local self-government — on the other for national autonomy as the surest guaranty of all rights — personal, local, and general.

The institution of negro slavery, the basis of the productive industries of the States of the South, which had from the organization of the Government been a source of friction between the slave-holding and nonslave-holding sections, and was in fact the underlying and potent cause of the war, went under in the strife and was by national edict forever prohibited.

The struggle being ended by the exhaustion of the insurgents, two conspicuous problems demanding immediate solution were developed: The status of the now ex-slaves, or freedmen — and the methods to be adopted for the rehabilitation of the revolted States, including the status of the revolted States themselves. The sword had declared that they had no constitutional power to withdraw from the Union, and the result demonstrated that they had not the physical power — and therefore that they were in the anomalous condition of States of though not States technically in the Union—and hence properly subject to the jurisdiction of the General Government, and bound by its judgment in any measures to be instituted by it for their future restoration to their former condition of co-equal States.

The now ex-slaves had been liberated, not with the consent of their former owners, but by the power of the conqueror as a war measure, who not unnaturally insisted upon the right to declare absolutely the future status of these persons without consultation with or in any way by the intervention of their late owners. The majority of the gentlemen in Congress representing the Northern States demanded the instant and complete enfranchisement of these persons, as the natural and logical sequence of their enfreedment. The people of the late slave States, as was to have been foreseen, and not without reason, objected—especially where, as was the case in many localities, the late slaves largely out-numbered the people of the white race: and it is apparent from subsequent developments that they had the sympathy of President Lincoln, at least so far as to refuse his sanction to the earlier action of Congress relative to restoration.

To add to the gravity of the situation and of the problem of reconstruction, the people of the States lately in rebellion were disfranchised in a mass, regardless of the fact that many of them refused to sanction the rebellion only so far as was necessary to their personal safety.

It was insisted by the dominant element of the party in control of Congress, that these States were dead as political entities, having committed political suicide, and their people without rights or the protection of law, as malcontents.

It is of record that Mr. Lincoln objected to this doctrine, and to all propositions that contemplated the treatment of the late rebellious States simply as conquered provinces and their people as having forfeited all rights under a common government, and under the laws of Nations entitled to no concessions, or even to consideration, in any proposed measures of restoration. That he had no sympathy with that theory is evidenced by the plan of restoration he attempted to establish in Louisiana.

It was at this point that differences arose between Mr. Lincoln and his party in Congress, which became more or less acute prior to his death and continued between Congress and Mr. Johnson on his attempt to carry out Mr. Lincoln's plans for restoration.

The cessation of hostilities in the field thus developed a politico-economic problem which had never before confronted any nation in such magnitude and gravity. The situation was at once novel, unprecedented, and in more senses than one, alarming. Without its due and timely solution there was danger of still farther disturbance of a far different and more alarming character than that of arms but lately ceased; and of a vastly more insidious and dangerous complexion. The war had been fought in the open. The record of the more than two thousand field and naval engagements that had marked its progress and the march of the Union armies to success, were heralded day by day to every household, and all could forecast its trend and its results. But the controversy now developed was insidious — its influences, its weapons, its designs, and its possible end, were in a measure hidden from the public — public opinion was divided, and its results, for good or ill, problematical. The wisest political sagacity and the broadest statesmanship possible were needed, and in their application no time was to be lost.

In his annual message to Congress, December 8th, 1863, Mr. Lincoln had to a considerable extent outlined his plan of Reconstruction; principally by a recital of what he had already done in that direction. That part of his message pertinent to this connection is reproduced here to illustrate the broad, humane, national and patriotic purpose that actuated him, quite as well as his lack of sympathy with the extreme partisan aims and methods that characterized the measures afterward adopted by Congress in opposition to his well-known wishes and views, and, also, as an important incident to the history of that controversy and of the time, and its bearing upon the frictions that followed between Congress and Mr. Lincoln's successor on that subject. Mr. Lincoln said:

When Congress assembled a year ago the war had already lasted twenty months, and there had been many conflicts on both land and sea, with varying results. The rebellion had been pressed back into reduced limits; yet the tone of public feeling and opinion, at home and abroad, was not satisfactory. With other signs, the popular elections, then just past, indicated uneasiness among ourselves, while, amid much that was cold and menacing, the kindest words coming from Europe were uttered in accents of pity that we were too blind to surrender a hopeless cause. Our commerce was suffering greatly by a few armed vessels built upon and furnished from foreign shores; and we were threatened with such additions from the same quarter as would sweep our trade from the sea and raise our blockade. We had failed to elicit from European Governments anything hopeful upon this subject. The preliminary Emancipation Proclamation, issued in September, was running its assigned period to the beginning of the new year. A month later that final proclamation came, including the announcement that colored men of suitable condition would be received into the army service. The policy of emancipation, and of employing black soldiers, gave to the future a new aspect, about which hope and fear and doubt contended in uncertain conflict. According to our political system, as a matter of civil administration, the General Government had no lawful power to effect emancipation in any State; and for a long time it had been hoped that the rebellion could be suppressed without resorting to it as a military measure. It was all the while deemed possible that the necessity for it might come, and that, if it should, the crisis of the contest would then be presented. It came, and, as was anticipated, was followed by dark and doubtful days. Eleven months have now passed, and we are permitted to take another review. The rebel borders are pressed still further back, and by the complete opening of the Mississippi the country dominated by the rebellion is divided into distinct parts, with no practical communication between them. Tennessee and Arkansas have been substantially cleared of insurgent control, and influential citizens in each, owners of slaves and advocates of slavery at the beginning of the rebellion, now declare openly for emancipation in their respective States. Of those States not included in the Emancipation Proclamation, Maryland and Missouri, neither of which three years ago would tolerate any restraint upon the extension of slavery into the new Territories, only dispute now as to the best mode of removing it within their own limits.

Of those who were slaves at the beginning of the rebellion, full one hundred thousand are now in the United States military service; about one half of which number actually bear arms in the ranks; thus giving the double advantage of taking so much labor from the insurgent cause, and supplying the places which must otherwise be filled with so many white men. So far as tested, it is difficult to say they are not as good soldiers as any. No servile insurrection, or tendency to violence or cruelty, has marked the measure of emancipation and arming the blacks. Those measures have been discussed in foreign countries, and contemporary with such discussion the tone of sentiment there is much improved. At home the same measures have been fully discussed, and supported, criticised, and denounced, and the annual elections following are highly encouraging to those whose official duty it is to bear the country through this great trial. Thus we have the new reckoning. The crisis which threatened to divide the friends of the Union is past.

Looking now to the present, and future, and with reference to a resumption of national authority within the States wherein that authority has been suspended, I have thought fit to issue a Proclamation, a copy of which is herewith transmitted. On examination of this Proclamation it will appear, as is believed, that nothing is attempted beyond what is amply justified by the Constitution. True, the form of an oath is given, but no man is coerced to take it. The man is only promised a pardon in case he voluntarily takes the oath. The Constitution authorizes the Executive to grant or withhold the pardon at his own absolute discretion, and this includes the power to grant on terms, as is fully established by judicial and other authorities.

It is also proffered that, if in any of the States named a State Government shall be, in the mode prescribed, set up, such Government shall be recognized and guaranteed by the United States, and that under it the State shall, on the constitutional conditions, be protected against invasion and domestic violence. The constitutional obligation of the United States to guarantee to every State in the Union a republican form of government, and to protect the State, in the cases stated, is explicit and full. But why tender the benefits of this provision only to a State Government set up in this particular way? This section contemplates a case wherein the element within a State favorable to a republican government, in the Union, may be too feeble for an opposite and hostile external to or even within the State; and such are precisely the cases with which we are dealing.

Any attempt to guaranty and protect a revived State Government, constituted in whole, or in preponderating part, from the very element against whose hostility it is to be protected, is simply absurd. There must be a test by which to separate the opposing elements, so as to build only from the sound; and that test is a sufficiently liberal one which accepts as sound whoever will make a sworn recantation of his former unsoundness.

But if it be proper to require, as a test of admission to the political body, an oath of allegiance to the Constitution of the United States, and to the Union under it, why also to the laws and Proclamation in regard to slavery? Those laws and Proclamations were enacted and put forth for the purpose of aiding in the suppression of the rebellion. To give them their fullest effect, there had to be a pledge — for their maintenance. In my judgment they have aided, and will further aid, the cause for which they were intended. To now abandon them would be not only to relinquish a lever of power, but would also be a cruel and an astounding breach of faith. I may add at this point, that while I remain in my present position, I shall not attempt to retract or modify the Emancipation Proclamation; nor shall I return to slavery any person who is free by the terms of the Proclamation, or by any of the acts of Congress. For these and other reasons it is thought best that support of these measures shall be included in the oath; and it is believed the Executive may lawfully claim it in return for pardon and restoration of forfeited rights, when he has clear constitutional power to withhold altogether or grant upon terms which he shall deem wisest for the public interest. It should be observed, also, that this part of the oath is subject to the modifying and abrogating power of legislation and supreme judicial decision.

The proposed acquiescence of the National Executive in any reasonable temporary State arrangement for the freed people is made with the view of possibly modifying the confusion and destitution which must, at best, attend all classes by a total revolution of labor throughout whole States. It is hoped that the already deeply afflicted people of those States may be somewhat more ready to give up the cause of their affliction, if, to this extent, this vital matter be left to themselves; while no power of the National Executive to prevent an abuse is abridged by the proposition.

The suggestion in the Proclamation as to maintaining the political frame-work of those States on what is called reconstruction, is made in the hope that it may do good without danger of harm. It will save labor and avoid great confusion.

But why any proclamation on this subject? This question is beset with the conflicting views that the step might be delayed too long or taken too soon. In some States the elements for resumption seem ready for action, but remain inactive apparently for want of a rallying point. Why shall A. adopt the plan of B., rather than B. that of A.? And if A. and B. should agree, how can they know but that the General Government here will reject their plan? By the Proclamation a plan is presented which may be accepted by them as a rallying point, and which they may be assured in advance will not be rejected here. This may bring them to act sooner than they otherwise would.

The objection to a premature presentation of a plan by the National Executive consists in the danger of committals on points which could be more safely left to further developments. Care has been taken to so shape the document as to avoid embarrassment from this source. Saying that, on certain terms, certain classes will be pardoned, with rights restored, it is not said that other classes on other terms will never be included. Saying that reconstruction will be accepted if presented in a specified way, it is not saying it will not be accepted in any other way.

The movements, by State action, for emancipation in several of the States not included in the Emancipation Proclamation, are matters of profound gratulation, and while I do not repeat in detail what I have heretofore so earnestly urged upon this subject, my general views and feelings remain unchanged, and I trust that Congress will omit no fair opportunity of aiding these important steps to a great consummation.

In the midst of other cares, however important, we must not lose sight of the fact that the war power is still our main reliance. To that power alone can we look, for a time, to give confidence to the people in the contested regions that the insurgent power will not again over-run them. Until that confidence shall be established, little can be done anywhere for what is called reconstruction. Hence our chiefest care must still be directed to the Army and Navy, who have thus far borne their hardest part nobly and well. And it may be esteemed fortunate that in giving the greatest efficiency to these indispensable arms, we do also honorably recognize the gallant men, from commander to sentinel, who compose them, to whom, more than to others, the world must stand indebted for the home of freedom disenthralled, regenerated, enlarged and perpetuated.

Abraham Lincoln. December 8, 1863.

The following is the Proclamation of Amnesty and Reconstruction referred to in the foregoing Message, and further illustrates Mr. Lincoln's plan for the restoration of the Union:

PROCLAMATION OF AMNESTY AND RECONSTRUCTION. BY THE PRESIDENT ON THE UNITED STATES OF AMERICA.

Whereas, in and by the Constitution of the United States, it is provided that the President "shall have the power to grant reprieves and pardons for offenses against the United States, except in cases of impeachment;" and

Whereas, a rebellion now exists whereby the loyal State governments of several States have for a long time been subverted, and many persons have committed, and are guilty of treason against the United States; and

Whereas, with reference to said rebellion and treason, laws have been enacted by Congress, declaring forfeitures and confiscations of property and liberation of slaves, all upon terms and conditions therein stated, and also declaring that the President was thereby authorized at any time thereafter, by proclamation, to extend to persons who may have participated in the existing rebellion, in any State or part thereof, pardon and amnesty, with such exceptions and at such times and on such conditions as he may deem expedient for the public welfare; and

Whereas, the Congressional declaration for limited and conditional pardon accords with well established judicial exposition of the pardoning power; and

Whereas, with reference to said rebellion, the President of the United States has issued several proclamations, with provisions in regard to the liberation of slaves; and

Whereas, it is now desired by some persons heretofore engaged in said rebellion to resume their allegiance to the United States, and to reinaugurate loyal State Governments within and for their respective States; therefore,

I, Abraham Lincoln, President of the United States, do proclaim, declare, and make known to all persons who have, directly or by implication, participated in the existing rebellion, except as hereinafter excepted, that a full pardon is hereby granted to them and each of them, with restoration of all rights of property, except as to slaves and in property cases where rights of third parties shall have intervened, and upon the condition that every such person shall take and subscribe an oath, and thenceforward keep and maintain said oath inviolate, and which oath shall be registered for permanent preservation, and shall be of the tenor and effect following, to-wit:

I, ___ __ ___, do solemnly swear, in presence of Almighty God, that I will henceforth faithfully support, protect, and defend the Constitution of the United States, and the Union of the States thereunder; and that I will, in like manner, abide by and faithfully support all acts of Congress passed during the existing rebellion with reference to slaves, so long and so far as not repealed, modified or held void by Congress, or by the decision of the Supreme Court; and that I will, in like manner, abide by and faithfully support all proclamations of the President made during the existing rebellion having reference to slaves, so long and so far as not modified or declared void by decision of the Supreme Court. So help me God.

The persons exempted from the benefits of the foregoing provisions are all who are, or shall have been, civil or diplomatic officers or agents of the so-called Confederate Government: all who have left judicial stations under the United States to aid the rebellion; all who are or shall have been military or naval officers of said so-called Confederate Government above the rank of Colonel in the army or Lieutenant in the Navy; all who have left seats in the United States Congress to aid the rebellion; all who resigned commissions in the army or navy of the United States and afterward aided the rebellion; and all who have engaged in any way in treating colored persons, or white persons in charge of such, otherwise than lawfully as prisoners of war, and which persons may have been found in the United States service as soldiers, seamen, or in any capacity.

And I do further proclaim, declare, and make known that whenever, in any of the States of Arkansas, Texas, Louisiana, Mississippi, Tennessee, Alabama, Georgia, Florida, South Carolina and North Carolina, a number of persons, not less than one-tenth in number of the votes cast in such State at the Presidential election of the year of our Lord one thousand eight hundred and sixty, each having taken the oath aforesaid and not having since violated it, and being a qualified voter by the election laws of the State existing immediately before the so-called act of secession, and excluding all others, shall reestablish a State government which shall be republican, and in no wise contravening said oath, such shall be recognized as the true government of the State, and the State shall receive thereunder the benefits of the constitutional provision which declares that "the United States shall guarantee to every state in this Union a republican form of government, and shall protect each of them against invasion; and, on the application of the legislature, or the executive (when the legislature cannot be convened) against domestic violence."

And I do further proclaim, declare, and make known, that any provision which may be adopted by such State government in relation to the freed people of such State, which shall recognize and declare their permanent freedom, provide for their education, and which may yet be consistent as a temporary arrangement with their present condition as a laboring, landless, and homeless class, will not be objected to by the National Executive.

And it is suggested as not improper that, in constructing a loyal State government in any State, the name of the State, the boundary, the subdivisions, the constitution, and the general code of laws, as before the rebellion, be maintained, subject only to the modifications made necessary by the conditions hereinbefore stated, and such others, if any, not contravening said conditions, and which may be deemed expedient by those framing the new State government.

To avoid misunderstanding, it may be proper to say, that whether members sent to Congress from any State shall be admitted to seats, constitutionally rests exclusively with the respective houses, and not to any extent with the Executive. And still further, that this proclamation is intended to present to the people of the States wherein the National authority has been suspended; and loyal State governments have been subverted, a mode in and by which the National authority and loyal State governments, may be re-established within said States, or, in any of them; and while the mode presented is the best the Executive can suggest, with his present impressions, it must not be understood that no other possible mode would be acceptable.

Given under my hand at the City of Washington, the eighth day of December, in the year of our Lord one thousand eight hundred and sixty-three, and of the Independence of the United States of America, the eighty-eighth.

[L. S.]

By the President: Abraham Lincoln. William H. Seward, Secretary of State.

How the revolted States could be most successfully and expeditiously restored to their constitutional relations to the Union on the cessation of hostilities, was the momentous question of the hour, upon which there were views and schemes as varied and antagonistic as were the mental differences and political disagreements of those who felt called upon to engage in the stupendous work. As history had recorded no similar conditions, and therefore no demand for the solution of such a problem, there were no examples or historic lights for the guidance of those upon whom the task had fallen.

It is apparent that Mr. Lincoln maintained the indestructibility of the States and the indivisibility of the Union—that the resolutions of secession were null and void, and that the States lately in rebellion were never in fact but only in theory out of the Union—that they retained inherently, though now dormant, their State autonomy and constitutional rights as before their revolutionary acts, except as to slavery, and that all their people had to do, to re-establish their former status, as he declared to the Emperor of the French when that potentate was about to recognize the Confederacy, was to resume their duties as loyal, law-abiding citizens, and reorganize their State Governments on a basis of loyalty to the Constitution and the Union. The terms he proposed to formally offer them were first illustrated in the case of Louisiana, early in 1863, and later in the foregoing Message and Proclamation; and clearly indicated what was to be his policy and process of reconstruction.

Messrs. Flanders and Hahn were admitted to the House of Representatives as members from Louisiana agreeably to the President's views thus outlined. They had been chosen at an election ordered by the Governor of the State (Gov. Shepley), who had undoubtedly been permitted, if not specially authorized by the President, to take this step, but they were the last to be received from Louisiana under Mr. Lincoln's plan, as the next Congress resolved to receive no more members from the seceded States till joint action by the two Houses therefor should be had.

Prior to the election at which these gentlemen were chosen, Mr. Lincoln addressed a characteristic note to Gov. Shepley, which was in effect a warning that Federal officials not citizens of Louisiana must not be chosen to represent the State in Congress, "We do not," said he, referring to the South, "particularly need members of Congress from those States to get along with legislation here. What we do want is the conclusive evidence that respectable citizens of Louisiana are willing to be members of Congress and to swear support to the Constitution, and that other respectable citizens are willing to vote for them and send them. To send a parcel of Northern men as Representatives, elected, as would be understood, (and perhaps really so) at the point of the bayonet, would be disgraceful and outrageous."

Mr. Lincoln would tolerate none of the "carpet-bagging" that afterwards became so conspicuous and offensive under the Congressional plan of Reconstruction.

These steps for reconstruction in Louisiana were followed by the assembling of a convention to frame a new constitution for that State. The convention was organized early in 1864, and its most important act was the prompt incorporation of an antislavery clause in its organic law. By a vote of 70 to 16 the convention declared slavery to be forever abolished in the State. The new Constitution was adopted by the people of the State on the 5th day of the ensuing September by a vote of 6,836 in its favor, to 1,566 against it. As the total vote of Louisiana in 1860 was 50,510, the new government had fulfilled the requirement of the President's Proclamation. It was sustained by more than the required one-tenth vote.

In a personal note of congratulation to Gov. Hahn, of Louisiana, the President, speaking of the coming convention, suggested that "some of the colored people be let in, as for instance, the very intelligent, and especially those who have fought gallantly in our ranks." "They would," said he, "probably help in some trying time in the future TO KEEP THE JEWEL OF LIBERTY IN THE FAMILY OF FREEDOM."

This action in regard to Louisiana was accompanied, indeed in some particulars preceded, by similar action in Arkansas. A Governor was elected, an anti-slavery Constitution adopted, a State Government duly installed, and Senators and Representatives in Congress elected, but were refused admission by Congress. Mr. Sumner, when the credentials of the Senators-elect were presented, foreshadowing the position to be taken by the Republican leaders, offered a resolution declaring that "a State pretending to secede from the Union, and battling against the General Government to maintain that position, must be regarded as a rebel State subject to military occupation and without representation on this floor until it has been readmitted by a vote of both Houses of Congress; and the Senate will decline to receive any such application from any such rebel State until after such a vote by both Houses."

A few weeks later, on the 27th of June, 1864, this resolution was in effect reported back to the Senate by the Judiciary Committee, to which it had been referred, and adopted by a vote of 27 to 6. The same action was had in the House of Representatives on the application of the Representatives-elect from Arkansas for admission to that body.

This was practically the declaration of a rupture between the President and Congress on the question of Reconstruction. It was a rebuke to Mr. Lincoln for having presumed to treat the seceded States as still in any sense States of the Union. It was in effect a declaration that those States had successfully seceded — that their elimination from the Union was an accomplished fact — that the Union of the States had been broken — and that the only method left for their return that would be considered by Congress was as conquered and outlying provinces, not even as Territories with the right of such to membership in the Union; and should be governed accordingly until such time as Congress should see fit (IF EVER, to use the language of Mr. Stevens in the House) to devise and establish some form whereby they could be annexed to or re-incorporated into the Union.

It was at this point — on the great question of Reconstruction, or more properly of Restoration — that the disagreements originated between the Executive and Congress which finally culminated in the impeachment of Mr. Lincoln's successor; and that condition of strained relations was measurably intensified when, on the following July 4th, a bill was passed by Congress making provision for the reorganization and admission of the revolted States on the extreme lines indicated by the above action of Congress and containing the very extraordinary provision that the President, AFTER OBTAINING THE CONSENT OF CONGRESS, shall recognize the State Government so established. That measure was still another and more marked rebuke by Congress to the President for having presumed to initiate a system of restoration without its consultation and advice. Naturally Mr. Lincoln was not in a mood to meekly accept the rebuke so marked and manifestly intended; and so the bill not having passed Congress till within the ten days preceding its adjournment allowed by the Constitution for its consideration by the President, and as it proposed to undo the work he had done, he failed to return it to Congress — "pocketed" it — and it therefore fell. He was not in a mood to accept a Congressional rebuke. He had given careful study to the duties, the responsibilities, and the limitations of the respective Departments of, the Government, and was not willing that his judgment should be revised, or his course censured, however indirectly, by any of its co-ordinate branches.

Four days after the session had closed, he issued a Proclamation in which he treated the bill merely as the expression of an opinion by Congress as to the best plan of Reconstruction — "which plan," he remarked, "it is now thought fit to lay before the people for their consideration."

He further stated in this Proclamation that he had already presented one plan of restoration, and that he was "unprepared by a formal approval of this bill to be inflexibly committed to any single plan of restoration, and was unprepared to declare that the free State Constitutions and Governments already adopted and installed in Louisiana and Arkansas, shall be set aside and held for naught, thereby repelling and discouraging the loyal citizens who have set up the same as to further effort, and unprepared to declare a constitutional competency in Congress to abolish slavery in the States, though sincerely hoping that a constitutional amendment abolishing slavery in all the States might be adopted."

While, with these objections, Mr. Lincoln could not approve the bill, he concluded his Proclamation with these words:

"Nevertheless, I am fully satisfied with the plan of restoration contained in the bill as one very proper for the loyal people of any State choosing to adopt it, and I am and at all times shall be prepared to give Executive aid and assistance to any such people as soon as military resistance to the United States shall have been suppressed in any such State and the people thereof shall have sufficiently returned to their obedience to the Constitution and laws of the United States—in which Military Governors will be appointed with directions to proceed according to the bill."

"It must be frankly admitted," says Mr. Blaine in reciting this record in his 'Thirty Years of Congress,' "that Mr. Lincoln's course was in some of its respects extraordinary. It met with almost unanimous dissent on the part of the Republican members, and violent criticism from the more radical members of both Houses. * * * Fortunately, the Senators and Representatives had returned to their States and Districts before the Reconstruction Proclamation was issued, and found the people united and enthusiastic in Mr. Lincoln's support."

In the last speech Mr. Lincoln ever made, (April 11th, 1865) referring to the twelve thousand men who had organized the Louisiana Government, (on the one-tenth basis) he said:

"If we now reject and spurn them, we do our utmost to disorganize and disperse them. We say to the white man, you are worthless, or worse. We will neither help you or be helped by you. To the black man we say, 'this cup of liberty which these, your old masters hold to your lips, we will dash from you, and leave you to the chances of gathering the spilled and scattered contents IN SOME VAGUE AND UNDEFINED WHEN AND WHERE AND HOW.' If this course, discouraging and paralyzing to both white and black, has any tendency to bring Louisiana into proper practical relations with the Union, I have so far been unable to perceive it. If, on the contrary, they reorganize and sustain the new Government of Louisiana, the converse of all this is made true. We encourage the hearts and nerve the arms of twelve thousand men to adhere to their work and argue for it, and proselyte for it, and fight for it, and grow it, and ripen it to a complete success. The colored man, too, in seeing all united for him, is inspired with vigilance and with energy and daring to the same end. Grant that he desires the elective franchise. HE WILL YET ATTAIN IT SOONER BY SAVING THE ALREADY ADVANCED STEPS TOWARD IT THAN BY RUNNING BACK OVER THEM. Concede that the new Government of Louisiana is only to what it should be as the egg to the fowl; we shall sooner have the fowl by hatching the egg than by smashing it."

It is manifest that Mr. Lincoln intuitively foresaw the danger of a great body of the people becoming accustomed to government by military power, and sought to end it by the speediest practicable means. As he expressed it, "We must begin and mould from disorganized and discordant elements: nor is it a small additional embarrassment that we, the loyal people, differ among ourselves as to the mode, manner, and measure of reconstruction."

Louisiana was wholly in possession of the Union forces and under loyal influence in 1863, and in his judgment the time had come for reconstructive action in that state—not merely for the purpose of strengthening and crystallizing the Union sentiment there, at a great gate-way of commerce, that would become a conspicuous object-lesson to foreign governments in behalf of more favorable influences abroad, but also to the encouragement of Union men and the discouragement of the rebellion in all the other revolted States. He had fortified his own judgment, as he frankly declared, "by submitting the Louisiana plan in advance to every member of the Cabinet, and every member approved it."

The steps taken in Louisiana were to be but a beginning. The nature of subsequent proceedings on his part must be governed by the success of this— that under then existing conditions it was inexpedient, in view of further possible complications, to forecast further proceedings, and especially to attempt to establish, at the outset, and under the chaotic conditions of the time, a general system of reconstruction applicable to all the States and to varying conditions. So the beginning was made in Louisiana. It is manifest that the purpose of this immediate action was two-fold—not only to restore Louisiana to the Union at the earliest practicable day—but also to so far establish a process of general restoration before Congress should reconvene at the coming December session, that there would be no sufficient occasion or excuse for interfering with his work by the application of the exasperating conditions that had been foreshadowed by that body.

On this point Mr. Welles, his Secretary of the Navy, testifies that at the close of a Cabinet meeting held immediately preceding Mr. Lincoln's death, "Mr. Stanton made some remarks on the general condition of affairs and the new phase and duties upon which we were about to enter. He alluded to the great solicitude which the President felt on this subject, his frequent recurrence to the necessity of establishing civil governments and preserving order in the rebel States. Like the rest of the Cabinet, doubtless, he had given this subject much consideration, and with a view of having something practical on which to base action, he had drawn up a rough plan or ordinance which he had handed to the President.

"The President said he proposed to bring forward that subject, although he had not had time as yet to give much attention to the details of the paper which the Secretary of War had given him only the day before; but that it was substantially, in its general scope, the plan which we had sometimes talked over in Cabinet meetings. We should probably make some modifications, prescribe further details; there were some suggestions which he should wish to make, and he desired all to bring their minds to the question, for no greater or more important one could come before us, or any future Cabinet. He thought it providential that, this great rebellion was crushed just as Congress had adjourned, AND THERE WERE NONE OF THE DISTURBING ELEMENTS OF THAT BODY TO HINDER AND EMBARRASS US. If we were wise and discreet, we should reanimate, the States and get their governments in successful operation, with order prevailing and the Union reestablished, BEFORE CONGRESS CAME TOGETHER IN DECEMBER. This he thought important. We could do better, accomplish more without than with them. There were men in Congress who, if their motives were good, were nevertheless impracticable, and who possessed feelings of hate and vindictiveness in which he did not sympathize and could not participate. Each House of Congress, he said, had the undoubted right to receive or reject members, the Executive had no control in this matter. But Congress had NOTHING TO DO WITH THE STATE GOVERNMENTS, which the President could recognize, and under existing laws treat as other States, give the same mail facilities, collect taxes, appoint judges, marshals, collectors, etc., subject, of course, to confirmation. There were men who objected to these views, BUT THEY WERE NOT HERE, AND WE MUST MAKE HASTE TO DO OUR DUTY BEFORE THEY CAME HERE."

The subjugated States were in a condition that could not be safely permitted to continue for any indefinite period. It would be inconsistent with the purpose of the war, incongruous to the American system and idea of government, and antagonistic to American political, or even commercial or social autonomy. Naturally upon Mr. Lincoln would fall largely the duty and responsibility of formulating and inaugurating some method of restoration. With the abolition of slavery, the most difficult of settlement of all the obstacles in the way of reconstruction had been removed. Naturally, too, during the later months of the war, when it became manifest that the end of the struggle was near, the question of reconstruction and the methods whereby it could be most naturally, speedily, and effectively accomplished, came uppermost in his mind. A humane, just man, and a sincere, broad-brained, patriot and far-seeing statesman, he instinctively rejected the many drastic schemes which filled a large portion of the public press of the North and afterwards characterized many of the suggestions of Congressional action. With him the prime purpose of the war was the preservation of the political, territorial and economic integrity of the Republic—in a word, to restore the Union, without needless humiliation to the defeated party, or the imposition of unnecessarily rigorous terms which could but result in future frictions—without slavery—and yet with sufficient safeguards against future disloyal association of the sections; and that purpose had been approved by an overwhelming majority of the people in his re-election in 1864.

In these purposes and methods Mr. Lincoln appears to have had the active sympathy and co-operation of his entire Cabinet, more especially of Mr. Stanton, his Secretary of War. Indeed, Mr. Stanton is understood, from the record, to have been the joint author, with Mr. Lincoln, of the plan of reconstruction agreed upon at the later meetings of the Cabinet immediately prior to Mr. Lincoln's death. Mr. Stanton proposed to put it in the form of a military order—Mr. Lincoln made an Executive order. The plan was embodied in what afterwards became known as the "North Carolina Proclamation," determined upon by Mr. Lincoln at his last Cabinet meeting and promulgated by Mr. Johnson shortly after his accession to the Presidency as Mr. Lincoln's successor, and is inserted in a subsequent chapter.

Mr. Lincoln unquestionably comprehended the peculiar conditions under which the Republican party had come to the control of the legislative branch of the Government, and fully realized the incapacity of the dominant element in that control for the delicate work of restoration and reconstruction—leading a conquered and embittered people back peacefully and successfully, without unnecessary friction, into harmonious relations to the Union.

No such responsibility, no such herculean task, had ever before, in the history of civilization, devolved upon any ruler or political party.

Mr. Lincoln seems to have realized the incapacity of party leaders brought to the surface by the tumult and demoralization of the time, whose only exploits and experiences were in the line of destruction and who must approach the task with divided counsel, to cope successfully with the delicate and responsible work of restoration the close of the war had made imperative. He comprehended the incongruities which characterized that great party better than its professed leaders, and foresaw the futility of any effort on its part, at that time and in its then temper, to the early establishment of any coherent or successful method of restoration. Hence, unquestionably, his prompt action in that behalf, and his failure to call the Congress into special session, to the end that there should be no time unnecessarily consumed and lost in the institution of some efficient form of civil government in the returning States—some form that would have the sanction of intelligent authority competent to restore and enforce public order, without the dangers of delay and consequent disorder that must result, and did afterwards result, from the protracted debates sure to follow and did follow the sudden precipitation of the questions of reconstruction and reconciliation upon a mass of Congressmen totally inexperienced in the anomalous conditions of that time, or in the methods most needed for their correction.

That Mr. Lincoln contemplated the ultimate and not remote enfranchisement of the late slaves, is manifest from his suggestion to Gov. Hahn, of Louisiana, hereinbefore quoted in connection with the then approaching Convention for the re-establishment of State Government there, and again still more manifest from his last public utterance on April 11, 1865, deprecating the rejection by Congress of his plan for the restoration of Louisiana, in which, he said, speaking of that action by Congress rejecting the Louisiana bill: "Grant that the colored male desires the elective franchise. He will attain it sooner by saving the already advanced steps towards it than by running back over them."

It is also apparent in the light of the succeeding history of that time and of that question, that if Mr. Lincoln's views had been seconded by Congress, the enfranchisement of the negro would have been, though delayed, as certain of accomplishment, and of a vastly higher and more satisfactory plane—and the country saved the years of friction and disgraceful public disorder that characterized the enforcement of the Congressional plan afterwards adopted.

As to the success of Mr. Lincoln's plans, had they been sanctioned, or even had they not been repudiated by Congress, Mr. Blaine, in his book, asserts that Mr. Lincoln, "By his four years of considerate and successful administration, by his patient and positive trust in the ultimate triumph of the Union, realized at last as he stood upon the edge of the grave—he had acquired so complete an ascendancy over the public, control in the loyal states, that ANY POLICY MATURED AND ANNOUNCED BY HIM WOULD HAVE BEEN ACCEPTED BY A VAST MAJORITY OF HIS COUNTRYMEN."

It was indicative of the sagacious foresight of Mr. Lincoln that he did not call the Congress into special session at the close of the war, as would have been natural and usual, before attempting the establishment of any method for the restoration of the revolted States. The fact that he did not do so, but was making preparations to proceed immediately in that work on his own lines and in accordance with his own ideas, and with the hearty accord of his entire Cabinet, of itself affords proof that he was apprehensive of obstruction from the same element of his party that subsequently arose in opposition to Mr. Johnson on that question, and that he preferred to put his plans into operation before the assembling of Congress in the next regular winter session, in order that he might be able then to show palpable results, and induce Congress to accept and follow up a humane, peaceful and satisfactory system of reconstruction. Mr. Lincoln undoubtedly hoped thus to avoid unnecessary friction. Having the quite unlimited confidence of the great mass of the people of the country, of both parties and on both sides of the line of hostilities, there seem to be excellent reasons for believing that he would have succeeded, and that the extraordinary and exasperating differences and local turmoils that followed the drastic measures which were afterward adopted by Congress over the President's vetoes, would have been in a very large degree avoided, and THERE WOULD HAVE BEEN NO IMPEACHMENT—either of Mr. Lincoln had he lived, or of Mr. Johnson after him.

It was the misfortune of the time, and of the occasion, which determined Mr. Lincoln to institute a plan of restoration during the interim of Congress, that the Republican party, then in absolute control of Congress, was in no sense equipped for such a work. Its first and great mission had been the destruction of slavery. Though not phrased in formal fashion, that was the logic of its creation and existence. It was brought into being purely as an anti-slavery party, illustrated in the fact that its membership included every pronounced anti-slavery man, known as abolitionists, in the United States. All its energies, during all its life up to the close of the war had been bent to that end. It had been born and bred to the work of destruction. It came to destroy slavery, and its forces had been nurtured, to the last day of the war, in pulling down—in fact, did not then wholly cease.

The work of restoration—the rebuilding of fallen States—had now come. The Republican party approached that work in the hot blood of war and the elation of victory—a condition illy fitting the demands of exalted statesmanship so essential to perfect political effort.

Never had nation or party thrust upon it a more delicate duty or graver responsibility. It was that of leading a conquered people to build a new civilization wholly different from the one in ruins. It was first to reconcile two races totally different from each other, so far as possible to move in harmony in supplanting servile by free labor, and the slave by a free American citizen. The transition was sudden, and the elements antagonistic in race, culture, self-governing power—indeed, in all the qualities which characterize a free people.

There was a wide margin for honest differences between statesmen of experience. A universal sentiment could not obtain. The accepted political leaders of the time were illy equipped to meet the issue—much less those who had been brought to prominence, and too often to control, in the hot blood of war and the frictions of the time, when intemperate denunciation and a free use of the epithets of "rebel," and "traitor," had become a ready passport to public honors. It was a time when the admonition to make haste slowly was of profound significance. A peril greater than any other the civil war had developed, overhung the nation. Greater than ever the demand for courage in conciliation—for divesting the issues of all mere partyism, and the yielding of something by the extremes, both of conservatism and radicalism.

CHAPTER II — THE BALTIMORE CONVENTION.

LINCOLN AND JOHNSON NOT NOMINATED AS REPUBLICANS.

Mr. Lincoln had been elected President in 1860, distinctively as a Republican. In 1864, however, the conditions had changed. The war had been in progress some three years, during which the insurgents had illustrated a measure of courage, endurance, and a command of the engineries of successful warfare that had not been anticipated by the people of the North. It was seen that to insure the success of the Union cause it was imperative that there should be thorough unity and cooperation of the loyal people of all parties—that it was no time for partisan division among those who hoped ever to see a restored Republic—that it was necessary to lay aside, as far as possible, mere partisan issues, and to unite, in the then approaching campaign, upon a non-partisan, distinctively Union ticket and platform.

Mr. Lincoln had given so satisfactory an administration so wisely, efficiently, and patriotically had he conducted his great office, that he was on all sides conceded to be the proper person for nomination and election. The Convention of 1861 was not called as a Republican Convention, but distinctively as a Union Convention.

"The undersigned," so ran the call, "who by original appointment, or subsequent delegation to fill vacancies, constitute the Executive Committee created by the National Convention held at Chicago on the 10th day of May, 1860, do hereby call upon all QUALIFIED VOTERS WHO DESIRE THE UNCONDITIONAL MAINTENANCE OF THE UNION, THE SUPREMACY OF THE CONSTITUTION, AND THE COMPLETE SUPPRESSION OF THE EXISTING REBELLION, WITH THE CAUSE THEREOF, by vigorous war, and all apt and effective means; to send delegates to a convention to assemble at Baltimore, on Tuesday, the 7th day of June, 1864, at 12 o'clock noon, for the purpose of presenting candidates for the offices of President and Vice President of the United States."

The delegates met pursuant to this call. Hon. Edwin D. Morgan, of New York, Chairman of the Union National Committee, called the Convention to order, and Robert J. Breckinridge, of Kentucky, was chosen temporary Chairman. In the course of his introductory address, Mr. Breckinridge said:

Passing over many things which it would be right for me to say, did the time serve, and were this the occasion—let me add,—you are a Union party. Your origin has been referred to as having occurred eight years ago. In one sense it is true. But you are far older than that. I see before me not only primitive Republicans and primitive Abolitionists, but I see also primitive Democrats and primitive Whigs. * * * As a Union party I will follow you to the ends of the earth, and to the gates of death. But as an Abolition party— as a Republican party—as a Whig party—as a Democratic party—as an American party, I will not follow you one foot.

Mr. William Dennison, of Ohio, was chosen President of the Convention. On taking the chair he said:

'In no sense do we meet as members or representatives of either of the old political parties which bound the people, or as the champions of any principle or doctrine peculiar to either. The extraordinary condition of the country since the outbreak of the rebellion has, from necessity, taken from the issues of these parties their practical significance, and compelled the formation of substantially new political organizations; hence the organization of the Union Party—if party it can be called—of which this Convention is for the purpose of its assembling, the accredited representative, and the only test of membership in which is an unreserved, unconditional loyalty to the Government and the Union.'

After perfecting its organization the Convention proceeded to ballot for a nominee for the Presidency, and Mr. Lincoln was unanimously nominated—the Missouri delegation at first casting its 22 votes for Gen. Grant, but afterwards changing them to Mr. Lincoln, giving him the total vote of the Convention—506—on the first and only ballot.

Nominations for the Vice Presidency being next in order, Mr. Lyman Tremaine, of New York, an old time Democrat, nominated Daniel S. Dickinson, another old time Democrat and a very distinguished citizen of that State. In his nominating speech Mr. Tremaine again emphasized that this Convention was a Union, and not a partisan body, in these words:

'It was well said by the temporary and by the permanent Chairman, that we meet not here as Republicans. If we do, I have no place in this Convention; but, like Daniel S. Dickinson, when the first gun was fired on Sumter, I felt that I should prove false to my revolutionary ancestry if I could have hesitated to cast partisan ties to the breeze, and rally around the flag of the Union for the preservation of the Government.'

The Indiana delegation nominated Andrew Johnson, also a Democrat, and the nomination was seconded by Mr. Stone, speaking for the Iowa delegation.

In the earlier proceedings of the Convention there had seemed a disposition to exclude the Tennessee delegation, and Parson Brownlow, an old line Whig, being called on for a speech, evidenced in the course of his remarks the small part which partisan considerations were permitted to play in the purposes and proceedings of the Convention. He said:

'There need be no detaining this Convention for two days in discussions of various kinds, and the idea I suggest to you as an inducement not to exclude our delegation is, that we may take it into our heads, before the thing is over, to present a candidate from that State in rebellion, for the second office in the gift of the people. We have a man down there whom it has been my good luck and bad fortune to fight untiringly and perseveringly for the past twenty-five years—Andrew Johnson. For the first time, in the Providence of God, three years ago we got together on the same platform, and we are fighting the devil, Tom Walker, and Jeff. Davis, side by side.'

Mr. Horace Maynard, a conspicuous Republican of Tennessee, said:

'Mr. President, we but represent the sentiment of those who sent here the delegation from Tennessee, when we announce that if no one else had made the nomination of Andrew Johnson, which is now before the Convention, it would have been our duty to make it by one of our own delegation. That citizen, known, honored, distinguished, has been presented to this Convention for the second place in the gift of the American people. It needs not that I should add words of commendation of him here. From the time he rose in the Senate of the United States, where he then was, on the 17th day of December, 1860, and met the leaders of treason face to face, and denounced them there, and declared that the laws of the country must and should be enforced, for which he was hanged in a effigy in the City of Memphis, in his own State, by the hands of a negro slave, and burned in effigy, I know not in how many places throughout that portion of the country—from that time, on during the residue of that session of the Senate until he returned to Tennessee after the firing upon Fort Sumter, when he was mobbed in the City of Lynchburg, Virginia—on through the memorable canvass that followed in Tennessee, till he passed through Cumberland Gap on his way North to invoke the aid of the Government for his people—his position of determined and undying hostility to this rebellion that now ravages the land, has been so well known that it is a part of the household knowledge of many loyal families in the country. * * * When he sees your resolutions that you have adopted here by acclamation, he will respond to them as his sentiments, and I pledge myself by all that I have to pledge before such an assemblage as this, that whether he be elected to this high place, or whether he retire to private life, he will adhere to those sentiments, and to the doctrine of those resolutions, as long as his reason remains unimpaired, and as long as breath is given him by his God.

Two ballots were taken on the nomination for Vice President. Mr. Johnson, whose nomination was known to be desired by Mr. Lincoln and his friends because of his prominence as a Southern Democrat and an influential supporter of the Union cause in his State, received 200 votes on the first ballot, and 404 on the second—the delegations of Maine, New Hampshire, Vermont, Connecticut, New York, New Jersey, Pennsylvania, Delaware, Maryland, Louisiana, Arkansas, Missouri, Tennessee, Ohio, Indiana, Illinois, Michigan, Iowa, Minnesota, Oregon, West Virginia, Kansas, Nebraska, Colorado, and Nevada, voting solidly for him—Massachusetts, Rhode Island, Kentucky, Wisconsin and Minnesota, only, being divided.

Thus a Republican and a Democrat were made the nominees of the Convention, and its non-partisan character found further expression in the first three Resolutions of the Platform adopted, which were as follows:

Resolved, 1st. That it is the highest duty of every American citizen to maintain against all their enemies the integrity of the Union and the paramount authority of the Constitution and laws of the United States; and that laying aside ALL DIFFERENCES OF POLITICAL OPINION, we pledge ourselves as Union men, animated by a common sentiment and aiming at a common object, to do everything in our power to aid the Government in quelling by force of arms the rebellion now raging against its authority, and in bringing to the punishment due to their crimes the rebels and traitors arrayed against it.

2nd. That we approve the determination of the Government of the United States not to compromise with Rebels, or to offer them any terms of peace, except such as may be based upon an unconditional surrender of their hostility and a return to their just allegiance to the Constitution and laws of the United States, and that we call upon the Government to maintain their position, and to prosecute the war with the utmost possible vigor to the complete suppression of the Rebellion, in full reliance upon the self-sacrificing patriotism, the heroic valor and the undying devotion of the American people to their country and its free institutions.

3rd. That as slavery was the cause, and now constitutes the strength, of this Rebellion, and as it must be, always and everywhere, hostile to the principles of Republican Government, justice and the National safety demand its utter and complete extirpation from the soil of the Republic; and that, while we uphold and maintain the acts and proclamation by which the Government in its own defense, has aimed a death blow at this gigantic evil, we are in favor, furthermore, of such an amendment to the Constitution, to be made by the people in conformity with its provisions, as shall terminate and forever prohibit the existence of slavery within the limits or jurisdiction of the United States.

So there seems to be good ground for saying that this was in no sense a partisan Convention, but, on the contrary, that it was a Convention of the loyal people of the Northern and Border States, of all parties, who were ready to lay aside party creeds and partisan considerations, the better to make common cause for the preservation of the Union.

Before the war, Mr. Johnson had been a Democratic Senator from Tennessee, and during the war, a gentleman of great influence in support of the Union cause. So pronounced and effective had been his loyalty that Mr. Lincoln appointed him a Brigadier General and Military Governor of Tennessee, to accept which he resigned his seat in the Senate, and so judicious and successful had been his administration of that office in behalf of the Union cause and of Union men, that Tennessee was the first of the revolted States to be readmitted to representation in Congress after the close of the war.

So it may be said of Mr. Johnson that he was a persistent and consistent Union Democrat of the old school — for war so long as war might be necessary to the preservation of the Union — for peace when the war was ended by the abandonment of the struggle by the insurgents — and for the restoration of the Union on terms consistent with then existing conditions — without slavery, which was dead — and the return of the people of the South to their loyalty to and support of the Government without debasing exactions — after they had laid down their arms. Aggressively radical so long as the people of the South continued in rebellion, he was considerate and merciful so soon as they yielded themselves to the authority of law and of the Union.

Like Mr. Lincoln, he opposed the idea strenuously advanced by Sumner, and Stevens, and that wing of the Republican party which they led, that the States in rebellion had committed suicide and were therefore dead and without rights, or entitled to consideration, even, in any proposition that might be adopted for their rehabilitation.

This record very effectually disposes of the criticisms of Mr. Johnson's course, so common after he came to the Presidency and growing out of his disagreements with the extremists of Congress, that he had deserted and betrayed the Republican party after it had elected him to the Vice Presidency and thus made him Mr. Lincoln's immediate successor—the facts of history showing that neither Mr. Lincoln nor Mr. Johnson were elected by the Republican party as Republicans, nor by the Democratic party as Democrats, but by a union of all parties of the North distinctively as a Union party and on a Union ticket and platform for the preservation of the Union and the destruction of slavery—and when those purposes were accomplished, the war ended and the Union party disbanded and was never heard of again. Mr. Lincoln, had he lived, would doubtless have still been a Republican, as Mr. Johnson was still a Democrat, as before the war—the purpose of that war and of the Convention that nominated him having been accomplished—and under no obligations, especially of a partisan character, to adopt or promote the partisan purposes relative to reconstruction or otherwise, that came to actuate the Republican party.

As stated. Mr..Johnson had, during the later years of the war, been acting as Military Governor of Tennessee, of which State he had been a citizen nearly all his life. His administration had been so efficient that Tennessee was practically restored to the Union at the close of the War, and so satisfactory to the loyal people of the country, that though an old line Democrat and a Southern man, Mr. Johnson's nomination by the National Convention for Vice President on the ticket with Mr. Lincoln for President, was, as has been shown, logical and consistent. Though a pronounced State Rights Democrat and a citizen of a Southern State in rebellion, he regarded himself as a citizen of the United States, to which he owed his first allegiance. State Rights meant to him, the rights of the States IN the Union, and not OUT of the Union.

In evidence of the confidence and esteem in which Mr. Johnson was generally held by those who knew him and knew of the valuable services he had rendered the cause of the Union, the following letter from Mr. Stanton, then secretary of War under Mr. Lincoln, is here reproduced. It was written to Mr. Johnson on his tender to the War Office of his resignation of the Military Governorship of Tennessee to accept the office of Vice President of the United States:

War Department, Washington, March 3, 1865.

Sir:—This Department has accepted your resignation as Brigadier General and Military Governor of Tennessee. Permit me on this occasion to tender to you the sincere thanks of this Department for your patriotic and able services during the eventful period through which you have exercised the highest trust committed to your charge. In one of the darkest hours of the great struggle for National existence, against rebellious foes, the Government called you from the comparatively safe and easy duties of civil life to place you in front of the enemy and in a position of personal toil and danger, perhaps more hazardous than was encountered by any citizen or military officer of the United States. With patriotic promptness you assumed the post, and maintained it under circumstances of unparalleled trial, until recent events have brought safety and deliverance to your State and to the integrity of the Constitutional Union, for which you so long and so gallantly periled all that is dear to man on earth. That you may be spared to enjoy the new honors and perform the high duties to which you have been called by the people of the United States, is the sincere wish of one who in every official and personal relation has found you worthy of the confidence of the Government and the honor and esteem of your fellow citizens.

Your obedient servant,

Edwin M. Stanton.

His Excellency, Andrew Johnson, Vice-President elect.

CHAPTER III — MR. JOHNSON'S ACCESSION TO THE PRESIDENCY.

THE RECONSTRUCTION ERA.

Mr. Johnson succeeded to the Presidential office on the death of Mr. Lincoln, April 15th, 1865. The conditions of the time were extraordinary. The war, so far as operations in the field were concerned, was at an end. The armies of the rebellion had been vanquished and practically disbanded. The States lately in revolt were prostrate at the feet of the conqueror, powerless for further resistance. But the general rejoicing over the happy termination of the strife had been inexpressibly saddened by the brutal assassination of the President who had so wisely and successfully conducted his great office and administered all its powers to the attainment of that happy result, and it was not unnatural or strange that the shocking event should greatly re-inflame the passions of the strife that the joys of peace had at last well nigh laid.

It was an especial misfortune that he who had so wisely and safely conducted the Nation through the conflict of arms and had foreshadowed his beneficent measures of peace and the restoration of the shattered Republic, was taken away as he and the Nation stood at last at the open door of successful rehabilitation on a broader and grander basis than had ever been reached in all previous efforts of man at Nation building. From day to day he had watched, with his hand on the key-board, the development and trend of events. They had resulted as he had planned, and he had become the most conspicuous, the best loved, and the most masterful of living man in the control of the future. In his death the Union lost its most sagacious and best trusted leader, and, the South its ablest, truest, and wisest friend.

It was under these circumstances that Mr. Johnson came to the Presidency as Mr. Lincoln's successor—without a moment of warning or an hour of preparation for the discharge of the crushing responsibilities that had so suddenly fallen to his direction.

Actuated, doubtless, and not unnaturally, by feelings of resentment over the manner and circumstances of Mr. Lincoln's death, Mr. Johnson at first gave expression to a spirit of hostility toward the leaders of the rebellion, and foreshadowed a somewhat rigorous policy in his methods of Reconstruction in accordance with the views of the leaders of the Republican party in Congress who had differed with Mr. Lincoln on that subject; but later on, under the advice of his Cabinet—notably, it is understood, of Mr. Seward—and under the responsibility of action—his views became modified, till in time, it is not impossible, but by no means certain, that he went even beyond the humane, natural and logical views and purposes of Mr. Lincoln in that regard.

This did not comport with the purposes of the Congressional faction that had opposed Mr. Lincoln's plans, which faction, under the pressure of the general indignation over his murder, quickly rose to the absolute control of Congress. Mr. Lincoln no longer stood in their way, and Mr. Johnson was then comparatively unknown to the great mass of the dominant party, and therefore at a corresponding disadvantage in the controversy. He had risen step by step to his new position from the humblest walks of Southern life, and each succeeding step to advancement had been made through personal conflicts such as few men in public life in this or any other country had ever borne. It was not unnatural, therefore, that he should have faith in himself, and in the superiority of his judgment, or little in that of others— and more especially when he was approached by those who had opposed Mr. Lincoln's plans in an attitude of dictation, and with suggestions and unsought advice as to the course he should pursue in the then absorbing question of the restoration of the States lately in rebellion—himself a citizen of one of those States, and for the preservation of which, as a State in the Union, he had staked his life.

As with Mr. Lincoln, so with Mr. Johnson—the first thing to be done, or sought, was the restoration of the Union by the return of the States in rebellion to their allegiance to the Constitution and laws of the country. Mr. Lincoln, to use one of his characteristic Western phrases, had "blazed the way," and Mr. Johnson took up that trail. A few weeks after his inauguration he issued a Proclamation outlining a plan for the reorganization of the State of North Carolina. That paper was confessedly designed as a general plan and basis for Executive action in the restoration of all the seceded States. Mr. Lincoln had, of course, foreseen that that subject would come up very shortly, in the then condition of affairs in the South, and it had therefore been considered in his later Cabinet meetings, as stated, more especially at the meeting immediately preceding his death, and a plan very similar to that afterwards determined upon by Mr. Johnson, if not identically so, was at that meeting finally adopted. That plan was set out in the North Carolina Proclamation, the essential features and general character of which became so conspicuous a factor in the subsequent controversies between the President and Congress. It was as follows:

Whereas: The Fourth Section of the Fourth Article of the Constitution of the United States declares that the United States shall guarantee to every State in the Union a Republican form of Government, and shall protect each of them against invasion and domestic violence; and whereas, the President of the United States is, by the Constitution, made Commander-in-Chief of the Army and Navy, as well as chief civil executive officer of the United States, and is bound by solemn oath faithfully to execute the office of President of the United States, and to take care that the laws be faithfully executed; and whereas, the rebellion which has been waged by a portion of the people of the United States against the properly constituted authority of the Government thereof in the most violent and revolting form, but whose organized and armed forces have now been almost entirely overcome has, in its revolutionary progress, deprived the people of the State of North Carolina of all civil government: and whereas, it becomes necessary and proper to carry out and enforce the obligations of the United States to the people of North Carolina in securing them it, the enjoyment of a republican form of Government:

Now, therefore, in obedience to the high and solemn duties imposed upon me by the Constitution of the United States, and for the purpose of enabling the loyal people of said State to organize a State Government; whereby justice may be established, domestic tranquility insured, I, Andrew Johnson, President of the United States and Commander-in-Chief of the Army and Navy of the United States, do hereby appoint William W. Holden Provisional Governor of the State of North Carolina, whose duty it shall be, at the earliest practicable period, to prescribe such rules and regulations as may be necessary and proper for convening it Convention, composed of delegates to be chosen by that portion of the people of the said State who are loyal all to the United States and no others, for the purpose of altering or amending the Constitution thereof; and with authority to exercise, within the limits of said State, all the powers necessary and proper to enable such loyal people of the State of North Carolina to restore said State to its constitutional relations to the Federal Government, and to present such a republican form of State Government as will entitle the said State to the guarantee of the United States therefor, and its people to protection by the United States against invasion, insurrection and domestic violence:

PROVIDED, that in any election that may be hereafter held for choosing delegates to any State Convention as aforesaid, no person shall be qualified as an elector, or shall be eligible as a member of such Convention, unless he shall have previously taken and subscribed to the oath of amnesty, as set forth in the President's Proclamation of May 29th, A. D. 1865, and is a voter qualified as prescribed by the Constitution and laws of the State of North Carolina in force immediately before the 20th of May, A. D. 1861, the date of the so-called ordinance of secession; and the said Convention, when convened, or the legislature that may be thereafter assembled, will prescribe the qualifications of electors, and the eligibility of persons to hold office under the Constitution and laws of the State—a power the people of the several States comprising the Federal Union have rightfully exercised from the origin of the Government to the present time. And I do hereby direct:

First—That the Military Commander of the Department, and all officers in the Military and Naval service, aid and assist the said Provisional Governor in carrying into effect this Proclamation, and they are enjoined to abstain from, in any way, hindering, impeding, or discouraging the loyal people from the organization of a State Government as herein authorized.

Second—That the Secretary of State proceed to put in force all laws of the United States, the administration whereof belongs to the State Department, applicable to the geographical limits aforesaid.

Third—That the Secretary of the Treasury proceed to nominate for appointment assessors of taxes, and collectors of customs and revenue, and such other officers of the Treasury Department as are authorized by law, and put in execution the revenue laws of the United States within the provisional limits aforesaid. In making appointments, the preference shall be given to qualified loyal persons residing in the districts where their respective duties are to be performed. But if suitable residents of the district shall not be found, then persons residing in other States or districts shall be appointed.

Fourth—That the Postmaster General proceed to establish postoffices and post routes, and put into execution the postal laws of the United States within the said State, giving to loyal residents the preference of appointments: but if suitable residents are not found, then to appoint agents, etc., from other States.

Fifth—That District Judges for the judicial districts in which North Carolina is included, proceed to hold courts within said State, in accordance with the provisions of the Act of Congress. The Attorney General will instruct the proper officers to libel, and bring to judgment, confiscation and sale, property subject to confiscation, and enforce the administration of justice within said State in all matters within the cognizance and jurisdiction of the Federal Courts.

Sixth—That the Secretary of the Navy take possession of all public property belonging to the Navy Department within said geographical limits, and put in operation all Acts of Congress in relation to naval affairs having application to said State.

Seventh—That the Secretary of the Interior put in force all laws relating to the Interior Department applicable to the geographical limits aforesaid.

In testimony whereof, I have hereunto set my hand and caused the seal of the United States to be affixed.

Done at the City of Washington, this 29th day of May, in the year, of our Lord 1865, and of the Independence of the United States the 89th.

By the President: Andrew Johnson. William H. Seward. Secretary of State.

North Carolina was the first of the revolted States to which this identical plan of reconstruction, or reorganization, was applied by Mr. Johnson. Its application to the several States then lately in revolt, was continued till the meeting of Congress in the following December, 1865.

On this matter Mr. Johnson, himself, testifies in his communication to the Senate in 1867, relating to the removal of Mr. Stanton, that "This grave subject (Reconstruction) had engaged the attention of Mr. Lincoln in the last days of his life, and the plan according to which it was to be managed had been prepared and was ready for adoption. A leading feature of that plan was that it was to be carried out by Executive authority. * * * The first business, transacted in the Cabinet after I became President was this unfinished business of my predecessor. A plan or scheme of reconstruction had been prepared for Mr. Lincoln by Mr. Stanton. It was approved, and at the earliest moment practicable was applied, in the form of a proclamation, to the State of North Carolina, and afterwards became the basis of action in turn for the other States."

Mr. Stanton also testified before the House Impeachment Committee of 1867, that he had "entertained no doubt of the authority of the President to take measures for the reorganization of the rebel States on the plan proposed, during the vacation of Congress, and agreed in the plan specified in the proclamation in the case of North Carolina."

In the first attempt to impeach the President, in 1867, Mr. Johnson's method of Reconstruction was the most conspicuous feature of the prosecution. It was insisted by the extremists that it was a departure from Mr. Lincoln's plan—an unwarranted assumption of authority by Mr. Johnson—that its purpose was the recognition of the people of the South as American citizens with the rights of such, and even as an act not far removed from treason. In reference to this action of the President, General Grant was called before the Committee and testified as follows:

Question: I wish to know whether, at or about the time of the war being ended, you advised the President that it was, in your judgment, best to extend a liberal policy towards the people of the South, and to restore as speedily as possible the fraternal relations that existed prior to the war between the sections?

Answer: I know that immediately after the close of the rebellion there was a very fine feeling manifested in the South, and I thought we ought to take advantage of it as soon as possible.

Ques. I understood you to say that Mr. Lincoln had inaugurated a policy intended to restore these governments?

Ans. Yes Sir.

Ques. You were present when the subject was brought before the Cabinet?

Ans. I was present, I think, twice before the assassination of Mr. Lincoln, when a plan was read.

Ques. I want to know whether the plan adopted by Mr. Johnson was substantially the plan which had been inaugurated by Mr. Lincoln as the basis for his future action.

Ans. Yes sir: substantially. I do not know but that it was verbatim the same.

Ques. I suppose the very paper of Mr. Lincoln was the one acted on?

Ans. I should think so. I think that the very paper which I heard read twice while Mr. Lincoln was President, was the one which was carried right through.

Ques. What paper was that?

Ans. The North Carolina Proclamation.

In additional testimony that Mr. Johnson was endeavoring to carry out Mr. Lincoln's methods of reconstruction, the following extracts from a speech by Gov. O. P. Morton, of Indiana, delivered at Richmond, that State, Sept. 29th, 1865, are here inserted:

An impression has gotten abroad in the North that Mr. Johnson has devised some new policy by which improper facilities are granted for the restoration of the rebel States, and that he is presenting improperly and unnecessarily hurrying forward the work of reconstruction, and that he is offering improper facilities for restoring those who have been engaged in the rebellion to the possession of their civil and political rights.

It is one of my purposes here this evening to show that so far as his policy of amnesty and reconstruction is concerned, he has absolutely presented nothing new, but that he has simply presented, and is simply continuing THE POLICY WHICH MR. LINCOLN PRESENTED TO THE NATION ON THE 8TH OF DECEMBER, 1863. Mr. Johnson's policy differs from Mr. Lincoln's in some restrictions it contains, which Mr. Lincoln's did not contain. His plan of reconstruction is absolutely and simply that of Mr. Lincoln, nothing more or less, with one difference only, that Mr. Lincoln required that one-tenth of the people of the disloyal States should be willing to embrace his plan of reconstruction, whereas Mr. Johnson says nothing about the number; but, so far as it has been acted upon yet, it has been done by a number much greater than one-tenth. * * * Their plans of amnesty and reconstruction cannot be distinguished from each other except in the particulars already mentioned, that Mr. Johnson proposed to restrict certain persons from taking the oath, unless they have a special pardon from him, whom Mr. Lincoln permitted to come forward and take the oath without it. * * * That was Mr. Lincoln's policy at the time he was nominated for re-election by the Union Convention at Baltimore, last summer; and in that convention the party sustained him and strongly endorsed his whole policy, of which this was a prominent part. MR. LINCOLN WAS TRIUMPHANTLY AND OVERWHELMINGLY RE-ELECTED UPON THAT POLICY.

In his last annual message to Congress, December, 1864, he again brings forward this same policy of his, and presents it to the Nation.

Again, on the 12th of April, 1865, only two days before his death, he referred to and presented this policy of amnesty and reconstruction. That speech may be called his last speech, his dying words to his people. It was after Richmond had been evacuated. It was the day after they had received the news of Lee's surrender. Washington City was illuminated. A large crowd came in front of the White House and Mr. Lincoln spoke to them from one of the windows. He referred to the organization of Louisiana under his plan of amnesty and reconstruction, and in speaking of it he gave the history of his policy. He said:

In my annual message of December, 1863, and accompanying the Proclamation, I presented a plan of reconstruction, as the phrase goes, which I promised if adopted by any State, would be acceptable and sustained by the Executive Government of this Nation. I distinctively stated that this was a plan which might possibly be acceptable, and also distinctively protested that the Executive claimed no right to say when or whether members should be admitted to seats in Congress from such States.

The new constitution of Louisiana, (said Mr. Lincoln) declaring emancipation for the whole State, practically applies the Proclamation to that part previously exempted. It does not adopt apprenticeship for freed people, and is silent, as it could not well be otherwise, about the admission of members to Congress. As it applied to Louisiana, every member of the Cabinet approved the plan of the message. * * * Now, we find Mr. Lincoln, just before his death; referring in warm and strong terms to his policy of amnesty and reconstruction, and giving it his endorsement; giving to the world that which had never been given before—the history of that plan and policy—stating that it had been presented and endorsed by every member of that able and distinguished Cabinet of 1863. Mr. Lincoln may be said to have died holding out to the Nation his policy of amnesty and reconstruction. It was held out by him at the very time the rebels laid down their arms. Mr. Lincoln died by the hand of an assassin and Mr. Johnson came into power. He took Mr. Lincoln's Cabinet as he had left it and he took Mr. Lincoln's policy of amnesty and reconstruction as he had left it, and as he had presented it to the world only two days before his death. MR. JOHNSON HAS HONESTLY AND FAITHFULLY ATTEMPTED TO ADMINISTER THAT POLICY, which had been bequeathed by that man around whose grave a whole world has gathered as mourners. I refer to these for the purpose of showing that Mr. Johnson's policy is not a new one, but that he is simply carrying out a policy left to him by his lamented predecessor—a policy that had been ENDORSED BY THE WHOLE NATION IN THE REELECTION OF MR. LINCOLN.

Again Gov. Morton said:

An impression has gotten abroad in the North that Mr. Johnson has devised some new policy by which improper facilities are granted for the restoration of the rebel States and that he is presenting improperly and unnecessarily hurrying forward the work of reconstruction, and that he is offering improper facilities for restoring those who have been engaged in rebellion, to the possession of their civil and political rights. It is one of my purposes here this evening to show that so far as his policy of amnesty and reconstruction is concerned, he has absolutely presented nothing new, that he has simply presented, and is SIMPLY CONTINUING THE POLICY WHICH MR. LINCOLN PRESENTED TO THE NATION ON THE 8TH OF DECEMBER, 1863.

The following are extracts from Mr. Johnson's Message to Congress, in December, 1865, on the re-assembling of that body—the first session of the

39th Congress. Indicating, as it did, a policy of reconstruction at variance with the views of the Congressional leaders, it may be said to have been another incident out of which arose the conditions that finally, led to his impeachment. Mr. Johnson said:

I found the States suffering from the effects of a civil war. Resistance to the General Government appeared to have exhausted itself. The United States had recovered possession of its forts and arsenals, and their armies were in the occupation of every State which had attempted to secede. Whether the territory within the limits of those States should be held as conquered territory, under Military authority emanating from the President as head of the Army, was the first question that presented itself for decision. Military Governments, established for an indefinite period, would have offered no security for the early suppression of discontent; would have divided the people into the vanquishers and the vanquished; and would have envenomed hatred rather than have restored affection. Once established, no precise limit to their continuance was conceivable. They would have occasioned an incalculable and exhausting expense. * * * The powers of patronage and rule which would have been exercised, under the President, over a vast and populous and naturally wealthy region, are greater than, under a less extreme necessity, I should be willing to entrust to any one man. They are such as, for myself, I should never, unless on occasion of great emergency, consent to exercise. The wilful use of such powers, if continued through a period of years, would have endangered the purity of the General Administration and the liberty of the States which remained loyal. * * * The policy of military rule over conquered territory would have implied that the States whose inhabitants may have taken part in the rebellion had, by the act of those inhabitants, ceased to exist. But the true theory is, that ALL PRETENDED ACTS OF SECESSION WERE, FROM THE BEGINNING, NULL AND VOID. THE STATES CAN NOT COMMIT TREASON, nor screen the individual citizens who may have committed treason, any more than they can make valid treaties, or engage in lawful commerce with any foreign power. The States attempting to secede placed themselves in a condition where their vitality was IMPAIRED, BUT NOT EXTINGUISHED—THEIR FUNCTIONS SUSPENDED, BUT NOT DESTROYED.

Reports had been circulated in the North, and found ready credence with a great many, that the people of the South were as a rule, insubordinate and indisposed to accept the changed conditions there, and that insubordination and turmoil were the rule. To ascertain the facts in this regard, during the later months of 1865 Mr. Johnson commissioned General Grant and others to make a tour of inspection and investigation of the condition of affairs in the Southern States, especially as to their disposition with reference to the acceptance by the people of those States, of their changed relations to the Union, and to report to him the results of their observations.

On the 10th of December, 1865, on motion of Mr. Cowan, of Pennsylvania, the following resolution was adopted by the Senate:

Resolved, That the President of the United States be, and he is hereby requested to furnish the Senate information of the state of that portion of the Union lately in rebellion; whether the rebellion has been suppressed and the United States put again in possession of the States in which it existed; whether the United States courts are restored, post offices re-established and the revenue collected; and also whether the people of those States have reorganized their State governments, and whether they are yielding obedience to the laws and Government of the United States. And at the same time furnish to the Senate copies of such reports as he may have received from such officers or agents appointed to visit that portion of the Union.

December 19th, 1865, in response to this resolution of the Senate, the President transmitted the following Message to the Senate inclosing Gen. Grant's Report:

In reply to the resolution adopted by the Senate on the 12th inst., I have the honor to state that the rebellion waged by a portion of the people against the properly constituted authorities of the Government of the United States has been suppressed; that the United States are in possession of every State in which the insurrection existed; and that, as far as could be done, the courts of the United States have been restored, postoffices re-established, and steps taken to put into effective operation the revenue laws of the country. As the result of the measures instituted by the Executive, with the view of inducing a resumption of the functions of the States comprehended in the inquiry of the Senate, the people in North Carolina, South Carolina, Georgia, Alabama, Mississippi, Louisiana, Arkansas, and Tennessee, have reorganized their respective State Governments, and 'are yielding their obedience to the laws and Government of the United States' with more willingness and greater promptitude than under the circumstances could reasonably have been anticipated. The proposed amendment to the Constitution, providing for the abolition of slavery forever within the limits of the country, has been ratified by each one of those States, with the exception of Mississippi, from which no official information has yet been received; and in nearly all of them measures have been adopted or are now pending, to confer upon freedmen rights and privileges which are essential to their comfort, protection and security. In Florida and Texas, the people are making considerable progress in restoring their State Governments, and no doubt is entertained that they will at the Federal Government. In that portion of the Union lately in rebellion, the aspect of affairs is more promising than, in view of all the circumstances, could have been expected. The people throughout the entire South evince a laudable desire to renew their allegiance to the Government, and to repair the devastations of war by a prompt and cheerful return to peaceful pursuits. An abiding faith is entertained that their actions will conform to their professions, and that, in acknowledging the supremacy of the Constitution and laws of the United States, their loyalty will be given unreservedly to the Government; whose leniency they cannot fail to appreciate, and whose fostering care will soon restore them to a condition of prosperity. It is true, that in some of the States the demoralizing effects of war are to be seen in occasional disorders; but these are local in character, not frequent in occurrence, and are really disappearing as the authority of the civil law is extended and sustained. * * * From all the information in my possession, and from that which I have recently derived from the most reliable authority, I am induced to cherish the belief that sectional animosity is surely and rapidly merging itself into a spirit of nationality, and that representation, connected with a properly adjusted system of taxation, will result in a harmonious restoration of the relations of the States and the National Union.

Andrew Johnson.

The following is General Grant's Report transmitted to Congress with the foregoing Message:

Headquarters Armies of the United States, Washington, D. C., Dec. 18, 1865.

Sir: — In reply to your note of the 16th inst., requesting a report from me giving such information as I may be possessed, coming within the scope of the inquiries made by the Senate of the United States, in their resolution of the 12th inst., I have the honor to submit the following:

With your approval, and also that of the Honorable Secretary of War, I left Washington City on the 27th of last month for the purpose of making a tour of inspection through some of the Southern States, or States lately in rebellion, and to see what changes were necessary to be made in the disposition of the Military forces of the country; how these forces could be reduced and expenses curtailed, etc., and to learn as far as possible, the feelings and intentions of the citizens of those States towards the General Government.

The State of Virginia being so accessible to Washington City, and information from this quarter therefore being readily obtained, I hastened through the State without conversing or meeting with any of its citizens. In Raleigh, North Carolina, I spent one day; in Charleston, South Carolina, I spent two days; Savannah and Augusta, Georgia, each one day. Both in traveling and while stopping, I saw much and conversed freely with the citizens of those States, as well as with officers of the Army who have been stationed among them. The following are the conclusions come to by me:

I am satisfied that the mass of the thinking men of the South accept the present situation of affairs in good faith. The questions which have heretofore divided the sentiments of the people of the two sections—Slavery and State Rights, or the right of a State to secede from the Union—they regard as having been settled forever by the highest tribunal—arms—that man can resort to. I was pleased to learn from the leading men whom I met, that they not only accepted the decision arrived at, as final, but that now, when the smoke of battle has cleared away, and time has been given for reflection, this decision has been a fortunate one for the whole country, they receiving like benefits from it with those who opposed them in the field and in council.

Four years of war, during which law was executed only at the point of the bayonet throughout the States in rebellion, have left the people possibly in a condition not to yield that ready obedience to civil authority the American people have been in the habit of generally yielding. This would render the presence of small garrisons throughout those States necessary until such time as labor returns to its proper channels and civil authority is fully established. I did not meet anyone, either those holding places under the Government or citizens of the Southern States, who think it practicable to withdraw the Military from the South at present. The white and black mutually require the protection of the General Government. There is such universal acquiescence in the authority of the General Government throughout the portions of the country visited by me, that the mere presence of a military force, without regard to numbers, is sufficient to maintain order. The good of the country and economy require that the force kept in the interior where there are many freedmen (elsewhere in the Southern States than at forts upon the sea coast, no more is necessary,) should all be white troops. The reasons for this are obvious without mentioning any of them. The presence of black troops, lately slaves, demoralizes labor both by their advice and by furnishing in their camps a resort for freedmen for long distances around. White troops generally excite no opposition, and therefore a small number of them can maintain order in a given district. Colored troops must be kept in bodies sufficient to defend themselves. It is not thinking men who would use violence towards any class of troops sent among them by the General Government, but the ignorant in some cases might, and the late slave seems to be imbued with the idea that the property of his late master should of right belong to him, or at least should have no protection from the colored soldiers. There is danger of collision being brought on by such causes.

My observations lead me to the conclusion that the citizens of the Southern States are anxious to return to self government within the Union as soon as possible; that while reconstructing they want and require protection from the Government; that they are in earnest in wishing to do what they think is required by the Government, not humiliating to them as citizens, and that if such is pointed out they would pursue it in good faith. It is to be regretted that there cannot be a greater commingling at this time between the citizens of the two sections, and particularly with THOSE ENTRUSTED WITH THE LAWMAKING POWER.

I did not give, the operation of the Freedmen's Bureau that attention I would have done if more time had been at my disposal. Conversations on the subject, however, with officers connected with the Bureau, led me to think that in some of the States its affairs have not been conducted with good judgment and economy, and that the belief, widely spread among the freedmen of the Southern States, that the land of their former masters will, at least in part, be divided among them, has come from the agents of this Bureau. This belief is seriously interfering with the willingness of the freedmen to make contracts for the coming year. In some form the Freedmen's Bureau is an absolute necessity until civil law is established and enforced, securing to the freedmen their rights and full protection. At present, however, it is independent of the Military establishment of the country, and seems to be operated by the different agents of the Bureau according to their individual notions, every where. Gen. Howard, the able head of the Bureau, made friends by the just and fair instructions and advice he gave; but the complaint in South Carolina was that, when he left, things went on as before. Many, perhaps the majority of the agents of the Bureau, advised the freedmen that by their industry they must expect to live. To this end they endeavor to secure employment for them: to see that both contracting parties comply with their agreements. In some instances; I am sorry to say, the freedman's mind does not seem to be disabused of the idea that a freedman has a right to live without care or provision for the future. The effect of the belief in the division of lands is idleness and accumulation in camps, towns, and cities. In such cases, I think it will be found that vice and disease will tend to the extermination, or great reduction of the colored race. It cannot be expected that the opinions held by men at the South can be changed in a day, and therefore the freedmen require for a few years not only laws to protect them, but the fostering care of those who will give them good counsel and in whom they can rely.

U. S. Grant, Lieutenant General.

This report was at once vigorously denounced in and out of Congress, by the extremists. Mr. Sumner characterized it in the Senate, as a "whitewashing report." The standing of General Grant in the country at large, however, was such that few had the indiscretion to attack him openly.

The controlling element of the party which had elected Lincoln and Johnson, had acquiesced for a time in the plan of reconstruction foreshadowed by Mr. Lincoln and adopted by Mr. Johnson, but during the summer of 1865, frictions developed between Mr. Johnson and those who on Mr. Lincoln's death had assumed the leadership in the work of reconstruction and other matters of administration, came to take the opposite ground, from the first occupied by Sumner and other extremists in Congress—that the States lately in rebellion had destroyed themselves by their own act of war, and had thereby forfeited all the rights of Statehood and were but conquered provinces, subject solely to the will of the conqueror.

From that point their ways parted and widened from month to month, till bitter hostility, political and personal, came to mark even their official intercourse.

Mr. Johnson was practically unknown to the great mass of the people of the North till he succeeded to the Presidency. He was in no sense regarded as or assumed to be the leader of the dominant party; while those who on Mr. Lincoln's death became leaders of the dominant party in opposition to Mr. Johnson's administration and policies, were widely known and of long public experience, and had correspondingly the confidence of their party.

So, in the strife that ensued, as it became embittered with the lapse of time, Mr. Johnson was at great disadvantage, and made little or no headway, but rather lost ground as the controversy progressed. His moderate, conservative views, radically expressed, in regard to what should be the methods of reconstruction and the restoration of the Union, found little favor with the mass of the veterans of the Union armies who had but lately returned from the victorious fields of the South, their blood not yet cooled after the fury and heat of the strife while to many, who had witnessed the horrors of war at a safe distance, with the cessation of hostilities in the field, to which they had been only anxious spectators, became suddenly enthused over issues that others had fought out in battle, and vigorously vicious towards Mr. Johnson for presuming to treat the conquered people of the South as American citizens and entitled to the rights of such, after having laid down their arms and peacefully returned to their homes and their respective callings.

This temper, permeating, as it did, the dominant party of practically every Northern State, was not unstintingly reflected upon the National Capitol in the return to Congress of a large majority in both Houses, of men who sympathized with and reflected back again upon their constituents the most extreme views as to what should be the policy of the Government towards the South.

These views characterized the legislation of the time. Partisan rancor was unbridled, and found expression not only in coercive legislation of various grades of severity, but in placing the Southern States generally under almost absolute military control, and in the practical abrogation of the common rights of American citizenship in most of them.

Quite every act of this sort of legislation was passed over the official protest of the President, and each of these protests seemed but to add emphasis to each succeeding act of Congress in that line, till it seemed that there could be no end to the strife, so long as Mr. Johnson remained in the Presidential office.

The ostensible basis of the disagreement which in a few months after the accession of Mr. Johnson to the Presidency began to develop between himself and the Republican leaders in Congress, was the plan of reconstruction put in operation by him during the recess of Congress that year, 1865, and outlined in his North Carolina Proclamation. It availed not, that that plan had been adopted originally by Mr. Lincoln a few days before his death—that it had been concurred in by his entire Cabinet and would undoubtedly have been carried out successfully by him had he lived that plan was made the ground of criticism of Mr. Johnson by the extreme party element in control of Congress, which persistently accused him of having abandoned the plan initiated by Mr. Lincoln, and of setting up another of his own, for purely personal and ambitious purposes, and to the detriment of the peace of the country.

Mr. Johnson may have been opinionated and headstrong, a characteristic of a great many people of strong convictions of duty and purpose; while the overwhelming numerical strength of the dominant party in and out of Congress made it seemingly indifferent, reckless and inconsiderate of the convictions, as of the rights and prerogatives of the Chief Executive treating him more as a clerk whose sole duty it was to register without suggestion the decrees of Congress.

That Mr. Lincoln, had he lived, would have pursued much the same policy of reconstruction, is clearly indicated by the established fact that he had determined to adopt precisely the initial measures thereto which Mr. Johnson did inaugurate and attempt to carry out. But Mr. Lincoln's superior ability in statecraft, his rare tact and knowledge of men, and his capacity for moulding and directing public opinion, seeming to follow where he actually led, would doubtless have secured a more favorable result. And more than all else, it can scarcely be doubted, that the unbounded confidence of the people in his patriotism and capacity to direct public affairs, would have enabled him to dictate terms of reconstruction strictly on the lines he had marked out, and would have commanded the general support of the country, regardless of partisan divisions, notwithstanding the well known fact that at the time of his death there were unmistakable indications of alienation from him of the extreme element of his party because of his conservative views as to the proper methods of reconstruction.

Meantime, in the effort to hamper the President, as far as it was possible for Congress to do, the Tenure-of-Office Act was passed, early in 1867. The ostensible purpose of that Act was to restrict the authority of the President in the selection of his Cabinet advisers, and his power over appointments generally. Its specific purpose, at least so far as the House of Representatives was concerned, and measurably so in the Senate, was to prevent his removal of the Secretary of War, Mr. Stanton, with the manifest if not avowed intent, as the sequel shows, to make that Secretary not only independent of his chief, but also to make him the immediate instrument of Congress in whatever disposition of the Army, or of military affairs generally relating to the government of the Southern States, the majority of Congress might dictate. In a word, the Congress, in that Act, virtually assumed, or attempted to assume, that control of the Army which the Constitution vests on the President.

The first effort to impeach the President, in 1867, was based upon a general accusation of high crimes and misdemeanors without literal specification. The second, in 1868, was based upon his alleged violation of the Tenure-of-Office Act, in the removal of Mr. Stanton.

While it is undoubted, as already shown, that Mr. Lincoln and Mr. Johnson were in accord as to the methods to be adopted for the restoration of the revolted States, it was Mr. Johnson's misfortune that he had not Mr. Lincoln's capacity for so great and so peculiar a task; though a gentleman of proven patriotism, ability, of a kindly, genial nature, and with record of valuable public service. Hampered by his lack of political finesse and intricate knowledge of state-craft, and in view of the conditions of that time, and the people with whom he had to deal, it was obvious from the outset that the result of the controversy could hardly be otherwise than disastrous to him. Mr. Lincoln would undoubtedly have been met by the same character of opposition, and from the same source. But there would have been the appearance at least of mutual concession, and while the APPEARANCE of concession would have been on Mr. Lincoln's side, the actual concession, so far as essentials were involved, would have been on the other.

Mr. Johnson was a Democrat of pronounced type and profound convictions, and in no sense did he depart from his faith. He belonged to the school of Jackson and Jefferson. He had not the electric intuitions and impetuous will of the former, nor the culture and genius of the latter. He adhered more religiously to the letter of the Constitution than either. To him it was the one law of supreme obligation, that never ceased its guarantees. As fittingly expressed by one of his Counsel, Mr. Groesbeck, in the trial: "He was not learned and scholarly—not a man of many ideas or of much speculation—but the Constitution had been the study of his life, and by a law of the mind he was only the truer to that which he did know."

As had Mr. Lincoln, Mr. Johnson keenly appreciated the importance of the people of the South returning at once to the Union, free and independent American citizens, clothed with all the rights, privileges and obligations common to such. In his Cabinet Councils, and to a degree supreme in that board sat William H. Seward, as he had throughout Mr. Lincoln's administration, than whom the Republic has produced no wiser, more sagacious, or patriotic statesman. He gave the subject his intense devotion in the maturity of his great powers.

There too, sat Secretary Welles, another of Mr. Lincoln's advisers, and a devoted friend of the Constitution and the sanctity of the Union.

Each of these men, thoroughly patriotic, and efficient, and untiring in the administration of their respective Departments, had commenced with the deluge of blood, and they now hoped to crown their official careers by a triumphant peace that would Honor their lives and glorify the Nation. These men had a salutary influence over Mr. Johnson, and greatly modified the asperities of his disposition.

Mr. Johnson believed, as did Mr. Lincoln, that the revolted States were still States of the Union—that all the pretended acts of secession were null and void, and that the loyal people therein had the right to reconstruct their State Governments on the basis proposed to them first by Mr. Lincoln, and after him by Mr. Johnson, and thus the right to representation in the General Government.

It was upon this question that parties divided during the reconstruction period. Mr. Lincoln, foreseeing danger in such a division, was anxious to bring those States into such relation that the people generally would consider them as virtually in the Union, without reference to the abstract question. It was with this view, undoubtedly, that he advocated the admission of Members and Senators whenever one-tenth of the voting population of 1860 should organize State Governments and ask for readmission. He would not only not countenance, but repelled the doctrine of "State Suicide," as it was called, and which came to characterize the methods of reconstruction subsequently adopted.

It is true, that on many occasions Mr. Johnson charged that the Congress was only a Congress of part of the States, and that its acts were therefore without validity. Yet he continued to execute those laws, and what to him was a very unpleasant duty, the law which set aside the State Governments organized under his own direction, so that notwithstanding his violent denunciations of the acts of Congress, and his personal opinions, he did not presume to act upon them. Angry and undignified language was uttered on both sides. Many of his speeches were violent and in bad taste and temper. So were a great many speeches uttered by senators and members of the House, and those bodies too often acted upon them.

It is therefore but repeating recorded history to say that Mr. Johnson was earnestly seeking to carry out Mr. Lincoln's plan of reconstruction, which was upon consultation with his entire Cabinet, more especially with Mr. Stanton, adopted by him as the basis for the restoration of the revolted States.

Yet, with these facts of record, that action was afterwards assailed by the Republican leaders in and out of Congress, who assumed to have become Mr. Lincoln's executors in the work of reconstruction, as not only an abandonment of the plan instituted by him, but a surrender of the issues fought out and the results accomplished by the war just closed notwithstanding very many of these critics of Mr. Johnson had but a few months before criticised Mr. Lincoln with quite equal severity for his suggestion of this same method of restoration.

Nor will it suffice to say that, though professing submission and loyalty, the people of the South were still hostile to the Union, and that there was no safety there for Union men. It is true that there came to be violence and disorder there upon the rejection by Congress of Mr. Johnson's plan of restoration.

These were the inevitable results of the conditions. There would also have been disorder and violence in the North and to a far greater degree, had the results of the war been reversed — an arbitrary and tyrannical system of restoration insisted upon — the established order of things destroyed homes broken up the people impoverished, and hordes of unscrupulous adventurers swarmed up from the South and overrun the country in pursuit of schemes of political chicanery and personal ambition, peculation and plunder, as was the South after the close of the war.

But when the fight was on, an overwhelmingly partisan House, as a last resort, in the hope of at once ending, by removal, all opposition on the part of the President to the views and aims of the dominant party in Congress, resorted to the first project of impeachment set out in the succeeding chapter.

CHAPTER IV — FIRST ATTEMPT TO IMPEACH THE PRESIDENT.

THE ASHLEY INDICTMENT.

The initiation of formal proceedings for the impeachment and removal of President Johnson occurred in the House of Representatives on January 7th, 1867, in the introduction of three separate resolutions for his impeachment, by Messrs. Loan and Kelso, of Missouri, and Mr. Ashley of Ohio. As Mr. Ashley's Resolution was the only one acted on by the House, only the proceedings had thereon are here given, as follows:

Mr. Speaker:—I rise to perform a painful but, nevertheless, to me, an imperative duty; a duty which I think ought not longer to be postponed, and which cannot, without criminality on our part, be neglected. I had hoped, sir, that this duty would have devolved upon an older and more experienced member of this House than myself. Prior to our adjournment I asked a number of gentlemen to offer the resolution which I introduced, but upon which I failed to obtain a suspension of the rules.

Confident, sir, that the loyal people of this country demand the adoption of some such proposition as I am about to submit, I am determined that no effort on my part shall be wanting to see that their expectations are not disappointed. * * * On my responsibility as a Representative, and in the presence of this House, and before the American people, I charge Andrew Johnson, Vice President and acting President of the United States, with the commission of acts which in contemplation of the Constitution, are high crimes and misdemeanors, for which, in my judgment, he ought to be impeached. I therefore submit the following:

I do impeach Andrew Johnson, Vice President and acting President of the United States, of high crimes and misdemeanors:

I charge him with a usurpation of power and violation of law:

In that he has corruptly used the appointing power;

In that he has corruptly used the pardoning power;

In that he has corruptly used the veto power;

In that he has corruptly disposed of public property of the United States;

In that he has corruptly interfered in elections, and committed acts which, in contemplation of the Constitution, are high crimes and misdemeanors: Therefore,

BE IT RESOLVED, That the Committee on the Judiciary be, and they are hereby, authorized to inquire into the official conduct of Andrew Johnson, Vice President of the United States, discharging the powers and duties of the office of President of the United States, and to report to this House, whether, in their opinion, the said Andrew Johnson, while in said office, has been guilty of acts which are designed or calculated to overthrow, subvert, or corrupt the Government of the United States, or any department or office thereof; and whether the said Andrew Johnson has been guilty of any act, or has conspired with others to do acts, which, in contemplation of the Constitution, are high crimes and misdemeanors, requiring the interposition of the constitutional power of this House; and that said committee have power to send for persons and papers, and to administer the customary oath to witnesses.

The question was taken on agreeing to the Resolution; and it was decided in the affirmative—yeas 107, nays 39, not voting 45.

On the 2nd of March, 1867, the subject of impeachment again came up in the House, and the following proceedings were had:

Mr. Wilson, of Iowa, (Rep.)—I am directed by the Committee on the Judiciary to present a report relative to the official conduct of the President of the United States.

Mr. Eldridge, (Dem.)—Mr. Speaker, I wish to raise a question of order: I see by the clock that it is almost three o'clock in the morning; and I believe this is the Sabbath day. I think we should not do any more business tonight, except it be business of necessity or charity.

The Speaker.—This, in parliamentary view, is Saturday. The clerk will read the report submitted by the gentleman from Iowa.

The clerk read as follows:

The Committee on the Judiciary, charged by the House with examination of certain allegations, of high crimes and misdemeanors against the President of the United States, submit the following report:

On the 7th day of January, 1867, the House, on the motion of the Hon. James M. Ashley, a Representative from the State of Ohio, adopted the following preamble and resolutions, to-wit:

The duty imposed upon this committee by this action of the House, was of the highest and gravest character. No committee during the entire history of the Government, has ever been charged with a more important trust. The responsibility which it imposed was of oppressive weight, and of a most unpleasant nature. Gladly would the committee have escaped from the arduous labor imposed upon it by the Resolution of the House; but once imposed, prompt, deliberate, and faithful action, with a view to correct results, became its duty, and to this end it has directed its efforts.

Soon after the adoption of the Resolution by the House, Hon. James M. Ashley communicated to the committee, in support of his charges against the President of the United States, such facts as were in his possession, and the investigation was proceeded with, and has been continued almost without, a day's interruption. A large number of witnesses have been examined, many documents collected, and everything done which could be done to reach a conclusion of the case. But the investigation covers a broad field, embraces many novel, interesting, and important questions, and involves a multitude of facts, while most of the witnesses are distant from the Capital, owing to which the committee, in view of the magnitude of the interests involved in its action, have not been able to conclude its labors, and is not therefore prepared to submit a definite and final report. If the investigation had even approached completeness, the committee would not feel authorized to present the result of the House at this late period of the session, unless the charges had been so entirely negative as to admit of no discussion, which, in the opinion of the committee, is not the case.

Certainly no affirmative report could be properly considered in the expiring hours of this Congress.

The committee not having fully investigated all the charges prepared against the President of the United States, it is deemed inexpedient to submit any conclusion beyond the statement that sufficient testimony has been brought to its notice to justify and demand a further prosecution of the investigation.

The testimony which the committee has taken will pass into the custody of the Clerk of the House, and can go into the hands of such committee as may be charged with the duty of bringing this investigation to a close, so that the labor expended upon it may not have been in vain.

The committee regrets its inability definitely to dispose of the important subject committed to its charge, and presents this report for its own justification, and for the additional purpose of notifying the succeeding Congress of the incompleteness of its labors, and that they should be completed.

James F. Wilson, Chairman. Francis Thomas, D. Morris, F. E. Woodbridge, George S. Boutwell, Thomas Williams, Burton C. Cook, William Lawrence,

Mr. Ancona, the only Democrat on the committee, presented a minority report, as follows:

The subscriber, one of the Judiciary Committee, to which was referred by the House the inquiry into the official conduct of His Excellency, the President of the United States, with a view to his impeachment upon certain charges made by Hon. James M. Ashley, begs leave to submit the following report:

The Committee refuses to allow a Report to be made giving to the House at this time upon grounds which are no doubt satisfactory to themselves; therefore, I cannot report the evidence upon which my conclusion is based, which I would gladly do did the Committee deem it expedient. The examination of witnesses and the records was commenced, as appears by the majority report, about the time of the reference, to-wit: on the 7th day of January, 1867, and continued daily. A large number of witnesses has been examined, and everything done that could be, to bring the case to a close, as appears by the majority report: and the majority have come to the conclusion "that sufficient testimony had been brought to its notice to justify and demand a further prosecution of the investigation." I have carefully examined all the evidence in the case, and do report that there is not one particle of evidence to sustain any of the charges which the House charged the Committee to investigate, and that the case is wholly without a particle of evidence upon which impeachment could be founded, and that with all the effort that has been made, and the mass of evidence that has been taken; the case is entirely void of proof. I furthermore report that the most of the testimony that has been taken is of a secondary character, and such as would not be admitted in a court of justice.

In view of this conclusion I can see no good in a continuation of the investigation. I am convinced that all the proof that can be produced has been before the Committee, as no pains have been spared to give the case a full investigation. Why, then, keep the country in a feverish state of excitement upon this question any longer, as it is sure to end, in my opinion, in a complete vindication of the President, if justice be done him by the committee, of which I have no doubt,

A. J. Rogers.

The two reports were ordered printed and laid on the table.

This session of the House, and with it the Thirty-Ninth Congress, ended a few hours later, the legislative day continuing till twelve o'clock, noon, on Sunday, March 3rd. The House adjourned sine die at that hour, when all unfinished business lapsed.

RENEWAL OF THE IMPEACHMENT.

The first session of the Fortieth Congress began on Monday, March 4th, 1867, and on the 7th, in the House of Representatives, Mr. Ashley (Rep.) offered the following Preamble and Resolutions:

Whereas the House of Representatives of the Thirty-Ninth Congress adopted, on the 7th of January, 1867, a Resolution authorizing an inquiry into certain charges preferred against the President of the United States; and whereas the Judiciary Committee, to whom said Resolution and charges were referred, with authority to investigate the same, were unable for want of time, to complete said investigation before the expiration of the Thirty-Ninth Congress; and whereas in the report submitted by said Judiciary Committee on the 2nd of March they declare that the evidence taken is of such a character as to justify and demand a continuation of the investigation by this Congress; therefore:

Be it Resolved by the House of Representatives, That the Judiciary Committee, when appointed, be, and they are hereby, instructed to continue the investigation authorized in said Resolution of Jan. 7th, 1867, and that they have power to send for persons and papers, and to administer the customary oath to witnesses; and that the committee have authority to sit during the sessions of the House and during any recess which Congress or this House may take.

Resolved, That the Speaker be requested to appoint the Committee on the Judiciary forthwith, and that the Committee so appointed be directed to take charge of the testimony taken by the Committee of the last Congress; and that said Committee have power to appoint a clerk at a compensation not to exceed six dollars per day, and employ the necessary stenographers.

At the close of the debate on Mr. Ashley's Resolution, it was adopted without a division, its form being changed to the following:

Resolved, That the Committee on Judiciary be requested to report on the charges against the President as aforesaid, on the first day of the meeting of the House after the recess hereafter to be determined.

Congress adjourned a few days later. It re-assembled on the 3rd of July, and on the 11th the following resolutions was offered by Mr. Stevens, (Rep.) of Pennsylvania:

Resolved, That the Committee on the Judiciary, to whom was referred the Resolution and Documents relative to the Impeachment of the President, be directed to report the evidence at this session, with leave to make further report if they shall deem proper.

That the impeachment enterprise was waning, and that its forces had received little encouragement during the recess of the Congress that had just closed, was evidenced by the fact that there could not be mustered ayes enough to put the resolution to a vote, and Mr. Wilson, of Iowa, moved the following substitute:

Resolved, That the Committee on Judiciary be, and they are hereby, authorized and directed to have the usual number of copies of the evidence taken by said committee relative to the Impeachment of the President, printed and laid on the desks of Members of the House on the first day of the next Congress, whether adjourned or regular.

The Resolution was adopted by a vote of 85 to 48, whereupon Mr. Stevens dejectedly remarked that, "after the vote which had been taken on this resolution, indicating the views of a majority of the House in regard to it, I am willing to abandon it. I therefore move that the Resolution as amended be laid on the table," which motion was agreed to.

On the 15th of July, 1867, Mr. Farnsworth, (Rep.) of Illinois, offered the following resolution and demanded the previous question thereon:

Resolved, That the Committee on the Judiciary be discharged from the further consideration of the question of the Impeachment of the President of the United States, and that the testimony already taken by said committee be printed for the use of the House.

The resolution was not seconded, and went over under the rules.

On the 25th of Nov. 1867, Mr. Boutwell (Rep.), on behalf of the Judiciary Committee, submitted the report of the majority of that committee, of the testimony taken in behalf of the proposed impeachment of the President. The report recommended his impeachment.

Mr. Wilson, submitted the report of the minority of the Committee (himself and Mr. Woodbridge), and moved the adoption of the following resolution:

Resolved, That the Committee on the Judiciary be discharged from the further consideration of the proposed impeachment of the President of the United States, and that the subject be laid upon the table.

Mr. Marshall, on behalf of himself and Mr. Eldridge, the two Democratic members of the committee, stated that though they had not signed the minority report submitted by Mr. Wilson, they joined in support of the resolution submitted by him, and asked leave to introduce and have printed separate views.

This, the first session of the Fortieth Congress, then adjourned, Dec. 2nd, 1867.

The second session of the Fortieth Congress was begun on the same day, and on the 5th, the impeachment question came up in its order in the House, on the resolution reported from the Judiciary Committee:

That Andrew Johnson, President of the United States, be impeached of high crimes and misdemeanors.

After a brief discussion of the order of business, the House adjourned for that day.

The debate was closed on the 6th, by Messrs. Boutwell and Wilson, the members of the Committee on the Judiciary having Charge of the impeachment measure. The closing passages of Mr. Boutwell's speech were as follows:

What is our position to-day? Can this House and the Senate, with the knowledge they have of the Presidents purposes and of the character of the men who surround him, give him the necessary power? (to remove alleged dishonest officials.) Do they not feel that if he be alloyed such power these places will be given to worse men? Hence, I say that with Mr. Johnson in office from this time until the 4th of March, 1869, there is no remedy for these grievances. These are considerations why we should not hesitate to do that which justice authorizes us to do if we believe that the President has been guilty of impeachable offenses.

Mr. Speaker, all rests here. To this House is given by the Constitution the sole power of impeachment; and this power of impeachment furnishes the only means by which we can secure the execution of the laws, and those of our fellow citizens who desire the administration of the law ought to sustain this House while it executes that great law which is in its hands and which is nowhere else, while it performs a high and solemn duty resting on it by which that man who has been the chief violator of law shall be removed, and without which there can be no execution of the law any where. Therefore the whole responsibility, whatever it may be, for the non-execution of the laws of the country, is, (in the presence of these great facts) upon this House. * * * I think that we can not do otherwise than believe, that he has disregarded that great injunction of the Constitution to take care that the laws be faithfully executed, that there is but one remedy. The remedy is with this House, and it is nowhere else. If we neglect or refuse to use our powers when the case arises demanding decisive action, the Government ceases to be a Government of law and becomes a Government of men.

Mr. Wilson, Chairman of the Committee, closed the debate in the following remarks:

The gentleman from Massachusetts has remarked that the President may interfere with the next Presidential election in the Southern States; that he may station soldiers at the voting places and overawe the loyal people of those States, especially the colored vote: and we must, I suppose, guard against the possibility of this by his impeachment and removal from office. This position, if I state it correctly, is startling. Are we to impeach the President for what he may do in the future? Do our fears constitute in the President high crimes and misdemeanors? Are we to wander beyond the record of this case and found our judgment on the possibilities of the future? This would lead us beyond the conscience of this House.

Sir, we must be guided by some rule in this grave proceeding—something more certain than an impossibility to arraign the President for a specific crime—and when the gentleman from Massachusetts, in commenting on one of the alleged offenses of the President, that we could not arraign him for the specific crime, he disclosed the weakness of the case we are now considering. If we cannot arraign the President for a specific crime, for what are we to proceed against him? For a bundle of generalities such as we have in the volume of testimony reported by the committee to the House in this case? If we cannot state upon paper a specific crime, how are we to carry this case to the Senate for trial?

At the close of his speech, Mr. Wilson moved to lay the subject of impeachment on the table, and the yeas and nays were ordered.

Several motions were then made—to adjourn, to adjourn to a day certain, etc.—which with roll calls practically consumed the day, and the motion of Mr. Wilson went over.

The next day, Dec. 7th, the question again came up in its order, and after several unsuccessful attempts to procure a vote on Mr. Wilson's motion to lay the Impeachment Resolution on the table, Mr. Wilson, by agreement, withdrew his motion, and called for the yeas and nays on the adoption of the resolution:

That Andrew Johnson, President of the United States, be impeached for high crimes and misdemeanors.

The yeas and nays were ordered, and the vote was yeas 57, nays 108.

So the resolution to impeach the President was rejected by the very emphatic vote of 67 to 108 — nearly two to one — and by a House two-thirds Republican.

So ended the first effort to impeach the President — the first formal action to that end having been taken on January 7, 1867, and the final vote at the close, and its abandonment, December 7, 1867.

For eleven months the overwhelming Republican majority of the House had been vigorously active in its search for evidence of criminality on the part of the President that would warrant the basing of an impeachment. No effort was left untried — no resource that promised a possible hope of successful exploitation was neglected. Republican partisans were set to the work of sleuth-hounds in the search for testimony in maintenance of the charges preferred, and an ever ready partisan press teemed from the beginning to the end of that time with animadversions upon Mr. Johnson's administration and denunciation of his alleged desertion of Mr. Lincoln's plan of restoration, of treachery to the party that had elected him, and a demand for his impeachment.

To be lukewarm in that controversy, or even to fail to join in the popular denunciation of Mr. Johnson was to put one's self at once under suspicion with the great mass of the dominant party, and without the pale of its consideration.

For eleven months the country was kept in the throes of partisan turmoil — and for what? Simply to depose a President who had disappointed the partisan and personal expectations and schemes of a rule or ruin faction which was able, under the peculiar conditions of the time, to subordinate to its purposes a large proportion of the dominant party of that day.

The following are the material portions of the testimony taken by the House Committee on the Judiciary under authority of the resolutions passed by the House of Representatives on March 7, 1867, for the impeachment of Andrew Johnson.

Eighty-nine witnesses were summoned before the committee. All of them were rigidly examined, and several of them were called and examined the second and third times. Their testimony fills more than twelve hundred octavo pages of print.

The first witness was Gen. L. C. Baker, of the War Department. His testimony related principally to a certain letter alleged to have been written by Mr. Johnson, in 1864.

The first question propounded to him by Mr. Ashley, was as follows:

I wish you to state to the committee the contents, as nearly as you can, of a letter which you have in your possession, written by Andrew Johnson, some time in the early part of 1864, to a Southern man, giving information as to the troops about the Capitol and elsewhere, and advice to Jefferson Davis. State where that letter is, and give the contents as nearly as you can, the history of it.

Mr. Baker answered that he knew there was a letter of that kind, purporting to have been written by Andrew Johnson, when he was acting Governor of Tennessee. That the letter was dated at Nashville and directed to Jefferson Davis, and related to some declared policy that had been adopted by the Confederacy—that the letter was being used to secure an appointment—that reference was made to troops, but nothing about localities where stationed, or numbers, and nothing about shipment of armor, and that the letter was stolen from Andrew Johnson's table and never sent.

The question was then asked of the witness by Mr. Ashley:

State whether the whole import of the letter written by Mr. Johnson, was not to turn the whole power which he possessed in Tennessee, in a certain contingency, over to the rebel cause?

Answer—No. I did not have that opinion of the letter exactly. From what I recollect of it, the thing was that he was making a proposition making suggestions as to what their policy should be.

Ques.—And if they accepted it?

Ans.—If they accepted it, my impression was that he was going with them.

Ques.—With the rebels?

Ans.—Yes sir.

Question by the Chairman.—If there are any other letters that you have seen of Mr. Johnson's written by him to any person connected with the Confederate Government, or proposing to change the Administration of the Government in their favor after he became President, or anything of a public nature affecting the interests of the United States, please state it and state all you know about such letters.

Ans.—I do not know of any letters of that character—or of any other letters.

This constituted the substance of Gen. Baker's testimony. His examination was very lengthy, embracing more of this character of testimony, and about pardon brokerage, and other alleged corrupt practices—all evidencing a determination and expectation to fix upon Mr.

Johnson a disposition to disloyalty and corruption, both before and after his succession to the Presidency, but no such testimony was obtained.

A considerable portion of the investigation was devoted to Mr. Johnson's business and personal affairs, such as could have no possible connection with or indicate implication in corrupt or disloyal practices of any sort.

A strenuous effort appears to have been made by the Committee throughout a long and searching examination of witnesses, and constitutes a conspicuous feature of that investigation, to establish the charges of corruption and disloyalty in the sale of public property, railways, etc., that had been constructed and equipped, or seized and operated, by the Government in connection with its military operations in the South. Such an accusation had been made with great pertinacity by Mr. Johnson's opponents, and was also then believed by a great many people to be true.

Among the parties examined by the committee, were Mr. James and Mr. Burns, of Nashville, Tenn., and Senator Fowler, of that State, and also the Secretary of war, Mr. Stanton. No facts whatever were elicited showing a privity to corruption in these matters on the part of Mr. Johnson.

The information obtained from Mr. Stanton, however, put an effectual estoppel to further investigation of the charge of corrupt or disloyal disposal of public property by the President. The following are extracts from Mr. Stanton's testimony, as given on February 11, 1867:

Shortly after the surrender of the rebel armies, the attention of the War Department was directed to the proper disposition to be made of the railroads and railroad stock throughout the rebel States which came into our possession, either by capture or construction. It was the subject of a good deal of consultation and conference between the Secretary of War and the Quartermaster General. It was the opinion of the Secretary of War that it was wholly impracticable for the General Government to operate these roads under any system, and that it would be greatly to the advantage of the country to make such disposition as would allow them, its speedily as possible, to become what they were designed for channels of commerce and trade between the States, and that any terms on which that could be done would be advantageous. This was especially the case in regard to the Western and Southwestern roads, where it was said there were large amounts of cotton that would be available to remove North, in exchange for supplies to go South, of which it was said they were greatly in want.

Ques. — In case of the construction of a railroad by the Government, the Government furnishing the material and the labor, what has been the custom of the Department in surrendering such roads to the companies claiming them?

Ans. — In all instances, I think such roads have been surrendered in the same manner as if they had been constructed by the companies. That subject was talked of a good deal in conference between myself and the Quartermaster General. My own views, that the great object on the part of the Government, was to get these roads operated; and that to go into an inquiry as to the cost of construction, would be impracticable, either as to the cost of construction or as to any certain rule of compensation, because many of them were constructed under the pressure of war, and for temporary Purposes. The object of arriving at the cash value or equivalent for the roads was not only impracticable, but really of very little practical interest in comparison with the great end of having the channels of commerce in the rebel states opened and carried on, with a view of getting out their produce, furnishing supplies, and getting commerce in its regular channels. In my own view, that appeared to be the most, certain and most speedy system of reconstruction we could adopt, and that it would tend more to establish harmony than any other thing that could be done by the Government. In view of all this, and after the most deliberate consideration we could give it, it was the opinion of the Quartermaster General and myself — certainly my own — that it would be impracticable to make any distinction: and so far as I know, no distinction was made in any part of the country in reference to roads built by the Government and roads that had been constructed by Companies before the war commenced.

Mr. Stanton was asked this question:

Suppose the Government, at his own expense, had constructed seventy miles of railroad in one of the rebel States, and that, at the close of the war, a company should apply to the Executive Department of the Government for a transfer of the road so constructed to it; by what authority or provision of law would Executive Department be authorized to transfer the road so constructed to the company making the application?

Mr. Stanton answered:

I do not know of any act of Congress that directly, in terms, would authorize any such transfer; but regarding the construction of the road, in time of war, simply as a means, or instrument, of carrying on war, when the war was over I would consider it strictly proven and within the scope of the power of the General Commanding, or especially of the President of the United States, as the Commander-in-Chief of the Army, to render that instrument as available for peace purposes as possible. And inasmuch as the road would be entirely useless unless it was operated, and it would be for the benefit and interest of the public, to have it operated as speedily as possible, I think it would be in the interest of a wise discretion, and exercising proper authority, to turn over that road to any company or individual who would operate it; for, in that way, he would be applying the war material to the only available use to which it could be applied. * * * I would regard the rolling stock as coming, to a certain extent, within the same principle. * * * No transfer of title was at any time made, so far as I know, or could be made, but only possession turned over. When the military use was no longer required, the railroads were turned over to their original owners, or their representatives, with permission to use them. These railroads, their plant and track fixtures, real property, of which the military authorities had only the possessory right and use, but the rolling stock and equipments, and iron not laid down, were personal property, which, by capture, or purchase, or construction, belonged to the United States. Sale could be made, and was made, of the personal property at values estimated by the proper officers. That which constituted real estate, to-wit, the railroad track, fixtures, etc., the military authorities might abandon altogether, or relinquish control and turn over possession to those who would make a beneficial use of it by working the road. Being in the nature of real estate, no title of the Government or of other persons could be divested and conveyed by military authority, but only the control relinquished and the use permitted during the existence of military authority in the department where the roads were situated.

The trend of a large portion of the testimony of witnesses called by this committee to testify as to the charges preferred against Mr. Johnson and relating to other allegations of the indictment, quite clearly indicated that the charges were based solely upon common street rumor, invented and given currency in partisan antagonism and for partisan purposes, and that the witnesses were called in the hope and expectation, on the part of the majority of the House, of developing proof of disloyalty and corruption on the part of the President, and, if not criminal connivance, at least, criminal knowledge of a conspiracy for the assassination of Mr. Lincoln.

But these expectations and hopes, in all respects, were so utterly disappointed, that there was pathos, at least, as the investigation was protracted from month to month, with no indication of the hoped for development, in the despondent inquiry of Mr. Thaddeus Stevens to one of his colleagues of the Impeachment Committee, as the inquest approached a close without results—"Well, HAVE YOU GOT ANYTHING, ANYHOW?" It was more an ejaculation of anger and disgust at failure, than a query of one seeking hoped for information.

CHAPTER V — THE TENURE-OF-OFFICE ACT.

ITS HISTORY AND PURPOSE — THE PRESIDENTS VETO MESSAGE.

Mr. Johnson's alleged violation of the act of Congress known as the Tenure-of-Office Act, constituted the ostensible basis of his impeachment in 1868. As stated, it had been passed for the purpose of restricting the power of the President over Executive appointments. That Act, therefore, becomes a very important and conspicuous incident in the impeachment affair, as its alleged violation constituted the only material accusation, set out in various forms, in the entire list of charges.

The proceedings had on the passage of that bill are inserted at some length here, as a technical knowledge of its history, character and purpose, is essential to a correct apprehension of the controversy that had arisen between the President and Congress.

The Tenure-of-Office bill was introduced in the Senate by Mr. Williams, of Oregon, Dec. 3rd, 1866, and on the 5th was referred to the Committee on Retrenchment. On the 10th Mr. Edmunds, in the name of the committee, reported it back to the Senate with the following remarks:

The joint select Committee on Retrenchment, to whom was referred the bill to regulate the tenure of offices, have had the same under consideration, and have instructed me to report the bill back, with a recommendation of certain amendments, which being adopted, the committee are of the opinion that the bill ought to pass. I beg leave to say in connection with this report that we have reported this bill and these amendments regulating removals from office and appointments to office so far as concerns officers whose nominations require the confirmation of the Senate, and have adopted what appears to us to be a feasible scheme in that respect, in no spirit of hostility to any party or administration whatever, but in what we conceive to be the true Republican interest of the country, under all administrations, under the domination of all parties in the growth which is before us in the future; and in that spirit I shall ask the attention of the Senate to the bill when it comes to be considered. I move that the amendment be printed, and that the bill be made the special order for Thursday next, at one o'clock.

On the 10th of January, 1867, on motion of Mr. Edmunds, the bill was taken up for consideration. As the first section of the bill was the only portion over which there was any serious controversy, or pertinent to this recital, only that section is produced here. It is as follows:

That every person (excepting the Secretaries of State, of the Treasury, of War, of the Navy, and of the Interior, the Postmaster General, and the Attorney General), holding any civil office to which he has been appointed by and with the advice and consent of the Senate, and every person who shall hereafter be appointed to any such office, and shall become duly qualified to act therein, is, and shall be, entitled to hold such office until a successor shall have been in like manner appointed and duly qualified, except as herein otherwise provided.

Mr. Howe objected to the exception of the Cabinet officers from the operation of the bill, and Mr. Edmunds responded that:

It did seem to the Committee, after a great deal of consultation and reflection, that it was right and just that the Chief Executive of the Nation, in selecting these named Secretaries, who, by law, and by the practice of the country, and officers analogous to whom by the practice of all other countries, are the confidential advisers of the Executive respecting the administration of all his Departments, should be persons who were personally agreeable to him, in whom he could place entire confidence and reliance, and that whenever it should seem to him that the state of relations, between him and any of them had become such as to render this relation of confidence and trust and personal esteem inharmonious, HE SHOULD IN SUCH CASE BE ALLOWED TO DISPENSE WITH THE SERVICES OF THAT OFFICER IN VACATION AND HAVE SOME OTHER PERSON ACT IN HIS STEAD. We thought that so much discretion, so much confidence, so much respect ought to be properly attributed to the Chief Magistrate of the Nation. It may happen that at some particular time — some people may suppose that it has happened now — the Chief Magistrate for the time being ought not to be invested with such powers; but the Committee have recommended the adoption of this rule respecting the tenure-of-office as a permanent and systematic, and as they believe, an appropriate regulation of the Government for all administrations and for all time; and it did appear to them (whether the reason may command itself to the Senate or not), that it was just to the Executive, and on the whole best for the interest of the Nation, that he should be allowed during a recess of the Senate to change his confidential advisers if it should appear to him to be fit, subject to that general responsibility which every officer must be held to the public and to the Senate when they meet again.

Mr. Williams said:

I prepared the original bill in this case, which contains in different words the exception contained in the amendment reported by the Committee. I do not regard the exception as of any real practical consequence, because I suppose if the President and any head of a Department should disagree so as to make their relations unpleasant, and the President should signify a desire that the head of a Department retire from the Cabinet, THAT WOULD FOLLOW WITHOUT ANY POSITIVE ACT OF REMOVAL ON THE PART OF THE PRESIDENT.

Mr. Fessenden said:

The Constitution imposes upon the President of the United States the duty of executing the laws; it does not impose that duty upon the Secretaries. They are creatures of the law and not of the Constitution directly. Some, and perhaps the greater part, of their functions are as advisers of the President and to aid him in executing the laws in their several Departments. There are some duties that are specifically conferred upon them by Congress. Their relation to the President, as has been well said by gentlemen, is that mostly of confidential advisers. With the exception of the particular duties imposed upon them by law, and on the Secretary of the Treasury more than on the others, they do nothing of their own motion, but act by order of the President in discharging the particular duties of their office. * * * That being the peculiar condition of affairs it has always been considered since the foundation of the Government, as a matter of course, as a general rule — there may have been one or two exceptions, and I think there have been, but I am not very positive on that point — that the President might select such persons as he pleased to be members of his Cabinet. Of course the confirmation of the Senate is necessary; but the general idea of the Senate has been, whether they liked the men or not, to confirm them without any difficulty, because in executing the great and varied interests of this great country it is exceedingly important that there should be the utmost harmony between those who are charged with that execution.

The bill passed as reported and went to the House. That body amended it by making Cabinet officers non-removable by the President without the consent of the Senate, and sent the bill back to the Senate, when Mr. Sherman said:

It (the Tenure-of-Office bill) ought to have been passed, and probably would have been passed, long ago, if a different condition of affairs had existed before. But when you propose to extend that principle to Cabinet officers, a very different state of affairs arises, and different circumstances apply to this subject. Now I say, that if a Cabinet officer should attempt to hold his office for a moment beyond the time when he retained the entire confidence of the President, I would not vote to retain him, NOR WOULD I COMPEL THE PRESIDENT TO LEAVE ABOUT HIM IN THESE HIGH POSITIONS A MAN IN WHOM HE DID NOT ENTIRELY TRUST, both personally and politically. It would be unwise to require him to administer the Government without agents of his own choosing. It seems to me, therefore, that it would be unwise for the Senate to engraft in this bill a provision that would enable a Cabinet officer to hold on to his office in violation of the will of his Chief. * * * Suppose the personal relations between a Cabinet officer and the President became so unpleasant that they could have no personal intercourse. The Senator from Wisconsin (Mr. Howe), says in such a case the Cabinet officer would resign. Suppose he should hold on to his power and position—what then? There is no power to remove him, and the President can have no intercourse with him. Would you compel such a state of affairs? It seems to me that it would be unwise to do so. That the Senate had no such purpose is shown by its vote twice to make this exception. That this provision does not apply to the present case, is shown by the fact that its language is so framed as NOT TO APPLY TO THE PRESENT PRESIDENT. * * * It would not prevent the present President from removing the present Secretary of War, the Secretary of the Navy, or the Secretary of State.

A considerable number of Senators participated in the debate, which was able and exhaustive to an exceptional degree, on both sides, and occupied several days in the various stages of the proceeding.

Mr. Edmunds closed the debate in the Senate with the following remarks:

I do not rise to prolong the debate, but only to express the hope that the debate on this question may terminate—that we may come to a vote. * * * While I should be glad to occupy some time in reply to some things that have fallen in the course of this debate, I feel it to be due to the business of the Senate to abstain. I hope the Senate will disagree to this amendment, (made by the House) and adhere to the bill as it stands.

The vote was then taken, and resulted in 17 for agreeing to the House amendment, and 28 against it.

The action of the Senate was reported to the House and Conference Committees were appointed by the two houses.

On the 18th of February, the following substitute for the first section of the bill was reported by the Committee of Conference and adopted by both Houses, and the bill went to the President:

Provided, That the Secretaries of State, of the Treasury, of War, of the Navy, and of the Interior, the Postmaster General and the Attorney General, shall hold their offices respectively FOR AND DURING THE TERMS OF THE PRESIDENT BY WHOM THEY MAY HAVE BEEN APPOINTED, and for one month thereafter, subject to removal by and with the advice and consent of the Senate.

On Monday, March 2nd, 1867, the President returned the bill to the Senate, in which house it had originated, with his objections thereto, as follows:

To the Senate of the United States:

I have carefully examined the bill to regulate the tenure of certain civil offices. The material portion of the bill is contained in the first section, and is of the effect following, namely:

"That every person holding any civil office to which he has been appointed by and with the advice and consent of the Senate, and every person who shall hereafter be appointed to any such office, and shall become duly qualified to act therein, is and shall be entitled to hold such office until a successor shall have been appointed by the President, with the advice and consent of the Senate, and duly qualified; and that the Secretaries of State, of the Treasury, of War, of the Navy, and of the Interior, the Postmaster General, and the Attorney General, shall hold their offices respectively for and during the term of the President by whom they may have been appointed, and for one month thereafter, subject to removal by and with the advice and consent of the Senate."

These revisions are qualified by a reservation in the fourth section, "that nothing contained in the bill shall be construed to extend the term of any office the duration of which is limited by law." In effect the bill provides that the President shall not remove from their places any of the civil officers whose terms of service are not limited by law without the advice and consent of the Senate of the United States. The bill, in this respect, conflicts, in my judgment, with the Constitution of the United States. The question, as Congress is well aware, is by no means a new one. That the power of removal is constitutionally vested in the President of the United States is a principle which has been not more distinctly declared by judicial authority and judicial commentators than it has been uniformly practiced upon by the legislative and executive departments of the Government. The question arose in the House of Representatives so early as the 16th day of June,

1789, on the bill for establishing an executive department, denominated "The Department of Foreign Affairs." The first clause of the bill, after recapitulating the functions of that officer and defining his duties, had these words: "To be removable from office by the President of the United States." It was moved to strike out these words, and the motion was sustained with great ability and vigor. It was insisted that the President could not constitutionally exercise the power of removal exclusive of the Senate; that the Federalist so interpreted the Constitution when arguing for its adoption by the several States; that the Constitution had nowhere given the President power of removal, either expressly or by strong implication; but on the contrary, had distinctly provided for removals from office by impeachment only. A construction which denied the power of removal by the President was further maintained by arguments drawn from the danger of the abuse of the power; from the supposed tendency of an exposure of public officers to capricious removal; to impair the efficiency of the civil service; from the alleged injustice and hardship of displacing incumbents, dependent upon their official stations, without sufficient consideration; from a supposed want of responsibility on the part the President, and from an imagined defect of guarantees against a vicious President, who might incline to abuse the power.

On the other hand, an exclusive power of removal by the President was defended as a true exposition of the text of the Constitution. It was maintained that there are certain causes for which persons ought to be removed from office without being guilty of treason, bribery, or malfeasance, and that the nature of things demands that it should be so. "Suppose," it was said, "a man becomes insane by the visitation of God, and is likely to ruin our affairs; are the hands of Government to be confined front warding off the evil? Suppose a person in office not possessing the talents he was judged to have at the time of the appointment, is the error not to be corrected; suppose he acquire vicious habits and incurable indolence, or totally neglect the duties of his office, which shall work mischief to the public welfare, is there no way to arrest the threatened danger? Suppose he become odious and unpopular by reason of the measures he pursues, and this he may do without committing any positive offense against the law, must he preserve his office in despite of the popular will? Suppose him grasping for his own aggrandizement and the elevation of his connections by every means short of the treason defined by the Constitution, hurrying your affairs to the precipice of destruction, endangering your domestic tranquility, plundering you of the means of defense, alienating the affections of your allies, and promoting the spirit of discord, must the tardy, tedious, desultory road, by way of impeachment, be traveled to overtake the man who, barely confining himself within the letter of the law, is employed in drawing off the vital principle of the Government?" The nature of things, the great objects of society, the express objects of the Constitution itself require that this thing should be otherwise. To unite the Senate with the President "in the exercise of the power" it was said, would involve us in the most serious difficulty. "Suppose a discovery of any of these events should take place when the Senate is not in session, how is the remedy to be applied? The evil could be avoided in no other way than by the Senate sitting always." In regard to the danger of the power being abused if exercised by one man, it was said "that the danger is as great with respect to the Senate, who are assembled from various parts of the continent, with different impressions and opinions;" that such a body is more likely to misuse the power of removal than the man whom the united voice of America calls to the presidential chair. As the nature of Government requires the power of removal, it was maintained "that it should be exercised in this way by the hand capable of exerting itself with effect, and the power must be conferred on the President by the Constitution as the executive officer of the Government." Mr. Madison, whose adverse opinion in the Federalist had been relied upon by those who denied the exclusive power, now participated in the debate. He declared that he had reviewed his former opinions, and he summed up the whole case as follows:

"The Constitution affirms that the executive power is vested in the President. Are there exceptions to this proposition? Yes, there are. The Constitution says that in appointing to office the Senate shall be associated with the President, unless, in the case of inferior officers, when the law shall otherwise direct. Have we (that is, Congress) a right to extend this exception? I believe not. If the Constitution has invested all executive power in the President, I return to assert that the Legislature has no right to diminish or modify his executive authority. The question now resolves itself into this: is the power of displacing an executive power? I conceive that if any power whatever is in the Executive, it is in the power of appointing, overseeing, and controlling those who execute the laws. If the Constitution had not qualified the power of the President in appointing to office by associating the Senate with him in that business, would it not be clear that he would have the right by virtue of his executive power to make such appointment? Should we be authorized, in defiance of that clause in the Constitution — the executive power shall be vested in the President — to unite the Senate with the President in the appointment to office? I conceive not. It is admitted that we should not be authorized to do this, I think it may be disputed whether we have a right to associate there in removing persons from office, the one power being as much of an executive nature as the other; and the first is authorized by being excepted out of the general rule established by the Constitution in these words: 'The executive power shall be vested in the President.'"

The question thus ably and exhaustively argued was decided by the House of Representatives, by a vote of 34 to 20, in favor of the principle that the executive power of removal is vested by the Constitution in the Executive, and in the Senate by the casting vote of the Vice President. The question has often been raised in subsequent times of high excitement, and the practice of the Government has nevertheless conformed in all cases to the decision thus early made. * * * Chancellor Kent's remarks on the subject are as follows:

"On the first organization of the Government it was made a question whether the power of removal in case of officers appointed to hold at pleasure resided nowhere but in the body which appointed, and, of course, whether the consent of the Senate was not requisite to remove. This was the construction given to the Constitution while it was pending for ratification before the State conventions by the author of the Federalist. But the construction which was given to the Constitution by Congress, after great consideration and discussion, was different. The words of the act (establishing the Treasury Department) are: 'And whenever the same shall be removed from office by the President of the United States, or in any other case of vacancy in the office, the assistant shall act.' This amounted to a legislative construction of the Constitution, and it has ever since been acquiesced in and acted upon as decisive authority in the case. It applies equally to every other officer of the Government appointed by the President, whose term of duration is not specially declared. It is supported by the weighty reason that the subordinate officers in the executive department ought to hold at the pleasure of the head of the Department, because he is invested generally with the executive authority, and the participation in that authority by the Senate was an exception to a general principle and ought to be taken strictly. The President is the great responsible officer for the faithful execution of the law, and the power of removal was incidental to that duty, and might often be requisite to fulfill it."

Thus has the important question presented by this bill been settled, in the language of the late Daniel Webster (who, while dissenting from it, admitted that it was settled), by construction, settled by precedent, settled by the practice of the Government, and settled by statute.

The events of the last war furnished a practical confirmation of the wisdom of the Constitution as it has hitherto been maintained in many of its parts, including that which is now the subject of consideration. When the war broke out rebel enemies, traitors, abettors, and sympathizers were found in every department of the Government, as well in the civil service as in the land and naval military service. They were found in Congress and among the keepers of the Capitol, in foreign missions, in each and all of the Executive Departments, in the judicial service, in the Post Office, and among the agents for conducting Indian affairs; and upon probable suspicion they were promptly displaced by my predecessor, so far as they held their offices under executive authority, and their duties were confided to new and loyal successors. No complaints against that power or doubts of its wisdom, were entertained in any quarter.

Having at an early period accepted the Constitution in regard to the executive office in the sense in which it was interpreted with the concurrence of its founders, I have found no sufficient grounds in the arguments now opposed to that construction or in any assumed necessity of the times for changing those opinions. For these reasons I return the bill to the Senate, in which House it originated, for the further consideration of Congress, which the Constitution prescribes. Insomuch as the several parts of the bill which I have not considered are matters chiefly of detail, and are based altogether upon the theory of the Constitution from which I am obliged to dissent, I have not thought it necessary to examine them with a view to make them an occasion of distinct and special objections. Experience, I think, has shown that it is the easiest, as it is also the most attractive, of studies to frame constitutions for the self-government of free States and nations.

But I think experience has equally shown that it is the most difficult of all political labors to preserve and maintain such free constitutions of self government when once happily established. I know no other way in which they can be preserved and maintained except by a constant adherence to them through the various vicissitudes of national existence, with such adaptations as may become necessary, always to be effected, however, through the agencies and in the forms prescribed in the original constitutions themselves. Whenever administration fails or seems to fail in securing any of the great ends for which Republican Government is established, the proper course seems to be to renew the original spirit and forms of the Constitution itself.

Andrew Johnson

The bill was promptly passed in both Houses over the President's veto and became a law.

As pertinent and incident to the history of this controversy, is the communication of the President notifying the Senate of the suspension of Mr. Stanton, Aug. 12, 1867. The President said:

The Tenure-of-Office Act did not pass without notice. Like other acts, it was sent to the President for approval. As is my custom I submitted it to the consideration of my Cabinet for their advice whether I should approve it or not. I was a grave question of constitutional law, in which I would of course rely mostly upon the opinion of the Attorney General, and of Mr. Stanton, who had once been Attorney General. EVERY MEMBER OF MY CABINET ADVISED ME THAT THE PROPOSED LAW WAS UNCONSTITUTIONAL. All spoke without doubt or reservation; but MR. STANTON'S CONDEMNATION OF THE LAW WAS THE MOST ELABORATE AND EMPHATIC. He referred to the Constitutional provisions, the debates in Congress, especially to the speech of Mr. Buchanan when a Senator, to the decisions of the Supreme Court, and to the usage from the beginning of the Government through every successive administration, all concurring to establish the right of removal as vested in the President. To all these he added the weight of his own deliberate judgment, and advised me that it was my duty to defend the power of the President from usurpation and veto the law.

During the recess of Congress in the Summer of 1867, the President suspended Mr. Stanton from the War Office and appointed Gen. Grant Secretary of War ad interim. Gen. Grant was then understood as supporting the President in his controversy with Mr. Stanton, and promptly accepted the appointment, holding it until the following December, when the change was duly reported to the Senate. The Senate refused to sanction Mr. Stanton's suspension, and he consequently resumed his position of Secretary of War and retained it until the close of the Impeachment trial — the Senate then, in effect, by rejecting the Impeachment, declaring that the President had the right to remove him.

Very naturally, after Mr. Stanton's restoration to the War Office by the refusal of the Senate to sanction his suspension, the relations between himself and the President were embittered and many efforts were made by mutual friends to induce Mr. Stanton to resign. Conspicuous among these were Gen. Grant, the General of the Army, and Gen. Sherman, the next in rank, as shown in the following note from Gen. Sherman to the President; but a few weeks before the crisis came. It explains itself, as showing the relations then subsisting between the parties mentioned:

332 K St., Washington, Jan, 18th.

I regretted, this morning, to say that I had agreed to go down to Annapolis, to spend Monday with Admiral Porter. Gen. Grant has to leave for Richmond on Monday morning at 6 o'clock. At a conversation with the General, after an interview wherein I offered to go with him on Monday morning to Mr. Stanton and say it was our joint opinion that he should resign, it was found impossible by reason of his going to Richmond and my going to Annapolis. The General proposed this course. He will tell you tomorrow and offer to go to Mr. Stanton to say that for the good of the service of the country he ought to resign—this on Sunday. On Monday, I will call on you, and if you think it necessary, I will do the same—call on Mr. Stanton and tell him he should resign. If he will not, then it will be time to consider ulterior measures. In the meantime, it also happens that no necessity exists for precipitating measures.

Yours truly, W. T. Sherman.

On Saturday, February 23, 1868, the day following the removal of Mr. Stanton, Mr. Johnson sent to the Senate the name of Mr. Thomas Ewing, senior, of Ohio, as his successor. The Senate had adjourned for the day when the President's Secretary reached the Capitol, between 12 and 1 o'clock, but the nomination was formally communicated on the following Monday. Of this nomination, Mr. Blaine has written, that "no name could have given better assurance of good intentions and upright conduct than that of Mr. Ewing. He was a man of lofty character, of great eminence in his profession of the law, and with wide and varied experience in public life. He had held high rank as a Senator in the Augustan period of the Senate's learning and eloquence, and he had been one of the ablest members of the distinguished Cabinets organized by the only two Presidents elected by the Whig Party. He had reached the ripe age of seventy-eight years, but still in complete possession of all his splendid faculties. He had voted for Mr. Lincoln at both elections, had been a warm supporter of the contest for the Union, and was represented by his own blood on many of the great battlefields of the war."

No notice was taken by the Senate of this nomination.

Here was offered an opportunity for the settlement of the dispute over the War Office on fair and honorable terms to all parties concerned. But that was not what the impeachers wanted. They wanted to get Mr. Johnson out. They thought they had a pretext that they could sustain by making it a party question, and did not want a settlement on any other terms—so no attention was given to Mr. Ewing's nomination. It was ignored and the impeachment movement went on.

CHAPTER VI — IMPEACHMENT AGREED TO BY THE HOUSE.

Mr. Johnson's veto of the Tenure-of-Office Bill, and the passage of that bill over his veto, of course intensified the antagonism between himself and Congress. He not unnaturally regarded that Act as an infringement of the Executive function which it was his duty to his office and to himself to resent. The culmination came upon his official notification to the Senate on February 21st, 1868, of his removal of Mr. Stanton from the office of Secretary of War, and his appointment of Gen. Lorenzo Thomas as Secretary ad interim, nothwithstanding the assumed interdiction of the Tenure-of-Office Act.

Immediately on receipt of this notification, the Senate went into executive session, and the following proceeding was had:

IN EXECUTIVE SESSION Senate of the United States February 21st, 1868

Whereas, The Senate have read and considered the communication of the President, stating that he had removed Edwin M. Stanton, Secretary of War, and had designated the Adjutant General of the Army to act as Secretary of War ad interim. interim... Therefore,

Resolved, by the Senate of the United States, That under the Constitution and laws of the United States, the President has no power to remove the Secretary of War and designate any other officer to perform the duties of that office ad interim.

The journal of the Senate shows that this Resolution was adopted by the following vote:

Yeas—Messrs. Cameron, Cattell, Cole, Conkling, Cragin, Drake, Ferry, Harlan, Morrill of Maine, Morrill of Vermont, Morton, Patterson of New Hampshire, Pomeroy, Ramsay, Ross, Sprague, Stewart. Sumner. Thayer, Tipton, Trumbull. Van Winkle, Wade, Willey Williams. Wilson. Yates—23.

Nays—Messrs. Buckalew, Davis, Doolittle, Edmunds, Hendricks, Patterson of Tennessee—6.

Absent or not voting—20. Note. (Note—It is due to myself to say here, that the entry of my name in the above vote, was incorrect. My distinct recollection is, that though present, I declined to vote, and from the consideration mentioned. I was totally unaware of my name being recorded as voting on the proposition until long after I left the Senate, when of course there was no opportunity to secure a correction of the journal.)

This was an extraordinary proceeding. A proposition to impeach the President had till recently been pending in the House for nearly a year, and the ingenuity of the majority had been taxed to the utmost to find some basis for an indictment upon which a successful impeachment might be possible. There is ground for the suggestion that much was hoped for in that direction from the Tenure-of-Office Bill, at least so far as the House was concerned. That hoped for opportunity had now come—nor is it an unreasonable surmise, that this very extraordinary action of the Senate was forced by outside as well as inside influences for the purpose of testing the Senate, and committing it in advance and in anticipation of the preferment of another impeachment by the House.

As to the question of the guilt or innocence of the President of the commission of an impeachable offense, this vote of the Senate was in the nature of a vote of "guilty." It was therefore to a degree an impeachment and conviction combined by the Senate, prior to the bringing of an accusation by the House of Representatives, the constitutional body for the preferment of an impeachment of the President—and was an improper, and not far removed from an indecent proceeding on the part of the Senate. In effect, the President was thereby condemned by the Senate without trial, and his later arraignment was simply to receive sentence-it being solely upon the removal of Mr. Stanton that the impeachment was brought by the House.

It is noticeable, and possibly indicative, that the names of twenty out of fifty-four members of the Senate do not appear in this list—a very unusual occurrence in divisions of that body; especially in the exciting conditions that then prevailed. The absentees, or at least abstentions from voting, were fifteen Republicans and five Democrats, more than one-third of the body. That very unusual absence or abstention from voting may well be attributed to the very proper hesitancy of Senators to commit themselves in advance, either way, on a proposition that was reasonably certain to lead to an impeachment of the President, then virtually pending and imminent in the House, and upon which the Senate was equally certain to be called upon to act.

The action of the President was also communicated to the House of Representatives by Mr. Stanton, at the same hour of the same day, February 21st, 1868, in the following communication, enclosing a copy of the President's notification of his dismissal.

War Department, Washington City, Feb. 21, 1868.

Sir:—Gen. Thomas has just delivered to me a copy of the enclosed order, which you will please communicate to the House of Representatives.

(Signed) E. M. Stanton, Secretary of War. Hon. Schuyler Colfax, Speaker House of Representatives.

This gave new life to the impeachment cause, which had a few weeks before been defeated in the House and since then had, for lack of material, been laming, to the discouragement of many of its advocates: and the gleeful ejaculations, on the floor of the House, in the lobbies, and on the streets, on receipt of this news, and more especially after the action of the Senate became known, which was not long in reaching the public, with a common greeting slid clasping of hands: "Well, we've got him now!"

The communication of Mr. Stanton to the House of Representatives was immediately, after reading, referred to the Committee on Reconstruction.

In the evening of the same day, Mr. Covode, of Pennsylvania, offered a resolution to impeach the President, which was also referred to the same Committee.

On the next day, Feb. 22d, 1868, Mr. Stevens, Chairman of that Committee, made the following report:

The Committee on Reconstruction, to whom was referred, on the 27th day of January last, the following resolution:

"Resolved, That the Committee on Reconstruction be authorized to inquire what combinations have been made or attempted to be made to obstruct the due execution of the laws; and to that end the committee have power to send for persons and papers and to examine witnesses oil oath, and report to this House what action, if any, they may deem necessary; and that said committee bade leave to report at any time."

And to whom was also referred, on the 21st day of February, instant, a communication from Hon. Edwin M. Stanton, Secretary of War, dated on said 21st day of February, together with a copy of a letter from Andrew Johnson, President of the United States, to the said Edwin M. Stanton, as follows:

Executive Mansion, Washington. D. C., Feb. 21, 1868.

Sir:-By virtue of the power and authority vested in me, as President, by the Constitution and laws of the United States, you are hereby removed from office as Secretary for the Department of War, and your functions as such will terminate upon the receipt of this communication.

You will transfer to Brevet Major General Lorenzo Thomas, Adjutant General of the Army, who has this day been authorized and empowered to act as Secretary of War ad interim, all records, books, papers, and other public property now in your custody and charge.

Respectfully yours. Andrew Johnson. Hon. Edwin M. Stanton, Washington, D. C.

And to whom was also referred by the House of Representatives the following resolution, namely:

"Resolved, That Andrew Johnson, President of the United States, be impeached of high crimes and misdemeanors."

Have considered the several subjects referred to them, and submit the following report:

That in addition to the papers referred to the committee, the committee find that the President, on the 21st day of February, 1868, signed and issued a commission or letter of authority to one Lorenzo Thomas, directing and authorizing said Thomas to act as Secretary of War ad interim, and to take possession of the books, records, and papers, and other public property in the War Department, of which the following is a copy:

Executive Mansion, Washington, Feb. 21, 1868.

Sir: — Hon. Edwin M. Stanton having been this day removed from office as Secretary for the Department of War, you are hereby authorized and empowered to act as Secretary of War ad interim, and will immediately enter upon the discharge of the duties pertaining to that office. Mr. Stanton has been instructed to transfer to you all the records, books, papers, and other public property now in his custody and charge.

Respectfully yours, Andrew Johnson.

To Brevet Major General Lorenzo Thomas, Adjutant General of the United States Army. Washington, District of Columbia.

Official copy respectfully furnished to Hon. Edwin M. Stanton.

L. Thomas. Secretary of War ad interim.

Upon the evidence collected by the committee, which is herewith presented, and in virtue of the powers with which they have been invested by the House, they are of the opinion that Andrew Johnson, President of the United States, be impeached of high crimes and misdemeanors. They therefore recommend to the House the adoption of the accompanying resolution. Thaddeus Stevens, George S. Boutwell, John A. Bingham, C. T. Hulburd, John F. Farnsworth, F. C. Beaman, H. E. Paine.

Resolution providing for the impeachment of Andrew Johnson, President of the United States.

Resolved, That Andrew Johnson, President of the United States, be impeached of high crimes and misdemeanors in office.

The following is a brief synopsis of the debate which ensued: Mr. Stevens, of Pennsylvania. Mr. Speaker, it is not my intention in the first instance to discuss this question; and if there be no desire on the other side to discuss it we are willing that the question should be taken upon the knowledge which the House already has. Indeed, the fact of removing a man from office while the Senate was in session without the consent of the Senate, if there were nothing else, is of itself, and always has been considered, a high crime and misdemeanor, and was never before practiced. But I will not discuss this question unless gentlemen on the other side desire to discuss it. It they do, I shall for the present give way to them and say what I have to say in conclusion.

Mr. Brooke, (Dem. of N. Y.) Mr. Speaker, I had hoped to have an opportunity, at least, to submit a minority report before we entered upon this august proceeding of impeaching the chief executive officer of this Government. But after a session of the Committee on Reconstruction, hardly an hour in length, violating an express rule of this House by sitting during the session—for Rule 72, provides that no committee shall sit during the session of the House without special leave—we have been summoned upon a very partial submission of facts, without any comprehension, in reality, of the charges which are made against the President of they United States, upon a new indictment, in a new form once more, and in a more alarming manner than ever, in this but a partial Congress, representing but a section of a portion of the people—in my judgment not representing the people of the United States at all—to act as a grand jury, with a large portion of that grand jury excluded from the jury-room here; and suddenly, impromptu perhaps, a vote is to be forced this very day—to impeach the President of the United States!

I am utterly inadequate to discharge the duty which has devolved upon me on this august day, the anniversary of the birthday of the Father of his country. I am utterly unable upon this occasion either to do my duty to the people or to express myself with that deep solemnity which I feel in rising to resist this untoward, this unholy, this unconstitutional proceeding. Indeed, I know not why the ghost of impeachment has appeared here in a new form. We have attempted to lay it hitherto, and we have successfully laid it upon the floor of this House. But a minority of the party on the other side, forcing its influence and its power upon a majority of a committee of this House, has at last succeeded in compelling its party to approach the House itself in a united, and therefore in a more solemn form, and to demand the impeachment of the President of the United States.

Sir, we have long been in the midst of a revolution. Long, long has our country been agitated by the throes of that revolution. But we are now approaching the last and the final stage of that revolution in which, like many revolutions that have preceded it, a legislative power not representing the people attempts to depose the executive power, and thus to overthrow that constitutional branch of the Government.

There is nothing new in all this. There is nothing new in what we are doing, for men of the present but repeat the history of the past. We are traversing over and over again the days of Cromwell and Charles I and Charles II, and we are traversing over and over again the scenes of the French revolution, baptized in blood in our introductory part, but I trust in God never again to be baptized by any revolutionary proceeding on the part of this House.

I have not and never have been a defender of all the opinions of General Jackson, but those on the other side who pretend to hold him as authority and those on this side who have ever held him as authority will find that in uttering the opinions which I have I but reutter the opinions which he advanced in his veto of July 10, 1832, when he said:

"The Congress, the Executive, and the court must each for itself be guided by its own opinion of the Constitution. Each public officer who takes the oath to support the Constitution swears that he will support it as he understands it, and not as it is understood by others."

The President of the United States has given his opinion upon the official tenure-of-office act and upon the Constitution of the United States by the appointment of Adjutant General Thomas as Secretary of War ad interim. and because of the exercise of that Constitutional right we are called upon here at once to pronounce him guilty of high crimes and misdemeanors and to demand his deposition and degradation therefor. * * * * *

Mr. Spalding, (Rep. of Ohio). Mr. Speaker, I feel myself to be in no proper frame of mind or heart to attempt rhetorical display on this occasion. I can appreciate the sentiments of the gentleman from New York [Mr. Brooks] when he says the question before us is filled with solemnity; but when he attempts by gasconade to deter members on this side of the House from the conscientious discharge of their duty I say to my friend that he has mistaken his calling. Sir, no more important duty could be devolved upon this House of Representatives than that of considering the question whether articles of impeachment shall be preferred against the Chief Magistrate of the United States; and for long months, ay, for more than a year, sir. I have resisted, with all my efforts and all my personal influence, the approach of that crisis which is now upon us and before us. The President has done many, very many, censurable acts: but I could not, on my conscience, say that he should be holden to answer upon a charge of "high crimes and misdemeanors" until something could be made tangible whereby he had brought himself in open conflict with the Constitution and laws of the Union.

It has seemed to me, sir, for weeks, that this high officer of our government was inviting the very ordeal which, I am sorry to say, is now upon us, and the dread consequences of which will speedily be upon him. He has thrown himself violently in contact with an Act of Congress passed on the 2d day of March last by the votes of the constitutional two-thirds of the Senate and two-thirds of the House of Representatives over his veto assigning his reasons for withholding his assent. Now, it matters not how many acts can be found upon the statute books in years gone by that would sanction the removal of a cabinet officer by the President; the gentleman from New York numbers three. He may reckon up thirty or three hundred and still if, within the last six or nine months, Congress has, in a constitutional manner, made an enactment that prohibits such removal, and the executive wantonly disregards such enactment and attempts to remove the officer, he incurs the penalty as clearly and as certainly as if there never had been any legislation to the contrary. That subsequent enactment, if it be constitutional, repeals, by its own force, all other prior enactments with which it may conflict; and in nothing is that enactment more significant than in this, that the President shall not remove any civil officer, who has been appointed by and with the advice and consent of the Senate, without the concurrence of that body, when it is itself in session.

Mr. Bingham, (Rep.) of Ohio. Mr. Speaker, all right-minded men must concede that the question under consideration is one of supreme moment to till the people of the Republic. I protest for myself, sir, that I am utterly incapable of approaching the discussion of this question in the spirit of a partisan. I repel, sir, the intimation of the gentleman from New York, Mr. Brooks, that I am careless of the obligation of my oath or unconcerned about the supremacy of the Constitution and the laws. I look upon the Constitution of the country as the very breath of the nation's life. I invoke this day upon the consideration of this great question the matchless name of Washington, as did the gentleman, and ask him, in the consideration of the matter now before us, to ponder upon those deathless words of the Father of our Country, wherein he declares that "the Constitution which at any time exists, till changed by an explicit and authentic act of the whole people, is sacredly obligatory upon all" — upon all sir, from the President to the humblest citizen — standing within the jurisdiction of the Republic. Washington but echoed the words that himself and his associates had imbedded in the text of the Constitution, that "this Constitution and the laws passed in pursuance thereof shall be the supreme law of the land." It shall be supreme over every officer; it shall be supreme over every State; it shall be supreme over every territory; it shall be supreme upon every deck covered by your flag in every zone all round the globe. Every man within its jurisdiction, official and unofficial, must bow to the supremacy of the Constitution.

The gentleman says that the issue involved is an issue about an office. I beg the gentleman's pardon. The issue involved is whether the supremacy of the Constitution shall be maintained by the people's Representatives. The President of the United States has assumed, sir, to set himself above the Constitution and the laws. He has assumed to defy the law, he has assumed to challenge the people's Representatives to sit in judgment upon his malfeasance in office. Every man who has considered it worth while to observe my conduct touching this question that has so long agitated this House and agitated this country may have discovered that I have kept myself back and have endeavored to keep others back from making any unnecessary issue between the President and Representatives of the people touching the manner in which he discharged the duties of his great office. I had no desire, sir, to have resort unnecessarily to this highest power reposed by the people in their Representatives and their Senators for the vindication of their own violated Constitution and violated laws. Notwithstanding there was much in the conduct of the President to endanger the peace and repose of the country, yet, so long as there was any doubt upon the question of his liability to impeachment within the text and spirit of the Constitution, I was unwilling to utter one syllable to favor such a proposition or to record a vote to advance it. * * *

Mr. Beck, (Dem. of Ky.) The single question upon which the decision of this House is now to be made is that the President has attempted to test the constitutionality of a law which he believes to be unconstitutional. All the testimony heretofore presented upon which to base an impeachment of the President was decided by even a majority of the Republican members of this House to be insufficient to justify impeachment. All questions growing out of the combinations and conspiracies lately charged upon the President were ruled by the Reconstruction Committee to be insufficient, and were not brought before this House. And the sole question now before us is, is there anything in this last act of the President removing Mr. Stanton and appointing Adjutant General Thomas Secretary of War ad interim to justify his impeachment by this House?

I maintain that the President of the United States is in duty bound to test the legality of every law which he thinks interferes with his rights and powers as the Chief Magistrate of this nation. Whenever he has powers conferred upon him by the Constitution of the United States, and an act of Congress undertakes to deprive him of those powers, or any of them, he would be false to his trust as the Chief Executive of this nation, false to the interests of the people whom he represents, if he did not by every means in his power seek to test the constitutionality of that law, and to take whatever steps were necessary and proper to have it tested by the highest tribunal in the land, and to ascertain whether he has a right under the Constitution to do what he claims the right to do, or whether Congress has the right to deprive him of the powers which he claims have been vested in him by the Constitution of the United States, and that is all that he proposes to do in this case. * * *

Mr. Logan, (Rep. of Ills.) Now, Mr. Speaker, let us examine this question for a moment. It seems to me very plain and easy of solution. It is not necessary, in order to decide whether this action of the President of the United States comes within the purview and meaning of this statute, for us to talk about revolutions or what this man or that man has said or decided. What has been the act of the President is the question. The law is plain. If the President shall appoint or shall give a letter of authority or issue a commission to any person, without the consent of the Senate, he is guilty of—what? The law says of a high misdemeanor. And, under and by virtue of the Constitution, the President can be impeached—for what? For high crimes or misdemeanors. This law declares the issuing a commission to, or giving a letter of authority to, or appointing to or removing from office, any person, without the advice and consent of the Senate of the United States, shall be a high misdemeanor, which is within the meaning and within the pale of the Constitution of the United States.

Now, what is the evidence presented to this body by one of its committees? It is of this character: The Secretary of War, Edwin M. Stanton, has been declared by a solemn vote of the Senate to be the Secretary of War, by virtue of—what? By virtue of an appointment to that office; by reason of the fact that Andrew Johnson did not relieve him from office when he had the right to present the name of somebody else—soon after his taking the presidential chair—not the right to turn him out, but the right to nominate some one else to the senate and ask them to confirm him to that office. That the President failed to do. Then, acting under the provisions of this statute, the President suspended Mr. Stanton as Secretary of War, but the Senate passed upon that act, and decided that the reasons given by the President for suspending Mr. Stanton were not satisfactory; and accordingly, by virtue of this law, Mr. Stanton was confirmed and reinstated in his position as Secretary of War.

Now, all this having been done, it cannot certainly be claimed that the President, in his recent course in regard to Mr. Stanton, has acted without any intention of violating the law. Nor can it be claimed that the President is ignorant of the law. * * *

Mr. Holman (Dem., Ind.) We have listened to much excited eloquence upon this question. It is too manifest that Congress, moving on with that impetus which is ever the result of excessive political power seeks to usurp those powers which are by the Constitution vested in the other Departments of the Government. I do not propose to discuss this subject or answer the speech of the gentleman from Illinois [Mr. Logan] with any words of my own. I have before me a paper which is full of mature wisdom and patriotic counsel, a speech that comes from the solemn past, yet speaks to every heart that beats for the Union of these States, and the prosperity of the American people; a voice that is answered back from every battlefield of the Revolution, and from the grave of every soldier who has fallen in defense of American liberty. I ask that this speech may be read to the House, as appropriate to this day, the 22nd of February, a day once so venerated. I ask that this immortal address to the American people, a speech that needs no revision: a speech in which there can be no interruptions made in this moment of passion, be read to the American Congress, for I can well afford to be silent while that great voice speaks to the Representatives of the people of this Republic.

The Clerk commenced the reading of Washington's Farewell Address.

Mr. Peters: I rise to a question of order. I insist that that address is not germane to the question before the House.

Mr. Holman: I insist that it is exceedingly germane.

Mr. Lawrence, of Ohio: Allow me to suggest that it is germane, for the reason that it relates to retirement from office. [Laughter.]

Mr. Peters: That is too remote.

The Speaker pro tempore, (Mr. Blaine, in the chair.) The Chair sustains the point of order.

Mr. Holman: I hope no gentleman will object to the completion of the reading: it will only occupy the time I am entitled to.

Mr. Peters: It is doubtless very instructive, and so would a chapter of the Bible be, but it has nothing to do with the question before the House, and I insist upon the point of order.

The Speaker pro tempore. Up to this point the discussion has been pertinent and germane to the question—very closely so—and the Chair is compelled to rule, the question of order being raised, that this is not germane or in order. The gentleman from Indiana will proceed in order.

Mr. Holman: I suppose, Mr. Speaker, the Constitution of the United States would scarcely be in order. I will not ask to have it read.

The debate continued in the vein illustrated in the foregoing extracts, from the morning of February 22, notwithstanding it was a National Holiday, such was the haste of the impeachers, to the evening of the 24th, almost without interruption. It was at times illustrated by marked ability, and on the Republican side by intense bitterness and partisan malignity. A large number of the members of the House participated in the debate.

Mr. Thaddeus Stevens then closed the debate in the following arraignment of the President:

Now in defiance of this law, (the Office-Tenure Act) Andrew Johnson, on the 21st day of February, 1868, issued his commission or letter of authority to one Lorenzo Thomas, appointing him Secretary of War ad interim. and commanded him to take possession of the Department of War and to eject the incumbent. E M. Stanton, then in lawful possession of said office. Here, if this act stood alone, would be an undeniable official misdemeanor—not only a misdemeanor per se, but declared to be so by the act itself, and the party made indictable and punishable in a criminal proceeding. If Andrew Johnson escapes with bare removal from office, if he be not FINED AND INCARCERATED IN THE PENITENTIARY AFTERWARD UNDER CRIMINAL PROCEEDINGS, he may thank the weakness or the clemency of Congress and not his own innocence.

We shall propose to prove on the trial that Andrew Johnson was guilty of misprision of bribery by offering to General Grant, if he would unite with him in his lawless violence, to assume in his stead the penalties and to endure the imprisonment denounced by the law Bribery is one of the offenses specifically enumerated for which the President may be impeached and removed from office. By the Constitution, article two, section two, the President has power to nominate and, by and with the advice and consent of the Senate, to appoint all officers of the United States whose appointments are not therein otherwise provided for and which shall be established by law, and to fill up all vacancies that may happen during the recess of the Senate, by granting commissions which shall expire at the end of their nest session. Nowhere, either in the Constitution or by statute, has the President power to create a vacancy during the session of the Senate and fill it without the advice and consent of the Senate, and yet, on the 21st day of February, 1868, while the Senate was in session, he notified the head of the War Department that he was removed from office and his successor ad interim appointed. Here is a plain, recorded violation of the Constitution and laws, which, if it stood alone, would make every honest and intelligent man give his vote for impeachment. The President had persevered in his lawless course through along series of unjustifiable acts. When the so called Confederate States of America were conquered and had laid down their arms and surrendered their territory to the victorious Union the government and final disposition of the conquered country BELONGED TO CONGRESS ALONE, according to every principle of the law of nations.

Neither the Executive nor the judiciary had any right to interfere with it except so far as was necessary to control it by military rule until the SOVEREIGN POWER OF THE NATION had provided for its civil administration. No power but Congress had any right to say WHETHER EVER OR WHEN they should be admitted to the Union as States and entitled to the privileges of the Constitution of the United States. And yet Andrew Johnson, with unblushing hardihood, undertook to rule them by his own power alone; to lead them into full communion with the Union: direct them what governments to erect and what constitutions to adopt, and to send Representatives and Senators to Congress according to his instructions. When admonished by express act of Congress, more than once repeated, he disregarded the warning and continued his lawless usurpation. He is since known to have obstructed the re-establishment of those governments by the authority of Congress, and has advised the inhabitants to resist the legislation of Congress. In my judgment his conduct with regard to that transaction was a high-handed usurpation of power which ought long ago to have brought him to impeachment and trial and to have removed him from his position of great mischief.

I trust that when we come to vote upon this question we shall remember that although it is the duty of the President to see that the laws be executed, THE SOVEREIGN POWER OF THE NATION RESTS IN CONGRESS, who have been placed around the executive as muniments to defend his rights, and as watchmen to enforce his obedience to the law and the Constitution. His oath to obey the Constitution and our duty to compel him to do it are a tremendous obligation, heavier than was ever assumed by mortal rulers. We are to protect or to destroy the liberty and happiness of a mighty people, and to take care that they progress in civilization and defend themselves against every kind of tyranny. As we deal with the first great political malefactor so will be the result of our efforts to perpetuate the happiness and good government of the human race. The God of our fathers, who inspired them with the thought of universal freedom, will hold us responsible for the noble institutions which they projected and expected us to carry out.

The Clerk then read the Resolution and the House proceeded to vote, as follows:

Resolution providing for the impeachment of Andrew Johnson, President of the United States:

Resolved, That Andrew Johnson, President of the United States, be impeached of high crimes and misdemeanors in office.

Yeas—Messrs. Allison, Ames, Anderson, Arnell, Delos R. Ashley, James M. Ashley, Bailey, Baker, Baldwin, Banks, Beaman, Beatty, Benton, Bingham, Blaine, Blair, Boutwell, Bromwell, Broomall. Buckland, Butler, Cake, Churchill, Reader W. Clarke, Sidney Clarke, Cobb, Coburn, Cook, Cornell, Covode, Cullom, Dawes, Dodge, Driggs, Eckley, Eggleston, Eliot, Farnsworth, Ferries. Ferry, Fields, Gravely, Griswold, Halsy, Harding, Higby, Hill, Hooper, Hopkins, Asahel W. Hubbard, Chester D. Hubbard, Hulburd, Hunter, Ingersoll, Jenckes, Judd, Julian, Kelley, Kelsey, Ketcham, Kitchen Laflin, George V. Lawrence, William Lawrence, Lincoln, Loan, Logan, Loughridge, Lynch, Mallory, Marvin, McCarthy, McClurg, Mercur, Miller, Moore, Moorhead, Morrell, Mullins, Myers, Newcomb, Nunn, O'Neill, Orth, Paine, Perham, Peters, Pike, Pile, Plants, Poland, Polsley, Price, Raum, Robertson, Sawyer, Schenck, Scofield, Selye, Shanks, Smith, Spalding, Starkweather, Aaron F. Stevens, Thaddeus Stevens, Stokes, Taffe, Taylor, Trowbridge, Twitchell, Upson, Van Aernam. Burt Van Horn, Van Wyck, Ward, Cadwalader C. Washburn, Elihu B. Washburn, Williams, Washburn, Welker, Thomas Williams, James F. Wilson, John T. Wilson, Stephen F. Wilson, Windom, Woodbridge and the Speaker—126.

Nays—Messrs. Adams, Archer, Axtell, Barnes, Barnum, Beck, Boyer, Brooks, Burr, Cary, Chanler, Eldridge, Fox, Getz, Glossbrenner, Galladay,

Grover, Haight, Holman, Hotchkiss, Richard D. Hubbard, Morrissey, Mungen, Niblack, Nicholson, Phelps, Pruyn, Randall, Ross, Sitgreaves, Stewart, Stone, Taber, Lawrence S. Trimble, Van Auken, Van Trump, Wood and Woodward—47.

On motion of Mr. Stevens the following resolutions were adopted:

Resolved, That a committee of two be appointed to go to the Senate and, at the bar thereof, in the name of the House of Representatives and of all the people of the United States, to impeach Andrew Johnson, President of the United States, of high crimes and misdemeanors in office, and acquaint the Senate that the House of Representatives will, in due time, exhibit particular articles of impeachment against him and make good the same; and that the committee do demand that the Senate take order for the appearance of said Andrew Johnson to answer to said impeachment.

Resolved, That a committee of seven be appointed to prepare and report articles of impeachment against Andrew Johnson, President of the United States, with power to send for persons, papers and records, and to take testimony under oath.

The Speaker announced the following committee under these resolutions:

Committee to Communicate to the Senate to the Senate the action of the House ordering AN IMPEACHMENT of the of the President of the United States.—-Thaddeus Stevens, of Pennsylvania, and John A. Bingham, of Ohio.

Committee to declare articles of Articles of Impeachment against the President of the United States.—George S. Boutwell of Massachusetts; Thaddeus Stevens, of Pennsylvania; John A. Bingham, of Ohio; James F. Wilson, of Iowa; John A. Logan, of Illinois; George W. Julian, of Indiana, and Hamilton Ward, of New York.

CHAPTER VII — IMPEACHMENT REPORTED TO THE SENATE.

THE PRESIDENT'S ANSWER.

On February 25th, 1868, Messrs. Stevens and Bingham, a committee of the House, appeared at the bar of the Senate, and Mr. Stevens said:

Mr. President, in obedience to the order of the House of Representatives, we appear before you, and in the name of the House of Representatives and of all the people of the United States, we do impeach Andrew Johnson, President of the United States, of high crimes and misdemeanors in office; and we further inform the Senate that the House of Representatives will in due time exhibit particular articles of impeachment against hint and make good the same; and in their name we demand that the Senate take order for the appearance of said Andrew Johnson to answer said impeachment.

The committee retired, and after debate the following resolution was adopted by the Senate:

Resolved, That the Message of the House of Representatives relating to the impeachment of Andrew Johnson. President of the United States, be referred to a select committee of seven, to consider and report thereon.

On the 26th, Mr. Howard, from the select committee appointed to consider and report upon the Message of the House of Representatives in relation to the impeachment of Andrew Johnson, President of the United States, reported the following resolution:

Whereas, the House of Representatives on the 25th day of the present month, by two of their members, Messrs. Thaddeus Stevens and John A. Bingham, at the bar of the Senate, impeached Andrew Johnson, President of the United States, of high crimes and misdemeanors in office, and informed the Senate that the House of Representatives will in due time exhibit particular articles of impeachment against him and make good the same; and likewise demanded that the Senate take order for the appearance of said Andrew Johnson, to answer to the said impeachment: Therefore,

Resolved, That the Senate will take proper order thereon, of which due notice shall be given to the House of Representatives.

On the 28th, Mr. Howard, of the Select Committee appointed to prepare rules for the government of trials of impeachment, reported a series of rules, which were adopted by the Senate on March 2nd, after a three days debate.

On the same day, the following gentlemen were elected by the House of Representatives as Managers to conduct the prosecution of the impeachment of the President before the Senate: Hons. Jno. A. Bingham, of Ohio; George S. Boutwell, of Massachusetts; James F. Wilson, of Iowa; Benj. F. Butler, of Massachusetts; John A. Logan, of Illinois; Thomas Wilson, of Pennsylvania, and Thaddeus Stevens, of Pennsylvania.

On March 3rd it was ordered by the Senate:

That the Secretary of the Senate inform the House of Representatives that the Senate is ready to receive the managers appointed by the House of Representatives to carry to the Senate articles of impeachment against Andrew Johnson, President of the United States.

In the Senate, on the 4th, the following formal proceedings were had:

The managers of the impeachment on the part of the House of Representatives appeared at the bar, and their presence was announced by the Sergeant-at-Arms.

The President pro tempore: The managers of the impeachment will advance within the bar and take the seats provided for them.

The managers came within the bar and took the seats assigned to them in the area in front of the Vice President's Chair.

The Speaker of the House of Representatives advanced and took a seat on the right of the President pro tempore of the Senate.

Mr. Manager Bingham:

Mr. President, the managers on the part of the House of Representatives, by order of the House, are ready at the bar of the Senate, whenever it may please the Senate to hear them, to present articles of impeachment and in maintenance of the impeachment preferred against Andrew Johnson, President of the United States, by the House of Representatives.

The President pro tempore:

The Sergeant-at-arms will make proclamation.

The Sergeant-at-arms:

Hear ye! Hear ye! All persons are commanded to keep silence, on pain of imprisonment, while the House of Representatives is exhibiting to the Senate of the United States, articles of impeachment against Andrew Johnson, President of the United States.

The managers then rose and remained standing, with the exception of Mr. Stevens, who was too feeble to do so, while Mr. Manager Bingham read the articles of impeachment, as follows:

Articles exhibited by the House of Representatives of the United States, in the name of themselves and all the people of the United States, against Andrew Johnson, President of the United States, in maintenance and support of their impeachment against him for high crimes and misdemeanors in ofce.

ARTICLE I.

That said Andrew Johnson, President of the United States, on the 21st day of February, in the year of our Lord eighteen hundred and sixty-eight, at Washington, in the District of Columbia, unmindful of the high duties of his office, of his oath of office, and of the requirement of the Constitution that he should take care that the laws be faithfully executed, did unlawfully, and in violation of the Constitution and laws of the United States issue an order in writing for the removal of Edwin M. Stanton from the office of Secretary for the Department of War, said Edwin M. Stanton having been theretofore duly appointed and commissioned by and with the advice and consent of the Senate of the United States, as such secretary, and said Andrew Johnson, President of the United States, on the twelfth day of August in the year of our Lord eighteen hundred and sixty-seven, and during the recess of said Senate, having suspended by his order Edwin M. Stanton from said office, and within twenty days after the first day of the next meeting of said Senate, that is to say, on the twelfth day of December in the year last aforesaid having reported to said Senate such suspension with the evidence and reasons for his action in the case and the name of the person designated to perform the duties of such office temporarily until the next meeting of the Senate, and said Senate thereafterwards, on the thirteenth day of January, in the year of our Lord eighteen hundred and sixty-eight, having duly considered the evidence and reasons reported by said Andrew Johnson for said suspension, and having refused to concur in said suspension, whereby and by force of the provisions of an act entitled "An Act regulating the tenure of certain civil offices," passed March second, eighteen hundred and sixty-seven, said Edwin M. Stanton did forthwith resume the functions of his office, whereof the said Andrew Johnson had then and there due notice, and said Edwin M. Stanton, by reason of the premises, on said 21st day of February, being lawfully entitled to hold said office of Secretary for the Department of War, which said order for the removal of said Edwin M. Stanton is in substance as follows, that is to say:

Executive Mansion, Washington, D. C., Feb. 21, 1868.

Sir: — By virtue of the power and authority vested in me as President by the Constitution and laws of the United States you are hereby removed from office as Secretary for the Department of War, and your functions as such will terminate upon the receipt of this communication.

You will transfer to Brevet Major General Lorenzo Thomas, Adjutant General of the army, who has this day been authorized and empowered to act as Secretary of War ad interim. all records, books, papers, and other public property now in your custody and charge.

Respectfully yours, Andrew Johnson. To the Hon. Edwin M. Stanton, Washington, D. C.

Which order was unlawfully issued with intent then and there to violate the act entitled "An Act regulating the tenure of certain civil offices," passed March 2d, 1867, and with the further intent contrary to the provisions of said act, in violation thereof, and contrary to the provisions of the Constitution of the United States, and without the advice and consent of the Senate of the United States, the said Senate then and there being in session, to remove said Edwin M. Stanton from the office of Secretary for the Department of War, the said. Edwin M. Stanton being then and there Secretary for the Department of War, and being then and there in the due and lawful execution and discharge of the duties of said office, whereby said Andrew Johnson. President of the United States, did then and there commit and was guilty of a high misdemeanor in office.

ARTICLE II.

That on the said twenty-first of February, in the year of our Lord one thousand eight hundred and sixty-eight, at Washington, in the District of Columbia, said Andrew Johnson, President of the United States, unmindful of the high duties of his office, of his oath of office, and in violation of the Constitution of the United States, and contrary to the provisions of an act entitled "An act regulating the tenure of certain civil offices," passed March second, eighteen hundred and sixty-seven, without the advice and consent of the Senate of the United States, said Senate then and there being in session, and without authority of law, did, with intent to violate the Constitution of the United States, and the act aforesaid, issue and deliver to one Lorenzo Thomas a letter of authority in substance as follows, that is to say:

Executive Mansion. Washington, D. C., February 21, 1868.

Sir: — The Hon. Edwin M. Stanton having been this day removed from office as Secretary for the Department of War, you are hereby authorized and empowered to act as Secretary of War ad interim, and will immediately enter upon the discharge of the duties pertaining to that office.

Mr. Stanton has been instructed to transfer to you all the records, books, papers, and other public property now in his custody and charge.

Respectfully yours, Andrew Johnson. To Brevet Major General Lorenzo Thomas. Adjutant General U. S. Army, Washington, D. C.

Then and there being no vacancy in said offce of Secretary for the Department of War, whereby said Andrew Johnson. President of the United States, did then and there commit and was guilty of a high misdemeanor in office.

ARTICLE III.

That said Andrew Johnson, President of the United States, on the twenty-first day of February, in the year of our Lord one thousand eight hundred and sixty-eight, at Washington, in the District of Columbia, did commit and was guilty of a high misdemeanor in office in this, that, without authority of law, while the Senate of the United States was then and there in session, he did appoint one Lorenzo Thomas to be Secretary for the Department of War ad interim, without the advice and consent of the Senate, and with intent to violate the Constitution of the United States, and no vacancy having happened in said office of Secretary for the Department of War during the recess of the Senate, and no vacancy existing in said office at the time, and which said appointment, so made by said Andrew Johnson, of said Lorenzo Thomas, is in substance as follows, that is to say:

Executive Mansion, Washington, D. C., Feb. 21, 1868. Sir:—The Hon. Edwin M. Stanton having been this day removed from office as Secretary for the Department of War, you are hereby authorized and empowered to act as Secretary of War ad interim, and will immediately enter upon the discharge of the duties pertaining to that office.

Mr. Stanton, has been instructed to transfer to you all the records, books, papers, and other public property now in his custody and charge.

Respectfully yours, Andrew Johnson. To Brevet Major General Lorenzo Thomas, Adjutant General, U. S. Army, Washington, D. C

ARTICLE IV.

That said Andrew Johnson, President of the United States, unmindful of the high duties of his office and of his oath of office, in violation of the Constitution and laws of the United States, on the twenty-first day of February, in the year of our Lord one thousand eight hundred and sixty-eight, at Washington, in the District of Columbia, did unlawfully conspire with one Lorenzo Thomas, and with other persons to the House of Representatives unknown, with intent, by intimidation and threats, unlawfully to hinder and prevent Edwin M. Stanton, then and there the Secretary for the Department of War, duly appointed under the laws of the United Stales, from holding said office of Secretary for the Department of War, contrary to and in violation of the Constitution of the United States, and of the provisions of an act entitled "An act to define and punish certain conspiracies," approved July thirty-first, eighteen hundred and sixty-one, whereby said Andrew Johnson, President of the United States, did then and there commit and was guilty of a high crime in office.

ARTICLE V.

That said Andrew Johnson, President of the United States, unmindful of the high duties of his office and of his oath of office, on the twenty-first day of February, in the year of our Lord one thousand eight hundred and sixty-eight, and on divers other days and times in said year, before the second day of March, in the year, of our Lord one thousand eight hundred and sixty-eight, at Washington, in the District of Columbia, did unlawfully conspire with one Lorenzo Thomas, and with other persons to the House of Representatives unknown, to prevent and hinder the execution of an act entitled "An act regulating the tenure of certain civil offices," passed March second, eighteen hundred and sixty-seven, and in pursuance of said conspiracy, did unlawfully attempt to prevent Edwin M. Stanton, then and there being Secretary for the Department of War, duly appointed and commissioned under the laws of the United States, from holding said office, whereby the said Andrew Johnson, President of the Unite States, did then and there commit and was guilty of a high misdemeanor in office.

ARTICLE VI.

That said Andrew Johnson, President of the United States, unmindful of the high duties of his office and of his oath of office, on the twenty-first day of February, in the year of our Lord one thousand eight hundred and sixty-eight, at Washington, in the District of Columbia, did unlawfully conspire with one Lorenzo Thomas by force to seize, take and possess the property of the United States in the Department of War, and then and there in the custody and charge of Edwin M. Stanton, Secretary for said Department, contrary to the provisions of an act entitled "An act to define and punish certain conspiracies," approved July thirty-one, eighteen hundred and sixty one, and with intent to violate and disregard an act entitled "An act regulating the tenure of certain civil offices," passed March second, eighteen hundred and sixty-seven, whereby said Andrew Johnson, President of the United States, did then and there commit a high crime in office.

ARTICLE VII.

That said Andrew Johnson, President of the United States, unmindful of the high duties of his office and of his oath of office, on the twenty-first day of February, in the year of our Lord one thousand eight hundred and sixty-eight, at Washington, in the District of Columbia, did unlawfully conspire with one Lorenzo Thomas with intent unlawfully to seize, take, and possess the property of the United States in the Department of War, in the custody and charge of Edwin M. Stanton Secretary for said Department, with intent to violate and disregard the act entitled "An act regulating the tenure of certain civil offices" passed March second, eighteen hundred and sixty-seven, whereby said Andrew Johnson, President of the United States, did then and there commit a high misdemeanor in office.

ARTICLE VIII.

That said Andrew Johnson, President of the United States, unmindful of the high duties of his office and of his oath of office, with intent unlawfully to control the disbursements of the moneys appropriated for the military service and for the Department of War, on the twenty-first day of February, in the year of our Lord one thousand eight hundred and sixty-eight, at Washington, in the District of Columbia, did unlawfully and contrary to the provisions of an act entitled "An act regulating the tenure of certain civil offices," passed March second, eighteen hundred and sixty-seven, and in violation of the Constitution of the United States, and without the advice and consent of the Senate of the United States, and while the Senate was then and there in session, there being no vacancy in the office of Secretary for the Department of War, and with intent to violate and disregard the act aforesaid, then and there issue and deliver to one Lorenzo Thomas a letter of authority in writing, in substance as follows, that is to say:

Executive Mansion, Washington, D. C., Feb. 21, 1868.

Sir: — The Hon. Edwin M. Stanton having been this day removed from office as Secretary for the Department of War, you are hereby authorized and empowered to act as Secretary of War ad interim, and will immediately enter upon the discharge of the duties pertaining to that office.

Mr. Stanton has been instructed to transfer to you all the records, books, papers, and other public property now in his custody and charge.

Respectfully yours, Andrew Johnson. To Brevet Major General Lorenzo Thomas, Adjutant General, United States Army, Washington, D. C.

Whereby said Andrew Johnson, President of the United States, did then and there commit and was guilty of a high misdemeanor in office.

ARTICLE IX.

That said Andrew Johnson, President of the United States, on the twenty-second day of February, in the year of our Lord one thousand eight hundred and sixty-eight, at Washington, in the District of Columbia, in disregard of the Constitution, and the laws of the United States duly enacted, as commander-in-chief of the army of the United States, dial bring before himself then and there William H. Emory, a major-general by brevet in the army of the United States, actually in command of the department of Washington and the military forces thereof, and did then and there, as such commander-in-chief, declare to and instruct said Emory that part of a law of the United states, passed March second, eighteen hundred and sixty-seven entitled "An act making appropriations for the support of the army for the year ending June thirtieth, eighteen hundred and sixty-eight and for other purposes," especially the second section thereof, which provides, among other things, that "all orders and instructions relating to military operations, issued by the President or Secretary of War, shall be issued through the General of the Army, and, in case of his inability, through the next in rank," was unconstitutional, and in contravention of the commission of said Emory, and which said provision of law had been theretofore duly and legally promulgated by General Orders for the government and direction of the army of the United States, as the said Andrew Johnson then and there well knew, with intent thereby to induce said Emory, in his official capacity as commander of the department of Washington, to violate the provisions of said act, and to take and receive, act upon, and obey such orders as he, the said Andrew Johnson, might make and give, and which should not be issued through the General of the army of the United States, according to the provisions of said act, and with the further intent thereby to enable him, the said Andrew Johnson, to prevent the execution of the act entitled "An act regulating the tenure of certain civil offices," passed March second eighteen hundred and sixty-seven and to unlawfully prevent Edwin M. Stanton then being Secretary for the Department of War, from holding said office and discharging the duties thereof, whereby said Andrew Johnson, President of the United States, did then and there commit and was guilty of a high misdemeanor in office.

And the House of Representatives by protestation saving to themselves the liberty of exhibiting at any time hereafter any further articles, or other accusation or impeachment against the said Andrew Johnson, President or the United States, and also of replying to his answers which he shall wake unto the articles herein preferred against him, and of offering proof to the same, and every part thereof, and to all and every other article, accusation, or impeachment which shall be exhibited by them, as the case shall require, do demand that the said Andrew Johnson may be put to answer the high crimes and misdemeanors in office herein charged against him, and that such proceedings, examinations, trials, and judgments may be thereupon had and given as may be agreeable to law and justice.

ARTICLE X.

That said Andrew Johnson, President of the United States, unmindful of the high duties of his office, and the dignity and proprieties thereof, and of the harmony and courtesies which ought to exist and be maintained between the executive and legislative branches of the government of the United States, designing and intending to set aside the rightful authority and powers of Congress, did attempt to bring into disgrace, ridicule, hatred, contempt and reproach, the Congress of the United States, and the several branches thereof, to impair and destroy the regard and respect of all the good people of the United States for the Congress and legislative powers thereof, (which all officers of the government ought inviolably to preserve and maintain.) and to excite the odium and resentment of all the good people of the United States against Congress and the laws by it duly and constitutionally enacted; and in pursuance of his said design and intent, openly and publicly, and before divers assemblages of the citizens of the United States, convened in divers parts thereof to meet and receive said Andrew Johnson as the Chief Magistrate of the United States, did, on the eighteenth day of August, in the year of our Lord one thousand eight hundred and sixty-six, and on divers other days and times, as well before as afterward, make and deliver, with a loud voice, certain intemperate, inflammatory, and scandalous harangues, and did therein utter loud threats and bitter menaces, as well against Congress as the laws of the United States duly enacted thereby, amid the cries, jeer, and laughter of the multitudes then assembled and in hearing.

ARTICLE XI.

That said Andrew Johnson, President of the United States, unmindful of the high duties of his office, and of his oath of offce, and in disregard of the Constitution and laws of the United States, did, heretofore, to wit, on the eighteenth day of August, A. D. eighteen hundred and sixty-six, at the City of Washington, and the District of Columbia, by public speech, declare and affirm, in substance, that the thirty-ninth Congress of the United States was not a Congress of the United States authorized by the Constitution to exercise legislative power under the same, but, on the contrary, was a Congress of only part of the States, thereby denying, and intending to deny, that the legislation of said Congress was valid or obligatory upon him, the said Andrew Johnson, except in so far as he saw fit to approve the same, and also thereby denying, and intending to deny, the power of the said thirty-ninth Congress to propose amendments to the Constitution of the United States; and, in pursuance of said declaration, the said Andrew Johnson, President of the United States, afterwards, to-wit, on the twenty first day of February, A. D. eighteen hundred and sixty-eight, at the city of Washington, in the District of Columbia, did, unlawfully, and in disregard of the requirements of the Constitution that he should take care that the laws be faithfully executed, attempt to prevent the execution of an act entitled "An act regulating the tenure of certain civil offices," passed March second, eighteen hundred and sixty-seven, by unlawfully devising and contriving, and attempting to devise and contrive means by which he should prevent Edwin M. Stanton from forthwith resuming the functions of the office of Secretary for the Department of War, notwithstanding the refusal of the Senate to concur in the suspension theretofore made by said Andrew Johnson of said Edwin M. Stanton from said office of Secretary for the Department of War; and, also, by further unlawfully devising and contriving, and attempting to devise and contrive means, then and there, to prevent the execution of an act entitled "An act making appropriations for the support of the army for the fiscal year ending June thirtieth, eighteen hundred and sixty-eight, and for other purposes," approved March second, eighteen hundred and sixty-seven; and also, to prevent the execution of an act entitled "An act to provide for the more efficient government of the rebel States," passed March second, eighteen hundred and sixty-seven, whereby the said Andrew Johnson, President of the United States, did then, to wit, on the twenty-first day of February, A. D. eighteen hundred and sixty-eight, at the city of Washington, commit, and was guilty of, a high misdemeanor in office.

Schuyler Colfax, Speaker of the House of Representatives. Attest: Edward McPherson, Clerk of the House of Representatives.

At the conclusion of the reading of the Articles of Impeachment, the President of the Senate responded that "the Senate will take order upon the subject of impeachment, of which proper notice will be given to the House of Representatives."

In addition to the Speaker and Managers, a large number of the members of the House of Representatives were present to witness the extraordinary and impressive proceedings, and at its close all withdrew and the Senate resumed the routine business of the day's session.

On Monday, March 23rd, 1868, the President, by his attorneys, appeared at the bar of the Senate and made answer to the several Articles of Impeachment, as follows:

(Answer to only the 1st, 2nd, 3rd, and 11th Articles, are here given, as the 2nd, 3rd and 11th were the only Articles put to vote—all others being abandoned, and as the 1st Article, though never put to vote, contained practically all there was of the impeachment.)

ANSWER TO ARTICLE I.

For answer to the first article he said: That Edwin M. Stanton was appointed Secretary for the Department of War on the 15th day of January, A. D. 1862, by Abraham Lincoln, then President of the United States, during the first term of his presidency, and was commissioned, according to the Constitution and laws of the United States, to hold the said office during the pleasure of the President; that the office of Secretary for the Department of War was created by an act of the first Congress in its first session, passed on the 7th day of August, A.D. 1789, and in and by that act it was provided and enacted that the said Secretary for the Department of War shall perform and execute such duties as shall from time to time be enjoined on and intrusted to him by the President of the United States, agreeably to the Constitution, relative to the subjects within the scope of said department; and furthermore, that the Secretary shall conduct the business of the said department in such a manner as the President of the United States shall, from time to time, order and instruct.

And this respondent further answering, says that by force of the act aforesaid and by reason of his appointment aforesaid the said Stanton became the principal officer in one of the executive departments of the government within the true, intent and meaning of the second section of the second article of the Constitution of the United States, and according to the true intent and meaning of that provision of the Constitution of the United States: and, in accordance with the settled and uniform practice of each and every President of the United States, the said Stanton then became, and so long as he should continue to hold the said office of Secretary for the Department of War must continue to be, one of the advisers of the President of the United States, as well as the person intrusted to act for and represent the President in matters enjoined upon him or entrusted to him by the President touching the department aforesaid, and for whose conduct in such capacity, subordinate to the President, the President is, by the Constitution and laws of the United States, made responsible.

And this respondent, further answering, says he succeeded to the office of President of the United States upon, and by reason of, the death of Abraham Lincoln, then President of the United States, on the 13th day of April, 1865, and the said Stanton was then holding the said office of Secretary for the Department of War under and by reason of the appointment and commission aforesaid; and, not having been removed from the said office by this respondent, the said Stanton continued to hold the same under the appointment and commission aforesaid, at the pleasure of the President, until the time hereinafter particularly mentioned: and at no time received any appointment or commission save as above detailed.

And this respondent, further answering, says that on and prior to the 5th day of August, A. D. 1867, this respondent, the President of the United States, responsible for the conduct of the Secretary for the Department of War, and having the constitutional right to resort to and rely upon the person holding that office for advice concerning the great and difficult public duties enjoined on the President by the Constitution and laws of the United States, became satisfied that he could not allow the said Stanton to continue to hold the office of Secretary for the Department of War without hazard of the public interest; that the relations between the said Stanton and the President no longer permitted the President to resort to him for advice, or to be, in the judgment of the President, safely responsible for his conduct of the affairs of the Department of War, as by law required, in accordance with the orders and instructions of the President; and thereupon, by force of the Constitution and laws of the United States, which devolve on the President the power and the duty to control the conduct of the business of that executive department of the government, and by reason of the constitutional duty of the President to take care that the laws be faithfully executed, this respondent did necessarily consider and did determine that the said Stanton ought no longer to hold the said office of Secretary for the Department of War. And this respondent, by virtue of the power and authority vested in him as President of the United States by the Constitution and laws of the United States, to give effect to such his decision and determination, did, on the 5th day of August, A. D. 1867, address to the said Stanton a note, of which the following is a true copy:

Sir: — Public considerations of a high character constrain me to say that your resignation as Secretary of War will be accepted.

To which note the said Stanton made the following reply:

War Department, Washington, August 5, 1867.

Sir:-Your note of this day has been received, stating that public considerations of a high character constrain you "to say that my resignation its Secretary of War will be accepted."

In reply I have the honor to say that public considerations of a high character, which alone have induced me to continue at the head of this department, constrain me not to resign the office of Secretary of War before the next meeting of Congress.

Very respectfully yours. Edwin M. Stanton.

This respondent, as President of the United States, was thereon of opinion that, having regard to the necessary official relations and duties of the Secretary for the Department of War to the President of the United States according to the Constitution and laws of the United States, and having regard to the responsibility of the President for the conduct of the said Secretary, and having regard to the permanent executive authority of the office which the respondent holds under the Constitution and laws of the United States, it was impossible, consistently with the public interests, to allow the said Stanton to continue to hold the said office of Secretary for the Department of War; and it then became the official duty of the respondent, as President of the United States, to consider and decide what act or acts should and might lawfully be done by him, as President of the United States, to cause the said Stanton to surrender the said office.

This respondent was informed and verily believed that it was practically settled by the first Congress of the United States, and had been so considered and uniformly and in great numbers of instances acted on by each Congress and President of the United States, in succession, from President Washington to, and including President Lincoln, and from the first Congress to the thirty-ninth Congress, that the Constitution of the United States conferred on the President, as part of the executive power and as one of the necessary means and instruments of performing the executive duty expressly imposed on him by the Constitution of taking care that the laws be faithfully executed, the power at any and all times of removing from office all executive officers for cause to be judged of by the President alone. This respondent had, in pursuance of the Constitution, required the opinion of each principal officer of the executive departments, upon this question of constitutional executive power and duty, and had been advised by each of them, including the said Stanton, Secretary for the Department of War, that under the Constitution of the United States this power was lodged by the Constitution in the President of the United States, and that consequently, it could be lawfully exercised by him, and the Congress could not deprive him thereof; and this respondent, in his capacity of President of the United States, and because in that capacity he was both enabled and bound to use his best judgment upon this question, did, in good faith and with an earnest desire to arrive at the truth, come to the conclusion and opinion, and did make the same known to the honorable the Senate of the United States by a message dated on the 2nd day of March, 1867, that the power last mentioned was conferred and the duty of exercising it, in fit cases, was imposed on the President by the Constitution of the United States, and that the President could not be deprived of this, power or relieved of this duty, nor could the same be vested by law in the President and the Senate jointly, either in part or whole.

This respondent was also then aware that by the first section of "An act regulating the tenure of certain civil offices," passed March 2, 1867, by a constitutional majority of both houses of Congress, it was enacted as follows:

"That every person holding any civil office to which he has been appointed by and with the advice and consent of the Senate, and every person who shall hereafter be appointed to any such office, and shall become duly qualified to act therein, is and shall be entitled to hold such office until a successor shall have been in like manner appointed and duly qualified, except as herein otherwise provided: Provided, That the Secretaries of State, of the Treasury, of War, of the Navy, and of the Interior, the Postmaster General, and the Attorney General shall hold their offices respectively for and during the term of the President by whom they may have been appointed, and one month thereafter, subject to removal by and with the advice and consent of the Senate."

This respondent was also aware that this act was understood and intended to be an expression of the opinion of the Congress by which that act was passed, that the power to remove executive officers for cause might, by law, be taken from the President and vested in him and the Senate jointly; and although this respondent had arrived at and still retained the opinion above expressed, and verily believed, as he still believes, that the said first section of the last mentioned act was and is wholly inoperative and void by reason of its conflict with the Constitution of the United States, yet, inasmuch as the same had been enacted by the constitutional majority in each of the two houses of that Congress, this respondent considered it to be proper to examine and decide whether the particular case of the said Stanton, on which it was this respondent's duty to act, was within or without the terms of that first section of the act; or, if within it, whether the President had not the power, according to the terms of the act, to remove the said Stanton from the office of Secretary for the Department of War, and having, in his capacity of President of the United States, so examined and considered, did form the opinion that the case of the said Stanton and his tenure of office were not affected by the first section of the last-named act.

And this respondent, further answering, says, that although a case thus existed which, in his judgment as President of the United States, called for the exercise of the executive power to remove the said Stanton from the office of Secretary for the Department of War, and although this respondent was of the opinion, as is above shown, that under the Constitution of the United States the power to remove the said Stanton from the said office was vested in the President of the United States; and also this respondent was also of the opinion, as is above shown, that the case of the said Stanton was not affected by the first section of the last named act, and although each of the said opinions had been formed by this respondent upon an actual case, requiring him, in his capacity of President of the United States to come to some judgment and determination thereon, yet this respondent, as President of the United States, desired and determined to avoid, if possible, any question of the construction and effect of the said first section of the last named act, and also the broader question of the executive power conferred on the President of the United States, by the Constitution of the United States, to remove one of the principal officers of one of the executive departments for cause seeming to him sufficient; and this respondent also desired and determined that if, from causes over which he could exert no control, it should become absolutely necessary to raise and have, in some way, determined either or both of the said last named questions, it was in accordance with the Constitution of the United States, and was required of the President thereby, that questions of so much gravity and importance, upon which the legislative and executive departments of the government had disagreed, which involved powers considered by all branches of the government, during its entire history down to the year 1867, to have been confided by the Constitution of the United States to the President, and to be necessary for the complete and proper execution of his constitutional duties, should be in some proper way submitted to that judicial department of the government instrusted by the Constitution with the power, and subjected by it to the duty, not only of determining finally the construction of and effect of all acts of Congress, but of comparing them with the Constitution of the United States and pronouncing them inoperative when found in conflict with that fundamental law which the people have enacted for the government of all their servants. And to these ends, first, that, through the action of the Senate of the United States, the absolute duty of the President to substitute some fit person in place of Mr. Stanton as one of his advisers, and as a principal subordinate officer whose official conduct he was responsible for and had lawful right to control, might, if, possible, be accomplished without the necessity of raising any one of the questions aforesaid; and, second, if this duty could not be so performed then that these questions, or such of them as might necessarily arise, should be judicially determined in manner aforesaid, and for no other end or purpose, this respondent, as

President of the United States, on the 12th day of August, 1867, seven days after the reception of the letter of the said Stanton of the 5th of August, hereinbefore stated, did issue to the said Stanton the order following namely:

Executive Mansion, Washington, August 12, 1867.

Sir: — By virtue of the power and authority vested in me as President by the Constitution and laws of the United States, you are hereby suspended from office as Secretary of War, and will cease to exercise any and all functions pertaining to the same.

You will at once transfer to General Ulysses S. Grant, who has this day been authorized and empowered to act as Secretary of War ad interim, all records, books, papers, and other public property now in your custody and charge. To Hon. Edwin M. Stanton, Secretary of War.

To which said order the said Stanton made the following reply:

War Department, Washington City, August 12, 1867.

Sir: — Your note of this date has been received, informing me that, by virtue of the powers vested in you as President by the Constitution and laws of the United States, I am suspended from office as Secretary of War, and will cease to exercise any and all functions pertaining to the same, and also directing me at once to transfer to General Ulysses S. Grant, who has this day been authorized and empowered to act as Secretary of War ad interim, all records, books, papers, and other public property now in my custody and charge. Under a sense of public duty I am compelled to deny your right, under the Constitution and laws of the United States, without the advice and consent of the senate, and without legal cause, to suspend me from office as Secretary of War, or the exercise of any or all functions pertaining to the same, or without such advice and consent to compel me to transfer to any person the records, books, papers, and public property in my custody as Secretary, But inasmuch as the General commanding the Armies of the United has been appointed ad interim and has notified me that he has accepted the appointment, I have no alternative but to submit, under protest, to superior force.

To the President.

And this respondent, further answering, says, that it is provided in and by the second section of "An act to regulate the tenure of certain civil offices," that the President may suspend an officer from the performance of the duties of the office held by him, for certain causes therein designated, until the next meeting of the Senate, and until the case shall be acted on by the senate; that this respondent, as President of the United States, was advised, and he verily believed and still believes, that the executive power of removal from office confided to him by the Constitution as aforesaid includes the power of suspension from office at the pleasure of the President, and this respondent, by the order aforesaid, did suspend the said Stanton from office, not until the next meeting of the Senate, or until the Senate should have acted upon the case, but by force of the power and authority vested in him by the Constitution and laws of the United States, indefinitely and at the pleasure of the President, and the order, in form aforesaid, was made known to the Senate of the United States on the 12th day of December, A. D. 1867, as will be more fully hereinafter stated.

And this respondent, further answering, says, that in and by the act of February 13, 1795, it was, among other things, provided and enacted that, in case of vacancy in the office of Secretary for the Department of War, it shall be lawful for the President, in case he shall think it necessary, to authorize any person to perform the duties of that office until a successor be appointed or such vacancy filled, but not exceeding the term of six months; and this respondent, being advised and believing that such law was in full force and not repealed, by an order dated August 12, 1867, did authorize and empower Ulysses S. Grant, General of the armies of the United States, to act as Secretary for the Department of War ad interim, in the form in which similar authority had theretofore been given, not until the next meeting of the Senate and until the Senate should act on the case, but at the pleasure of the President, subject only to the limitation of six months in the said last-mentioned act contained; and a copy of the last-named order was made known to the Senate of the United States on the 12th day of December, 1867, as will be hereinafter more fully stated: and in pursuance of the design and intention aforesaid, if it should become necessary to submit the said question to a judicial determination, this respondent, at or near the date of the last-mentioned order, did make known such his purpose to obtain a judicial decision of the said question, or such of them as might be necessary.

And this respondent, further answering, says, that in further pursuance of his intention and design, if possible, to perform what he judged to be his imperative duty, to prevent the said Stanton from longer holding the office of Secretary for the Department of War, and at the same time avoiding, if possible, any question respecting the extent of the power of removal from executive office confided to the President by the Constitution of the United States, and any question respecting the construction and effect of the first section of the said "act regulating the tenure of certain civil offices," while he should not, by any act of his, abandon and relinquish, either a power which he believed the Constitution had conferred on the President of the United States, to enable him to perform the duties of his office, or, a power designedly left to him by the first section of the act of Congress last aforesaid, this respondent did, on the 12th day of December, 1867, transmit to the senate of the United States a message a copy whereof is hereunto annexed and marked B, wherein he made known the orders aforesaid and the reasons which had induced the same, so far as this respondent then considered it material and necessary that the same should be set forth, and reiterated his views concerning the constitutional power of removal vested in the President, and also expressed his views concerning the construction of the said first section of the last mentioned act, as respected the power of the President to remove the said Stanton from the said office of Secretary for the Department of War, well hoping that this respondent could thus perform what he then believed, and still believes, to be his imperative duty in reference to the said Stanton, without derogating from the powers which this respondent believed were confided to the President, by the Constitution and laws, and without the necessity of raising, judicially, any questions respecting the same.

And this respondent, further answering, says, that this hope not having been realized, the President was compelled either to allow the said Stanton to resume the said office and remain therein contrary to the settled convictions of the President, formed as aforesaid respecting the powers confided to him and the duties required of him by the Constitution of the United States, and contrary to the opinion formed as aforesaid, that the first section of the last mentioned act did not affect the case of the said Stanton, and contrary to the fixed belief of the President that he could no longer advise with or trust or be responsible for the said Stanton, for the said office of Secretary for the Department of War, or else he was compelled to take such steps as might, in the judgment of the President, be lawful and necessary to raise, for a judicial decision, the questions affecting the lawful right of the said Stanton to resume the said office, or the power of the said Stanton to persist in refusing to quit the said office if he should persist in actually refusing to quit the same; and to this end, and to this end only, this respondent did, on the 21st day of February, 1868 issue the order for the removal of the said Stanton, in the said first article mentioned and set forth, and the order authorizing the said Lorenzo F. Thomas to act as Secretary of War ad interim, in the said second article set forth.

And this respondent, proceeding to answer specifically each substantial allegation in the said first article, says: He denies that the said Stanton, on the 21st day of February, 1868, was lawfully in possession of the said ofce of Secretary for the Department of War. He denies that the said Stanton, on the day last mentioned, was lawfully entitled to hold the said office against the will of the President of the United States. He denies that the said order for the removal of the said Stanton was unlawfully issued. He denies that the said order was issued with intent to violate the act entitled "An act to regulate the tenure of certain civil offices." He denies that the said order was a violation of the last mentioned act. He denies that the said order was a violation of the Constitution of the United States, or of any law thereof, or of his oath of office. He denies that the said order was issued with an intent to violate the Constitution of the United States or any law thereof, or this respondent's oath of office; and he respectfully, but earnestly insists that not only was it issued by him in the performance of what he believed to be an imperative official duty, but in the performance of what this honorable court will consider was, in point of fact, an imperative official duty. And he denies that any and all substantive matters, in the said first article contained, in manner and form as the same are therein stated and set forth, do, by law, constitute a high misdemeanor in office, within the true intent and meaning of the Constitution of the United States.

ANSWER TO ARTICLE II.

And for answer to the second article, this respondent says that he admits he did issue and deliver to said Lorenzo Thomas the said writing set forth in said second article, bearing date at Washington, District of Columbia, February 21, 1868, addressed to Brevet Major General Lorenzo Thomas, Adjutant General United States army, Washington, District of Columbia, and he further admits that the same was so issued without the advice and consent of the Senate of the United States, then in session; but he denies that he thereby violated the Constitution of the United States, or any law thereof, or that he did thereby intend to violate the Constitution of the United States or the provisions of any act of Congress; and this respondent refers to his answer to said first articles for a full statement of the purposes and intentions with which said order was issued, and adopts the same as part of his answer to this article; and he further denies that there was then and there no vacancy in the said office of Secretary for the Department of War, or that he did then and there commit or was guilty of a high misdemeanor in office; and this respondent maintains and will insist:

1. That at the date and delivery of said writing there was a vacancy existing in the office of Secretary for the Department of War.

2. That notwithstanding the Senate of the United States was then in session, it was lawful and according to long and well established usage to empower and authorize the said Thomas to act as Secretary of War ad interim.

3. That if the said act regulating the tenure of civil offices be held to be a valid law, no provision of the same was violated by the issuing of said order or by the designation of said Thomas to act as Secretary of War ad interim.

ANSWER TO ARTICLE III.

And for answer to said third article, this respondent says that he abides by his answer to said first and second articles in so far as the same are responsive to the allegations contained in the said third article, and, without here again repeating the same answer, prays the same be taken as an answer to this third article as fully as if here again set out at length; and as to the new allegation contained in said third article, that this respondent did appoint the said Thomas to be Secretary for the Department of War ad interim, this respondent denies that he gave any other authority to said Thomas than such as appears in said written authority set out in said article, by which he authorized and empowered said Thomas to act as Secretary for the Department of War ad interim; and he denies that the same amounts to an appointment, and insists that it is only a designation of an officer of that department to act temporarily as Secretary for the Department of War ad interim, until an appointment should be made. But whether the said written authority amounts to an appointment or to a temporary authority or designation, this respondent denies that in any sense he did thereby intend to violate the Constitution of the United States, or that he thereby intended to give the said order the character or effect of an appointment in the constitutional or legal sense of that term. He further denies that there was no vacancy in said office of Secretary for the Department of War existing at the date of said written authority.

ANSWER TO ARTICLE XI.

And in answer to the eleventh article, this respondent denies that on the 18th day of August, in the year 1866, at the City of Washington, in the District of Columbia, he did, by public speech or otherwise, declare or affirm, in substance or at all, that the thirty-ninth Congress of the United States was not a Congress of the United States authorized by the constitution to exercise legislative power under the same, or that he did then and there declare or affirm that the said thirty-ninth Congress was a Congress of only part of the States in any sense or meaning other than that ten States of the Union were denied representation therein; or that he made any or either of the declarations or affirmations in this behalf, in the said article alleged, as denying or intending to deny that the legislation of said thirty-ninth Congress was valid or obligatory upon this respondent, except so far as this respondent saw fit to approve the same; and as to the allegation in said article, that he did thereby intend or mean to be understood that the said Congress had not power to propose amendments to the Constitution, this respondent says that in said address he said nothing in reference to the subject of amendments of the Constitution, nor was the question of the competency of the said Congress to propose such amendments, without the participation of said excluded States at the time of said address in any way mentioned or considered or referred to by this respondent, nor in what he did say had he any intent regarding the same, and he denies the allegation so made to the contrary thereof. But this respondent, in further answer to, and in respect of, the said allegations of the said eleventh article hereinbefore traversed and denied, claims and insists upon his personal and official right of freedom of opinion and freedom of speech, and his duty in his political relations as President of the United States to the people of the United States in the exercise of such freedom of opinion and freedom of speech, in the same manner, form and effect as he has in this behalf stated the same in his answer to the said tenth article, and with the same effect as if he here repeated the same; and he further claims and insists, as in said answer to said tenth article he has claimed and insisted, that he is not subject to question, inquisition, impeachment, or inculpation, in any form or manner, of or concerning such rights of freedom of opinion or freedom of speech or his alleged exercise thereof.

And this respondent further denies that on the 21st day of February, in the year 1868, or at any other time, at the City of Washington, in the District of Columbia, in pursuance of any such declaration as is in that behalf in said eleventh article alleged, or otherwise, he did unlawfully, and in disregard of the requirement of the Constitution that he should take care that the laws should be faithfully executed, attempt to prevent the execution of an act entitled "An act regulating the tenure of certain civil offices," passed March 2, 1867, by unlawfully devising or contriving, or attempting to devise or contrive, means by which he should prevent Edwin M. Stanton from forthwith resuming the functions of Secretary for the Department of War, or by lawfully devising or contriving, or attempting to devise or contrive, means to prevent the execution of an act entitled "An act making appropriations for the support of the army for the fiscal year ending June 30, 1868, and for other purposes," approved March 2, 1867, or to prevent the execution of an act entitled "An act to provide for the more efficient government of the rebel States," passed March 2, 1867.

And this respondent, further answering the said eleventh article, says that he has, in his answer to the first article, set forth in detail the acts, steps, and proceedings done and taken by this respondent to and toward or in the matter of the suspension or removal of the said Edwin M. Stanton in or from the office of Secretary for the Department of War, with the times, modes, circumstances, intents, views, purposes, and opinions of official obligation and duty under and with which such acts, steps, and proceedings were done and taken; and he makes answer to this eleventh article of the matters in his answer to the first article, pertaining to the suspension or removal of said Edwin M. Stanton, to the same intent and effect as if they were here repeated and set forth.

And this deponent, further answering the said eleventh article, denies that by means or reason of anything in said article alleged, this respondent, as President of the United States, did, on the 21st day of February, 1868, or at any other day or time, commit, or that he was guilty of, a high misdemeanor in office.

And this respondent, further answering the said eleventh article, says that the same and the matters therein contained do not charge or allege the commission of any act whatever by this respondent, in his office of President of the United States, nor the omission by this respondent of any act of official obligation or duty in his office of President of the United States; nor does the said article nor the matters therein contained name designate, describe, or define any act or mode or form of attempt, device, contrivance, or means, or of attempt at device, contrivance or means, whereby this respondent can know or understand what act or mode or form of attempt, device, contrivance or means, or of attempt at device, contrivance, or means are imputed to or charged against this respondent, in his office of President of the United States, or intended so to be, or whereby this respondent can more fully or definitely make answer unto the said article than he hereby does.

And this respondent, in submitting to this honorable court this his answer to the articles of impeachment exhibited against him, respectfully reserves leave to amend and add to the same from time to time, as may become necessary or proper, and when and as such necessity and propriety shall appear. Andrew Johnson Henry Stanbery, B. R. Curtis, Thomas A. R. Nelson, William M. Evarts. W. S. Groesbeck. Of Counsel.

CHAPTER VIII — ORGANIZATION OF THE COURT ARGUMENT OF COUNSEL

On Thursday, March 5th, 1868, the Senate of the United States was organized for the trial of the charges brought against Andrew Johnson, President of the United States, by the House of Representatives — Honorable Salmon P. Chase, Chief Justice of the United States, presiding.

The following gentlemen appeared as managers of the prosecution on the part of the House:

Hon. John A. Bingham, of Ohio; Hon. George S. Boutwell, of Massachusetts; Hon. James F. Wilson, of Iowa; Hon. John A. Logan, of Illinois; Hon. Thomas F. Williams, of Pennsylvania; Hon. Benjamin F. Butler, of Massachusetts; and Hon. Thaddeus Stevens, of Pennsylvania.

The following gentlemen appeared as counsel for the President:

Messrs. Henry Stanbery, of Kentucky; Benjamin R. Curtis, of Massachusetts; Thomas A. R. Nelson, of Tennessee; William M. Evarts, of New York, and William S. Groesbeck, of Ohio.

The following gentlemen comprised the United States Senate, sitting for the trial of the President:

California-Cornelius Cole, (R)-John Conness, (R). Connecticut-James Dixon, (D)-Orris S. Ferry, (R). Delaware-Willard Saulsbury, (D)-James A. Bayard, (D). Illinois-Lyman Trumbull, (R)-Richard Yates, (R). Indiana-Oliver P. Morton, (R)-Thomas A. Hendricks, (D). Iowa-James W. Grimes, (R)-James Harlan, (R). Kansas-Samuel C. Pomeroy, (R)-Edmund G. Ross, (R). Kentucky-Thomas C. McCreary, (D)-Garrett Davis, (D). Massachusetts-Charles Sumner, (R)-Henry Wilson, (R). Maine-William Pitt Fessenden, (R)-Lot M. Morrill, (R). Maryland-Reverdy Johnson, (D)-George Vickers, (D). Michigan-Zachariah Chandler, (R)-Jacob M. Howard, (R). Missouri-John B. Henderson, (R)-Charles D. Drake, (R). Minnesota-Alexander Ramsay, (R)-Daniel S. Norton, (D). New York-Roscoe Conkling, (R)-Edwin D. Morgan, (R). Nevada-James W. Nye, (R)-William M. Stewart, (R). Nebraska-Thomas W. Tipton, (R)-John M. Thayer, (R). New Jersey-Alexander G. Cattell, (R)-F. T. Frelinghuysen, (R). New Hampshire-Alexander H. Craigin, (R)-Jas. W.

Patterson, (R). Ohio-John Sherman, (R)-Benjamin F. Wade, (R). Oregon-Henry W. Corbett, (R)-Geo. H. Williams, (R). Pennsylvania-Simon Cameron, (R)-Charles R. Buckalew, (D). Rhode Island-Henry B. Anthony, (R)-William Sprague, (R). Tennessee—David T. Patterson, (D)-Joseph S. Fowler, (R). Vermont-George F. Edmunds, (R)-Justin S. Morrill, (R). West Virginia-W. T. Willey,(R)-Peter (3. Van Winkle, (R). Wisconsin-James R. Doolittle, (D)-Timothy O. Howe, (R). [Forty-two Republicans and twelve Democrats.]

The House bringing the Impeachment was three-fourths Republican — the Senate that tried it was more than three-fourths Republican—the managers on the part of the House were all Republicans—the counsel for the President were three Democrats and one Republican—the President on trial was a Democrat—the interrogatories propounded to witnesses were generally received or rejected, according as their probable answers would make for or against the President—the people of the country at large were, as a rule, rigidly divided on party lines relative to the case, Republicans demanding the conviction of the President and Democrats urging his acquittal. The Chief Justice presiding in the trial was the only strictly nonpartisan factor in the case.

The answer of the President to the Articles of Impeachment having been presented on the 23rd of March, 1868—the replication of the House duly made, and all the preliminary steps completed, the proceedings in the actual trial commenced on the 30th day of March, 1868. Gen. Butler, one of the managers on the part of the House, made the opening argument for the prosecution, from which the following extracts are taken:

The first eight articles set out in several distinct forms the acts of the respondent removing Mr. Stanton from office, and appointing Mr. Thomas, ad interim, differing in legal effect in the purposes for which and the intent with which, either or both of the acts were done, and the legal duties and rights infringed, and the acts of Congress violated in so doing.

All the articles allege these acts to be in contravention of his oath of office, and in disregard of the duties thereof.

If they are so, however, the President might have the POWER to do them under the law; still, being so done, they are acts of official misconduct, and as we have seen, impeachable.

The President has the legal power to do many acts which, if done in disregard of his duty, or for improper purposes, then the exercise of that power is an official misdemeanor.

Ex. gr: he has the power of pardon; if exercised in a given case for a corrupt motive, as for the payment of money, or wantonly pardoning all criminals, it would be a misdemeanor. Examples might be multiplied indefinitely.

Article first, stripped of legal verbiage, alleges that, having suspended Mr. Stanton and reported the same to the Senate, which refused to concur in the suspension, and Stanton having rightfully resumed the duties of his office, the respondent, with knowledge of the facts, issued an order which is recited for Stanton's removal, with intent to violate the act of March 2, 1867, to regulate the tenure of certain civil offices, and with the further intent to remove Stanton from the office of Secretary of War, then in the lawful discharge of its duties, in contravention of said act without the advice and consent of the Senate, and against the Constitution of the United States.

Article 2 charges that the President, without authority of law, on the 21st of February, 1868, issued letter of authority to Lorenzo Thomas to act as Secretary of War ad interim, the Senate being in session, in violation of the tenure-of-office act, and with intent to violate it and the Constitution, there being no vacancy in the office of Secretary of War.

Article 3 alleges the same act as done without authority of law, and alleges an intent to violate the Constitution.

Article 4 charges that the President conspired with Lorenzo Thomas and divers other persons, with intent, by INTIMIDATION AND THREATS, to prevent Mr. Stanton from holding the office of Secretary of War, in violation of the Constitution and of the act of July 31, 1861.

Article 5 charges the same conspiracy with Thomas to prevent Mr. Stanton's holding his office, and thereby to prevent the execution of the civil tenure act.

Article 6 charges that the President conspired with Thomas to seize and possess the property under the control of the War Department by FORCE, in contravention of the act of July 31, 1861, and with intent to disregard the civil tenure-of-office act.

Article 7 charges the same conspiracy, with intent only to violate the civil tenure-of-office act.

Articles 3d, 4th, 5th, 6th and 7th may all be considered together, as to to the proof to support them.

It will be shown that having removed Stanton and appointed Thomas, the President sent Thomas to the War Office to obtain possession; that having been met by Stanton with a denial of his rights, Thomas retired, and after consultation with the President, Thomas asserted his purpose to take possession of the War Office by force, making his boast in several public places of his intentions so to do, but was prevented by being promptly arrested by process from the court.

This will be shown by the evidence of Hon. Mr. Van Horn, a member of the House, who was present when the demand for possession of the War office was made by General Thomas, already made public.

By the testimony of the Hon. Mr. Burleigh, who, after that, in the evening of the twenty-first of February, was told by Thomas that he intended to take possession of the War Office by force the following morning, and invited him up to see the performance. Mr. Burleigh attended, but the act did not come off, for Thomas had been arrested and held to bail.

By Thomas boasting at Willard's hotel on the same evening that he should call on General Grant for military force to put him in possession of the office, and he did not see how Grant could refuse it. Article 8 charges that the appointment of Thomas was made for the purpose of getting control of the disbursement of the moneys appropriated for the military service and Department of War.

In addition to the proof already adduced, it will be shown that, after the appointment of Thomas, which must have been known to the members of his cabinet, the President caused a formal notice to be served on the Secretary of the Treasury, to the end that the Secretary might answer the requisitions for money of Thomas, and this was only prevented by the firmness with which Stanton retained possession of the books and papers of the War office. It will be seen that every fact charged in Article 1 is admitted by the answer of the respondent; the intent also admitted as charged; that is to say, to set aside the civil tenure-of-office act, and to remove Mr. Stanton from the office of the Secretary for the Department of War without the advice and consent of the Senate, and, if not justified, contrary to the provisions of the Constitution itself.

The only question remaining is, does the respondent justify himself by the Constitution and laws?

On this he avers, that by the Constitution, there is "conferred on the President as a part of the executive power, the power at any and all times of removing from office all executive officers for cause, to be judged of by the President alone, and that he verily believes that the executive power of removal from office, confided to him by the Constitution, as aforesaid, includes the power of suspension from office indefinitely."

Now, these offices, so vacated, must be filled, temporarily at least, by his appointment, because government must go on; there can be no interregnum in the execution of the laws in an organized government; he claims, therefore, of necessity, the right to fill their places with appointments of his choice, and that this power can not be restrained or limited in any degree by any law of Congress, because, he avers, "that the power was conferred, and the duty of exercising it in fit cases was imposed on the President by the Constitution of the United States, and that the President could not be deprived of this power, or relieved of this duty, nor could the same be vested by law in the President and the Senate jointly, either in part or whole."

This, then, is the plain and inevitable issue before the Senate and the American people:

Has the President, under the Constitution, the more than kingly prerogative at will to remove from office and suspend from office indefinitely, all executive officers of the United States, either civil, military or naval, at any and all times, and fill the vacancies with creatures of his own appointment, for his own purposes, without any restraint whatever, or possibility of restraint by the Senate or by Congress through laws duly enacted?

The House of Representatives, in behalf of the people join this issue by affirming that the exercise of such powers is a high misdemeanor in office.

If the affirmative is maintained by the respondent, then, so far as the first eight articles are concerned—unless such corrupt purposes are shown as will of themselves make the exercise of a legal power a crime—the respondent must go, and ought to go quit and free.

Therefore, by these articles and the answers thereto, the momentous question, here and now, is raised whether the PRESIDENTIAL OFFICE ITSELF (IF IT HAS THE PREROGATIVES AND POWER CLAIMED FOR IT) OUGHT, IN FACT, TO EXIST AS APART OF THE CONSTITUTIONAL GOVERNMENT OF A FREE PEOPLE, while by the last three articles the simpler and less important inquiry is to be determined, whether Andrew Johnson has so conducted himself that he ought longer to held any constitutional office whatever. The latter sinks to merited insignificance compared with the grandeur of the former.

If that is sustained, then a right and power hitherto unclaimed and unknown to the people of the country is engrafted on the Constitution most alarming in its extent, most corrupting in its influence, most dangerous in its tendencies, and most tyrannical in its exercise.

Whoever, therefore, votes "not guilty" on these articles votes to enchain our free institutions, and to prostrate them at the feet of any man who, being President, may choose to control them.

A few days after this, Judge Curtis, of the President's counsel, spoke on behalf of the President. The first and principal Government of the Articles of Impeachment against Mr. Johnson was violation of the Office-

Tenure Act, which had been passed the year before for the undisguised purpose of restricting the President's power to remove his Cabinet officers, particularly, his War Minister, Mr. Stanton. It was apparent that Mr. Butler had been embarassed in his plea by the proviso of that Act, that members of the Cabinet should hold "during the term of the President by WHOM THEY MAY HAVE BEEN APPOINTED and for one month longer."

Mr. Butler had asked — By whom was Mr. Stanton appointed? By Mr. Lincoln. Whose presidential term was he holding tinder when the bullet of Booth became a proximate cause of this trial? Was not this appointment in full force at that hour. Had any act of the respondent up to the 12th day of August last vitiated or interfered with that appointment? Whose Presidential term is the respondent now serving out? His own, or Mr. Lincoln's. If his own, he is entitled to four years up to the anniversary of the murder, because each presidential term is four years by the Constitution, and the regular recurrence of those terms is fixed by the Act of May 8, 1792. If he is serving out the remainder of Mr. Lincoln's term, then his term of office expires on the 4th of March, 1869, if it does not before.

Judge Curtis struck his first blow at the weak point of General Butler's speech. He said:

There is a question involved which enters deeply into the first eight Articles of Impeachment and materially touches two of the others; and to that question I desire in the first place to invite the attention of the court, namely — whether MR. STANTON'S CASE COMES UNDER THE TENURE-OF-OFFICE ACTS? * * * I must ask your attention therefore to the construction and application of the first section of that act, as follows: "that every person holding an official position to which he has been appointed by and with the advice and consent of the Senate, and every person who shall hereafter be appointed to any such office and shall become duly qualified to act therein, is and shall be entitled to hold such office until a successor shall have been in like manner appointed and duly qualified, except as herein OTHERWISE PROVIDED." Then comes what is otherwise provided. "PROVIDED, HOWEVER, That the Secretaries of State, Treasury, War, Navy, and Interior Departments, the Postmaster General and Attorney General, shall hold their offices respectively for AND DURING THE TERM OF THE PRESIDENT BY WHOM THEY MAY HAVE BEEN APPOINTED."

The first inquiry which arises on this language, is as to the meaning of the words "for and during the term of the President." Mr. Stanton, as appears by the commission which has been put in the case by the Honorable Managers, was appointed in January, 1862, during the first term of President

Lincoln. Are the words "during the term of the President," applicable to Mr. Stanton's case? That depends upon whether an expounder of this law, judicially, who finds set down in it as a part of the descriptive words, "DURING THE TERMS OF THE PRESIDENT," HAS ANY RIGHT TO ADD, "AND DURING ANY OTHER TERM FOR WHICH HE MAY BE AFTERWARDS ELECTED."

I respectfully submit no such judicial interpretation can be put on the words. Then, if you please, take the next step: "During the term of the President by whom he was appointed." At the time when this order was issued for the removal of Mr. Stanton, was he holding the term of the President by whom he was appointed? The Honorable Managers say yes; because, as they, say, Mr. Johnson is merely serving out the residue of Mr. Lincoln's term. But is that so under the provisions of the Constitution of the United States? * * Although the President, like the Vice President, is elected for a term of four years, and each is elected for the same term, the President is not to hold the office absolutely during four years. The limit of four years is not an absolute limit. Death is a limit. "A conditional limitation," as the lawyers call it, is imposed on his tenure of office. And when the President dies his term of four years, for which he was elected and during which he was to hold provided he should so long live, terminates, and the office devolves upon the Vice President. For what period of time? FOR THE REMAINDER OF THE TERM FOR WHICH THE VICE PRESIDENT WAS ELECTED. And there is no more propriety, under the provisions of the Constitution of the United dictates, in calling the term during which Mr. Johnson holds the office of President, after it was devolved upon him, a part of Mr. Lincoln's term, then there would be propriety in saying that one sovereign who succeeded another sovereign by death, holds his predecessor's term.** They (the Cabinet officers) were to be the advisers of the President; they were to be the immediate confidential assistants of the President, for whom he was to be responsible, but in whom he was expected to repose a great amount of trust and confidence; and therefore it was that this Act has connected the tenure-of-office of these Secretaries to which it applies with the President by whom they were appointed. It says, in the description which the Act gives of the future tenure-of-office of Secretaries, that a controlling regard is to be had to the fact that the Secretary whose tenure is to be regulated was appointed by some particular President; and during the term of that President he shall continue to hold his office; but as for Secretaries who are in office, not appointed by the President, we have nothing to say; we leave them as they heretofore have been. I submit to Senators that this is the natural, and, having regard to the character of these officers, the necessary conclusion, that the tenure-of-office of a Secretary here described is a tenure during the term of service of the President by whom he was appointed; that it was not the intention of Congress to compel a President of the United States to continue in office a Secretary not appointed by himself. * * *

Shortly after this, occurred one of the most amusing and interesting incidents of the trial. Mr. Boutwell, who was altogether a matter-of-fact man, though at times indulging in the heroics, ventured, in the course of his argument, upon a flight of imagination in depicting the punishment that should be meted out to Mr. Johnson for venturing to differ with Congress upon the constitutionality of an act of that body. He said:

Travelers and astronomers inform us that in the Southern heavens, near the Southern cross, there is a vast space which the uneducated call the "hole in the sky," where the eye of man, with the aid of the powers of the telescope, has been unable to discover nebulae, or asteroid, or comet, or planet, or star, or sun. In that dreary, cold, dark region of space, which is only known to be less infinite by the evidences of creation elsewhere, the great author of celestial mechanism has left the chaos which was in the beginning. If this earth were capable of the sentiments and emotions of justice and virtue which in human mortal beings are the evidences and pledge of our divine origin and immortal destiny, it would heave and throb with the energy of the elemental forces of nature, and project this enemy (referring to President Johnson) of two races of men into that vast region, there forever to exist in a solitude eternal as life or as the absence of life, emblematical of, if not really, that outer darkness of which the Savior of mankind spoke in warning to those who are enemies to themselves and of their race and of God.

Mr. Evarts followed Mr. Boutwell, and in the course of his argument referred to this paragraph in Mr. Boutwell's speech in the following humorously sarcastic vein, during the delivery of which, the Senate was repeatedly convulsed with laughter. Mr. Evarts said:

I may as conveniently at this point of the argument as at any other pay some attention to the astronomical punishment which the learned and honorable manager Mr. Boutwell, thinks should be applied to this novel case of impeachment of the President. Cicero, I think it is, who says that a lawyer should know everything, for sooner or later, there is no fact in history, science or human knowledge that will not come into play in his arguments. Painfully sensitive of my ignorance, being devoted to a profession which "sharpens and does not enlarge the mind," I yet can admire without envy the superior knowledge evinced by the honorable manager. Indeed, upon my soul, I believe he is aware of an astronomical fact which many professors of the science are wholly ignorant of; but nevertheless, while some of his colleagues were paying attention to an unoccupied and unappropriated island on the surface of the seas, Mr. Manager Boutwell, more ambitious, had discovered an untenanted and unappropriated region in the skies, reserved, he would have us think, in the final councils of the Almighty as the place of punishment for deposed and convicted American Presidents.

At first, I thought that his mind had become so enlarged that it was not sharp enough to observe that the Constitution has limited the punishment, but on reflection I saw that he was as legal and logical as he was ambitious and astronomical; for the Constitution has said "remove from office," and has put no limit to the distance of removal so that it may be without the shedding of a drop of his blood or taking a penny of his property, or confining his limbs. Instant removal from office and transportation to the skies. Truly this is a great undertaking, and if the learned manager can only get over the obstacle of the laws of nature, the Constitution will, not stand in his way.

He can contrive no method but that of a convulsion of the earth that shall project the deposed President to this indefinitely distant space; but a shock of nature of so vast an energy and for so great a result on him might unsettle even the footing of the firm members of Congress. We certainly need not resort to so perilous a method as that. How shall we accomplish it? Why, in the first place, nobody knows where that space is but the learned manager himself, and he is the necessary deputy to execute the judgment of the court. Let it then be provided that, in case of your sentence of deposition and removal from office, the honorable and astronomical manager shall take into his own hands the execution of the sentence. With the President made fast to his broad and strong shoulders, and having already assayed the flight by imagination, better prepared than anybody else to execute it in form, taking the advantage of ladders as far as ladders will go to the top of this great capitol, and spurning there with his foot the crest of Liberty, let him set out upon his flight while the two houses of Congress and all the people of the United States shall shout—"Sic itur ad astra!" But here a distressing doubt strikes me. How will the manager get back. He will have got far beyond the reach of gravitation to restore him, and so ambitious a wing as his should never stoop to a downward flight. Indeed, as he passes through the constellations, the famous question of Carlyle (by which he derides the littleness of human affairs upon the scale of the measure of the heavens,) "What thinks Bootes as he drives his hunting dogs up the zenith in their leash of sidereal fire?" will force itself on his notice. What, indeed, will Bootes think of this new constellation? Besides, reaching this space beyond the power of Congress ever to send for persons and papers, how shall he return, and how decide in the contest there become personal and perpetual — the struggle of strength between him and the President? In this new revolution thus established forever, who shall decide which is the sun and which is the moon? Who determine the only scientific test, which reflects hardest upon the other?

Gen. Logan, one of the managers, appeared for the prosecution, upon the close of the examination of witnesses. The following is a brief extract from his very long and labored argument, and relates to the Tenure-of-Office Act:

It is a new method of ascertaining the meaning of a law, plain upon its face, by resorting to legislative discussions, and giving in evidence opinions affected by the law. As a matter of fact; it is well known the act was intended to prevent the very thing Mr. Johnson attempted in the matter of Mr. Stanton's removal. I think this manner of defense will not avail before the Senate. The law must govern in its natural and plain intendment, and will not be frittered away by extraneous interpretation. The President in his veto message admits substantially this construction.

The proviso does not change the general provisions of the Act, except by giving a more definite limit to the tenure-of-office, but the last paragraph of the Act puts the whole question back into the hands of the Senate according to the general intention of the Act, and provides that even the Secretaries are subject to removal by and with the advice and consent of the Senate.

The Act first provides that all persons holding civil offices at the date of its passage appointed by and with the advice and consent of the Senate, shall only be removed in the same manner. This applies to the Secretary of War. This proviso merely gives a tenure running with the term of the President and one month thereafter, subject to removal by and with the advice and consent of the Senate. The law clearly gives Mr. Stanton a right to the office from the 4th of March, 1865, till one month after the 4th of March, 1869, and he can only be disturbed in that tenure by the President by and with the advice and consent of the Senate.

Yet, although Mr. Stanton was appointed by Mr. Lincoln in his first term, when there was no tenure-of-office fixed by law, and continued by Mr. Lincoln in his second term, it is argued that his term expired one month after the passage of the Tenure-of-Office Act, March 2nd, 1867, for the reason that Mr. Lincoln's term expired at his death. This is false reasoning; the Constitution fixed the term of the President at four years, and by law the commencement of his term is the 4th of March. Will it be said that when Mr. Johnson is deposed by a verdict of the Senate, that the officer who will succeed him will serve for four years? Certainly not. Why? Because he will have no Presidential term, and will be merely serving out a part of the unexpired term of Mr. Lincoln, and will go out of office on the 4th of March, 1869, at the time Mr. Lincoln would have retired by expiration of his term, had he lived. * * *

The only question, then, which remains, is simply this: Has the accused violated that (Tenure-of-Office) Act? No one knows better than this accused the history of, and the purpose to be secured by, that Act. It was ably and exhaustively discussed on both sides, in all aspects. In the debates of Congress it was subsequently reviewed and closely analyzed in a Veto Message of the respondent. No portion of that Act escaped his remark, and no practical application which has been made of it since did he fail to anticipate. He knew before he attempted its violation that more than three-fourths of the Representatives of the people in Congress assembled had set their seal of disapprobation upon the reasons given in the Veto Message and had enacted the law by more than the constitutional number of votes required. Nay, more; he was repeatedly warned, by investigations made looking toward just such a proceeding as now being witnessed in this court, that the people had instructed their Representatives to tolerate no violation of the laws constitutionally enacted.

Mr. Groesbeck, in behalf of the defense, said in closing his argument:

What is to be your judgment, Senators, in this case? Removal from office and perpetual disqualification? If the President has committed that for which he should be ejected from office it were judicial mockery to stop short of the largest disqualifications you can impose. It will be a heavy judgment. What is his crime in its moral aspects, to merit such a judgment? Let us look to it.

He tried to pluck a thorn out of his very heart, for the condition of things in the War Department, and consequently in his Cabinet, did pain him as a thorn in his heart. You fastened it there, and you are now asked to punish him for attempting to extract it. What more? He made an ad interim appointment to last for a single day. You could have terminated it whenever you saw fit. You had only to take up the nomination which he had sent to you, which was a good nomination, and act upon it and the ad interim vanished like smoke. He had no idea of fastening it upon the department. He had no intention of doing anything of that kind. He merely proposed that for the purpose, if the opportunity should occur, of subjecting this law to a constitutional test. That was all the purpose it was to answer. It is all for which it was intended. The thing was in your hands from the beginning to the end. You had only to act upon the nomination, and the matter was settled. Surely that was no crime.

I point you to the cases that have occurred — of ad interim appointment after ad interim appointment; but I point especially to the case of Mr. Holt, where the Senate in its legislative capacity examined it, weighed it, decided upon it, heard the report of the President and received it as satisfactory. That is, for the purpose of this trial, before the same tribunal, res adjudicate, I think, and it will be so regarded.

What else did he do? He talked with an officer about the law. That is the Emory Article. He made intemperate speeches, though full of honest, patriotic sentiments; when reviled, he should not revile again; when smitten upon one cheek he should turn the other.

"But," the gentleman who spoke last on the part of the managers, "he tried to defeat pacification and restoration." I deny it in the sense in which he presented it — that is, as a criminal act. Here, too, he followed precedent and trod the path in which were the footsteps of Lincoln, and which was bright with the radiance of his divine utterance, "charity for all, malice toward none." He was eager for pacification. He thought that the war was ended. The drums were all silent — the arsenals were all shut; the roar of the canon had died away to the last reverberation; the armies were disbanded; not a single army confronted us in the field. Ah, he was too eager, too forgiving, too kind. The hand of conciliation was stretched out to him and he took it? It may be he should have put it away; but was it a crime to take it? Kindness, forgiveness a crime! Kindness a crime! Kindness is omnipotent for good, more powerful than gunpowder or canon. Kindness is statesmanship. Kindness is the highest statesmanship of heaven itself. The thunders of Sinai do but terrify and distract; alone they accomplish little; it is the kindness of Calvary that subdues and pacifies.

What shall I say of this man? He is no theorist; he is no reformer; I have looked over his life. He has ever walked in beaten paths, and by the light of, the Constitution. The mariner, tempest-tossed in mid-sea, does not more certainly turn to his star for guidance than does this man in trial and difficulty to the star of the Constitution. He loves the Constitution. It has been the study of his life. He is not learned and scholarly like many of you; he is not a man of many ideas or of much speculation but by a law of the mind he is only the truer to that he does know. He is a patriot, second to no one of you in the measure of his patriotism. He loves his country; he may be full of error; I will not canvass now his views; but he loves his country; he has the courage to defend it, and I believe to die for it if need be. His courage and patriotism are not without illustration. My colleague (Mr. Nelson) referred the other day to the scenes which occurred in this Chamber when he alone of twenty-two Senators remained; even his State seceded, but he remained. That was a trial of his patriotism, of which many of you, by reason of your locality and of your life-long associations, know nothing. How his voice rang out in this hall in the hour of alarm for the good cause, and in denunciation of the rebellion! But he did not remain here; it was a pleasant, honorable, safe, and easy position; but he was wanted for a more difficult and arduous and perilous service. He faltered not, but entered upon it. That was a trial of his courage and patriotism of which some of you who now sit in judgment on more than his life, know nothing. I have, often thought that those who, dwelt at the North, safely distant from the collisions and strifes of the war, knew little of its actual, trying dangers. We who lived on the border know more. Our horizon was always red with flame; and it sometimes burned so near us that we could feel its heat upon the outstretched hand. But he was wanted for a greater peril, and went into the very furnace of the war, and there served his country long and well. Who of you have done more? Not one. * * * It seems cruel, Senators, that he should be dragged here as a criminal, or that any one who served his country and bore himself well and bravely through that trying ordeal, should be condemned upon miserable technicalities.

If he has committed any gross crime, shocking alike and indiscriminately the entire public mind, then condemn him; but he has rendered services to the country that entitle him to kind and respectful consideration. He has precedents for everything he has done, and what excellent precedents! The voices of the great dead come to us from the grave sanctioning his course. All our past history approves it. How can you single out this man, now in this condition of things, and brand him before the world, put your brand of infamy upon him because he made an ad interim appointment for a day, and possible may have made a mistake in attempting to remove Stanton? I can at a glance put my eye on Senators here who would not endure the position he occupied. You do not think it is right yourselves. You framed this civil tenure law to give each President his own Cabinet, and yet his whole crime is that he wants harmony and peace in his.

Senators, I will not go on. There is a great deal that is crowding on my tongue for utterance, but it is not from my head; it is rather from my heart; and it would be but a repetition of the vain things 1 have been saying the past half hour But I do hope you will not drive the President out and take possession of his office. I hope this, not merely as counsel for Andrew Johnson, for Andrew Johnson's administration is to me but as a moment, and himself as nothing in comparison with the possible consequences of such an act. No good can come of it, Senators, and how much will the heart of the nation be refreshed if at last the Senate of the United States can, in its judgment upon this case, maintain its ancient dignity and high character in the midst of storms, and passion, and strife.

A somewhat startling incident, which for the moment threatened unpleasant results, occurred in the course of the trial. In his opening speech for the prosecution, Mr. Manager Boutwell used this language, speaking of the President:

The President is a man of strong will, of violent passions, of unlimited ambition, with capacity to employ and use timid men, adhesive, subservient men, and corrupt men, as the instruments of his designs. It is the truth of history that he has injured every person with whom he has had confidential relations, and many have escaped ruin only by withdrawing from his society altogether. He has one rule of his life: he attempts to use every man of power, capacity, or influence within his reach. Succeeding in his attempts, they are in time, and usually in a short time, utterly ruined. If the considerate flee from him, if the brave and patriotic resist his schemes or expose his plans, he attacks them with all the energy and patronage of his office, and pursues them with all the violence of his personal hatred. He attacks to destroy all who will not become his instruments, and all who become his instruments are destroyed in the use. He spares no one. * * * Already this purpose of his life is illustrated in the treatment of a gentleman who was of counsel for the respondent, but who has never appeared in his behalf.

The last paragraph of the above quotation manifestly referred to a disagreement between the President and Judge Black, which led to the retirement of that gentleman from the Management of the Defense of the President, a few days prior to the beginning of the trial.

To this criticism of the President, Judge Nelson, of Counsel for Defense, responded a few days later, with the following statement:

It is to me, Senators, a source of much embarrassment how to speak in reply to the accusation which has thus been preferred against the President of the United States. * * *

In order that you may understand what I have to say about it I desire to refer the Senate to a brief statement which I have prepared on account of the delicacy of the subject; and, although I have not had time to write it out as I would have desired to do, it will be sufficient to enable you to comprehend the facts which I am about to state. You will understand, Senators, that I do not purport to give a full history of what I may call the Alta Vela case, as to which a report was made to the Senate by the Secretary of State upon your call. A mere outline of the case will be sufficient to explain what I have to say in reference to Judge Black:

Under the guano act of 1856, William T. Kendal on the one side, and Patterson and Marguiendo on the other, filed claims in the Secretary of State's office to the island which is claimed by the government of St. Domingo.

On the 17th of June, 1867, the examiner of claims submitted a report adverse to the claim for damages against the Dominican government. On the 22d of July, 1867, Mr. Black addressed a letter to the President, (page 10) and another on the 7th of August, 1867. On page 13 it is said that Patterson and Marguiendo acquiesce in the decision. On page 13 it is shown that other parties are in averse possession. On page 15 it is asserted that the contest is between citizens of the United States, and can be settled in the courts of the United States. The contest now seems to be between Patterson and Marguiendo and Thomas B. Webster & Co.

On the 14th of December, 1859, Judge Black, as Attorney General, rejected the claim of W. J. Kendall to an island in the Carribean Sea, called Cayo Verde, and Mr. Seward seems to regard the two cases as resting on the same principle in his report of 17th of January, 1867.

On the 22d of July, 1867, Judge Black addressed a letter to the President enclosing a brief. On the 7th of August, 1867, he addressed another communication to the President. On the 7th of February, 1868, an elaborate an able communication was sent to the President, signed by W. J. Shaffer, attorney for Patterson and Marguiendo, and Black, Lamon &, Co., counsel, in which they criticised with severity the report of Mr. Seward and asked the President to review his decision.

According to the best information I can obtain, I state that ON THE 9TH OF MARCH, 1868, General Benjamin F. Butler addressed a letter to

J. W. Shaffer, in which he stated that he was "clearly of the opinion that, under the claim of the United States its citizens have the exclusive right to take guano there," and that he had never been able to understand why the executive did not long since assert the rights of the government, and sustain the rightful claims of its citizens to the possession of the island IN THE MOST FORCIBLE MANNER consistent with the dignity and honor of the Nation.

The letter was concurred in and approved of by John A. Logan, J. A. Garfield, W. H. Koontz, J. K. Moorhead and John A. Bingham, on the same day, 9th of March, 1868.

This letter expressing the opinion of Generals Butler, Logan and Garfield was placed in the hands of the President by Chauncey F. Black, who, on the 16th of March, 1868, addressed a letter to him in which he enclosed a copy of the same with the concurrence of Thaddeus Stevens, John A. Bingham, J. G. Blaine, J. K. Moorhead and William H. Koontz.

After the date of this letter, and while Judge Black was the counsel of the respondent in this cause, he had an interview with the President, in which he urged immediate action on his part and the sending an armed vessel to take possession of the island; and because the President refused to do so, Judge Black, on the 19th of March, 1868, declined to appear further as his counsel in this case.

Such are the facts in regard to the withdrawal of Judge Black, according to the best information I can obtain.

The island of Alta Vela, or the claim for damages, is said to amount in value to more than a million dollars, and it is quite likely that an extensive speculation is on foot. I have no reason to charge that any of the managers are engaged in it, and presume that the letters were signed, as such communications are often signed, by members of Congress, through the importunity of friends.

Judge Black no doubt thought it was his duty to other clients to press this claims but how did the President view it?

Senators, I ask you for a moment to put yourself in the place of the President of the United States, and as this is made a matter of railing accusation against him, to consider how the President of the United States felt it.

There are two or three facts to which I desire to call the attention of the Senate and the country in connection with these recommendations. They are, first, that they were all gotten up after this impeachment proceeding was commenced against the President of the United States.

Another strong and powerful fact to be noticed in vindication of the President of the United States, in reference to this case which has been so strongly preferred against him, is that these recommendations were signed by four of the honorable, gentlemen to whom the House of Representatives have intrusted the duty of managing this great impeachment against him.

Of course exception was taken to this statement, and to the revisal inferences therefrom, and the authenticity of the signatures mentioned at first denied, and then an effort made to explain them away, but it is unsuccessful.

The incident left a fixed impression, at least in the minds of many of the Senators, that an effort had been made to coerce the President, in fear of successful impeachment, into the perpetration of a cowardly and disgraceful international act, not only by his then Chief of Counsel, but also by a number of his active prosecutors on the part of the House.

It would be difficult to fittingly characterize this scandalous effort to pervert a great State trial into an instrumentality for the successful exploitation of a commercial venture which was by no means free from the elements of international robbery.

Yet to Mr. Johnson's lasting credit, he proved that he possessed the honesty and courage to dare his enemies to do their worst—he would not smirch his own name and disgrace his country and his great office, by using its power for the-promotion of an enterprise not far removed from a scheme of personal plunder, let it cost him what it might. It was a heroic act, and bravely, unselfishly, modestly performed.

CHAPTER IX — EXAMINATION OF WITNESSES AND THEIR TESTIMONY.

The initial proceedings to the taking of testimony, while to a degree foreshadowing a partisan division in the trial, also demonstrated the presence of a Republican minority which could not at all times, be depended upon to register the decrees of the more radical portion of the body. The first development of this fact came in the defeat of a proposition to amend the rules in the interest of the prosecution, and again on the examination of Mr. Burleigh, a delegate from Dakota Territory in the House of Representatives and a witness brought by the prosecution on March 31st. Mr. Butler, examining the witness, asked the question:

Had you on the evening before seen General Thomas? * * * Had you a communication with him?

Answer. Yes sir.

Mr. Stanbery objected, and the Chief Justice ruled that the testimony was competent and would be heard "unless the Senate think otherwise."

To this ruling Mr. Drake objected and appealed from the decision of the Chair to the Senate. It appeared to be not to the ruling per se, that Mr. Drake objected, but to the right of the Chair to rule at all upon the admissibility of testimony. Mr. Drake representing the extremists of the dominant side of the Chamber. There seemed to be apprehension of the effect upon the Senate of the absolute judicial fairness of the rulings of the Chief Justice, and the great weight they would naturally have, coming from so just and eminent a jurist. After discussion, Mr. Wilson moved that the Senate retire for consultation.

The vote on this motion was a tie, being twenty-five for and twenty-five against retiring, whereupon the Chief Justice announced the fact of a tie and voted "yea;" and the Senate retired to its consultation room, where, after discussion and repeated suggestions of amendment to the rules, the following resolution was offered by Mr. Henderson:

Resolved, That rule 7 be amended by substituting therefor the following:

The presiding officer of the Senate shall direct all necessary preparations in the Senate Chamber, and the presiding officer in the trial shall direct all the forms of proceeding while the Senate are sitting for the purpose of trying an impeachment, and all forms during the trial not otherwise provided for. And the presiding officer on the trial may rule all questions of of evidence and incidental questions, which ruling shall stand as the judgment of the Senate, unless some member of the Senate shall ask that a formal vote be taken thereon, in which case it shall be submitted to the Senate for decision; or he may, at his option, in the first instance, submit any such question to a vote of the members of the Senate.

Mr. Morrill, of Maine, moved to amend the proposed rule by striking out the words "which ruling shall stand as the judgment of the Senate," which was rejected without a division.

Mr. Sumner then moved to substitute the following:

That the chief justice of the United States, presiding in the Senate on the trial of the President of the United States, is not a member of the Senate, and has no authority under the Constitution to vote on any question during the trial, and he can pronounce decision only as the organ of the Senate, with its assent.

It is not insisted here that there was any sinister purpose in this proposition, yet the possibilities, in case of its adoption, were very grave. Like the wasp, the sting was in the tail — "he (the chief justice;) can pronounce decision only as the organ of the Senate, WITH ITS ASSENT!" Had that rule been adopted, suppose the Senate, with, its vote of forty-two Republicans and twelve Democrats, upon failure of conviction by a two-thirds vote had refused or refrained on a party vote from giving "its assent" to a judgment of acquittal?

The vote upon this proposed amendment was as follows:

For its adoption — Messrs. Cameron, Cattell, Chandler, Conkling, Conness, Corbett, Cragin, Drake, Howard, Morgan, Morrill of Maine, Morton, Nye, Pomeroy, Ramsay, Stewart, Sumner, Thayer, Tipton, Trumbull, Williams, Wilson — 22 — all Republicans.

Against its adoption — Messrs. Bayard, Buckalew, Cole, Davis, Dixon, Doolittle, Edmunds, Ferry, Fessenden, Fowler, Frelinghuysen, Henderson, Hendricks, Howe, Johnson, McCreery, Morrill of Vermont, Norton, Patterson of New Hampshire, Patterson of Tennessee, Ross, Sherman, Sprague, Van Winkle, Vickers, Willey — 26 — 15 Republicans and 11 Democrats.

So the resolution was rejected—every aye vote a Republican, and all but one, Mr. Trumbull, afterwards voting to impeach the President at tHe close of the trial—eleven Democrats and fifteen Republicans voting nay.

Mr. Drake then offered the following:

It is the judgment of the Senate that under the Constitution the Chief Justice presiding over the Senate in the pending trial has no privilege of ruling questions of law arising thereon, but that all such questions shall be submitted to a decision by the Senate alone.

It would be difficult to formulate a proposition better calculated to taint the proceedings with a partisan bias than this one by Mr. Drake. The impeachment movement was in a very large sense, if not entirely, a partisan enterprise. It had its origin in partisan differences, and was based mainly on differences as to public policies at issue between the two great parties of the country—and while it was expected that every political friend of the President would vote against the impeachment, it was DEMANDED, and made a test of party fealty, that every Republican Senator should vote for his conviction. Therefore, and perhaps it was not illogical from these premises, party leaders of Mr. Drake's inclination should not relish the influence the legal, unbiased and non-partisan rulings of the Chief Justice might have upon his more conservatively inclined fellow partisans of the body.

Mr. Drake called for the yeas and nays, which were ordered, and the vote was yeas 20, nays 30. The personality of this vote was very much the same as on the previous proposition.

The rule proposed by Mr. Henderson was then adopted. The conference closed shortly after, and the session of the Senate was resumed.

The next day, April 1st, Mr. Sumner renewed in the Senate his proposition submitted at the Conference the day before but not acted upon, to change the rules of the Senate in the following form:

It appearing from the reading of the Journal yesterday that on a question where the Senate were equally divided, the Chief Justice, presiding on the trial of the President, gave a casting vote; it is hereby ordered that, in the judgment of the Senate, such vote was without authority under the Constitution of the United States.

The proposition was put to vote with the following result:

Yeas—Messrs. Cameron, Chandler, Cole, Conkling, Conness, Cragin, Drake, Howard, Howe, Morgan, Morrill of Maine, Morton, Norton, Ramsay,

Stewart, Sumner, Thayer, Tipton, Trumbull, Williams, Wilson—21—10 Republicans and 1 Democrat.

Nays—Messrs. Anthony, Bayard, Buckalew, Corbett, Davis, Dixon, Doolittle, Edmunds, Ferry, Fessenden, Fowler, Frelinghuysen, Grimes, Henderson, Hendricks, Johnson, McCreery, Morrill of Vermont, Patterson of Tennessee, Ross, Sherman, Sprague, Van Winkle, Vickers, Willey—26—16 Republicans and 10 Democrats.

So the proposed order was rejected. The trial then proceeded. The answers to a very large proportion of the interrogatories propounded to the witnesses, on both sides, were unimportant, having very little bearing, either way, upon the case. Twenty-eight of those interrogatories, however, were more or less important, and were challenged, seven by the defense, and twenty-one by the prosecution. For convenience of reference, these interrogatories are numbered from one to twenty-eight, inclusive, with the answers thereto, when permitted to be answered, as follows:

Question submitted by Mr. Butler, of the prosecution, April 1st, 1868, to Mr. Walter A. Burleigh, witness on the stand, called for the prosecution:

No. 1.

You said yesterday, in answer to my question, that you had a conversation with General Lorenzo Thomason the evening of the 21st of February last. State if he said anything as to the means by which he intended to obtain or was directed by the President to obtain possession of the War Department. If so, state all he said, as nearly as you can?

Mr. Stanbery objected.

Mr. Drake called for the yeas and nays, which were ordered, and the vote was as follows:

Yeas—Anthony, Cameron, Cattell, Chandler, Cole, Conkling, Conness, Corbett, Cragin, Drake, Edmunds, Ferry, Fessenden, Fowler, Frelinghuysen, Grimes, Henderson, Howard, Howe, Morgan, Morrill of Maine, Morrill of Vermont, Morton, Nye, Patterson of New Hampshire, Pomeroy, Ramsay, Ross, Sherman, Sprague, Stewart, Sumner, Thayer, Tipton, Trumbull, Van Winkle, Willey, Williams, Wilson—39—all Republicans.

Nays-Bayard, Buckalew, Davis, Dixon, Doolittle, Hendricks, Johnson, McCreery, Norton, Patterson of Tennessee, Vickers—11—all Democrats.

So, the Senate decided that the question should be answered.

General Butler repeated the interrogatory, and Mr. Burleigh's answer was as follows:

On the evening of February 21st last, I learned that General Thomas had been appointed Secretary of War ad interim, I think while at the Metropolitan Hotel. I invited Mr. Leonard Smith, of Leavenworth, Kas., to go with me up to his house and see him. We took a carriage and went up. I found the General there ready to go out with his daughters to spend the evening at some place of amusement. I told him I would not detain him if he was going out; but he insisted on my sitting down and I sat down for a few moments. I told him I had learned he had been appointed Secretary of War. He said he had; that he had been appointed that day, I think; that after receiving his appointment from the President he went to the War Office to show his authority, or his appointment, to Secretary Stanton, and also his order to take possession of the office; that the Secretary remarked to him that he supposed he would give him time to remove his personal effects, or his private papers, or something to that effect; and the answer was "certainly." He said that in a short time the Secretary asked him if he would give him a copy of his order, and he replied "certainly," and gave it to him. He said that it was no more than right to give him time to take out his personal effects. I asked him when he was going to assume the duties of the office. He remarked that he should take possession the next morning at ten o'clock, which would be the 22nd; and I think in that connection he stated that he had issued some order in regard to the observance of the day; but of that I am not sure. I remarked to him that I should be up at that end of the avenue the next day, and he asked me to come in and see him. I asked him where I could find him and he said in the Secretary's room up stairs. I told him I would be there. Said he, "be there punctually at 10 o'clock." Said I, "you are going to take possession to-morrow?" "Yes." Said he, "suppose Stanton objects to it—resists?" "Well," said he, "I expect to meet force by force. Or use force."

Mr. Conkling: "Repeat that."

The witness. I asked him what he would do if Stanton objected, or resisted. He said he would use force, or resort to force. Said I, "Suppose he bars the doors?" His reply was. "I will break them down." I think that was about all the conversation that we had there in that connection.

No. 2.

The next disputed interrogatory put by General Butler to the witness was:

Shortly after this conversation about which you have testified, and after the President restored Major General Thomas to the office of Adjutant

General, if you know the fact that he was so restored, were you present in the War Department, and did you hear Thomas make any statements to the officers and clerks, or either of them, belonging to the War Office, as to the rules and orders of Mr. Stanton or of the War Office which he, Thomas, would make, revoke, relax, or rescind, in favor of such officers or employes when he had control of the affairs therein? If so, state as near as you can when it was such conversation occurred, and state all he said, as near as you can.

Mr. Howard demanded the yeas and nays and they were ordered and were as follows:

Yeas—Anthony Cameron, Cattell, Chandler, Cole, Conkling, Conness, Corbett, Cragin, Drake, Henderson Howard, Howe, Morgan, Morrill of Vermont, Morton, Nye, Patterson of New Hampshire, Pomeroy, Ramsey, Ross, Sprague, Stewart, Sumner, Thayer, Tipton, Trumbull, Wilson—28— all Republicans.

Nays—Bayard, Buckalew, Davis, Dixon, Doolittle, Edmunds, Ferry, Fessenden, Fowler, Frelinghuysen, Grimes, Hendricks, Johnson, McCreery, Morrill of Maine, Norton, Patterson of Tennessee, Sherman, Van Winkle, Vickers, Willey, Wilson—22—11 Republicans, 11 Democrats.

So the Senate decided that the question should be answered.

Mr. Butler: With the leave of the President, I will put this question by portions.

Did you hear Thomas make any statement to the officers or clerks, or either of them, belonging to the War Office, as to the rules and orders of Mr. Stanton, or of the office, which he, Thomas, would revoke, relax, or rescind, in favor of such officers and employes when he had control therein?

Answer: The General remarked to me that he had made an arrangement to have all the heads, or officers in charge of the different departments of the office come in with their clerks that morning, as he wanted to address them. He stated that the rules which had been adopted for the government of the clerks by his predecessor were of a very arbitrary character, and he proposed to relax them. I suggested to him that perhaps I had better go. He said, "no, not at all—remain," and I sat down and he had some three or four officers—four or five, perhaps—come in, and each one brought in a roomful of clerks, and he made an address to each company as they came in, stating to them that he did not propose to hold them strictly to the letter of the instructions; but when they wanted to go out they could go out, and when they wanted to come in they could come in; that he regarded them all as gentlemen, and supposed they would do their duty, and he should require them to do their duty; but so far as their little indulgences were concerned—I suppose such as going out across the street or something of that kind—he did not intend to interfere with them; all he expected was that they would do their duty. I waited until he concluded, and we took a walk, and I came away.

Mr. Samuel Wilkinson testified in response to an interrogatory by Mr. Butler:

I asked him (Thomas) to tell me what had occurred that morning between him and the Secretary of War in his endeavor to take possession of the War Department. He hesitated to do so till I told him that the town was filled with rumors of the change that had been made, of the removal of Mr. Stanton and the appointment of himself. He then said that since the affair had become public he felt relieved to speak to me with freedom about it. He drew from his pocket a copy, or rather the original, of the order of the President of the United States, directing him to take possession of the War Department immediately. He told me that he had taken as a witness of his action General Williams, and had gone up into the War Department and had shown to Edwin M. Stanton the order of the President, and had demanded by virtue of that order the possession of the War Department and its books and papers. He told me that Edwin M. Stanton, after reading the order, had asked him if he would allow him sufficient time for him to get together his books, papers, and other personal property and take away with him; that he told him that he would allow to him all necessary time to do so, and had then withdrawn from Mr. Stanton's room. He further told me, that day being Friday, that the next day would be what he called a dies non, being the holiday of the anniversary of Washington's birthday, when he had directed that the War Department should be closed, that the day thereafter would be Sunday, and that on Monday morning he should demand possession of the War Department and of its property, and if that demand was refused or resisted he should apply to the General-in-Chief of the Army for a force sufficient to enable him to take possession of the War Department; and he added that he did not see how the General of the Army could refuse to obey his demand for that force. He then added that under the order that the President had given to him he had no election to pursue any other course than the one that he indicated; that he was a subordinate officer directed by an order from a superior officer, and that he must pursue that course.

Hon. T. W. Ferry, called by the Prosecution, testified from memoranda taken down at the time of the demand of General Thomas for possession of the War Office (Mr. Ferry being present), as follows:

War Department Washington, Feb. 22, 1867.

In the presence of Secretary Stanton, Judge Kelley, Morehead, Dodge, Van Wyck, Van Horn, Delano, and Freeman Clarke, at 25 minutes past 12 m., General Thomas, Adjutant-General, came into the Secretary of War Office, saying, "Good morning," the Secretary replying "Good morning, sir." Thomas looked around and said, "I do not wish to disturb you gentlemen, and will wait." Stanton said, "Nothing private here; what do you want?" Thomas demanded of Secretary Stanton the surrender of the Secretary of War Office. Stanton denied it to him, and ordered him back to his own office as Adjutant-General. Thomas refused to go. "I claim the office of Secretary of War, and demand it by order of the President."

Stanton: "I deny your authority to act, and order you back to your own office."

Thomas: "I will stand here. I want no unpleasantness in the presence of these gentlemen."

Stanton: "You can stand there if you please, but you can not act as Secretary of War. I am Secretary of War. I order you out of this office and to your own." Thomas: "I refuse to go, and will stand here."

Stanton: "How are you to get possession? Do you intend to use force?"

Thomas: "I do not care to use force, but my mind is made up as to what I shall do. I want no unpleasantness, though. I shall stay here and act as Secretary of War."

Stanton: "You shall not, and I order you, as your superior, back to your own office."

Thomas: "I will not obey you, but will stand here and remain here."

Stanton: "You call stand there if you please. I order you out of this office to your own. I am Secretary of War, and your superior."

Thomas then went into opposite room across hall (General Schriver's) and commenced ordering General Schriver and General Townsend. Stanton entered, followed by Moorhead and Ferry, and ordered those generals not to obey or pay any attention to General Thomas' orders; that he denied his assumed authority as Secretary of War ad interim, and forbade their obedience of his directions. "I am Secretary of War, and I now order you, General Thomas out of this place to your own quarters."

Thomas: "I will not go, I shall discharge the functions of Secretary of War."

Stanton: "You will not."

Thomas: "I shall require the mails of the War Department to be delivered to me and shall transact the business of the office."

Stanton: "You shall not have them, and I order you to your room."

No. 3.

On Tuesday, April 2nd, the prosecution put in evidence a letter from the President to Gen. Grant, dated Feb. 10, 1868, in answer to a prior letter front the General. The President's letter, as introduced in evidence, purported to contain certain enclosures relating to the subject matter of the President's letter. The following is that portion of the President's letter which speaks of the enclosures accompanying and included therein:

GENERAL: The extraordinary character of your letter of the 3rd instant would seem to preclude any reply on my part; but the manner in which publicity has been given to the correspondence of which that letter forms a part, and the grave questions which are involved, induce me to take this mode of giving, as a proper sequel to the communications which have passed between us, the statements of the five members of the cabinet who were present on the occasion of our conversation on the 14th ultimo. Copies of the letters which they have addressed to me upon the subject are accordingly herewith enclosed.

Counsel for the President objected that the letter introduced by the prosecution was not evidence in the case unless the managers should also produce the enclosures therein referred to and made a part of the same. The following was the vote on sustaining the objection:

Yeas—Bayard, Conkling, Davis, Dixon, Doolittle, Fowler, Grimes, Henderson, Hendricks, Johnson, McCreery, Morrill of Vermont Norton, Patterson of Tennessee, Ross, Sprague, Trumbull, Van Winkle, Vickers and Willey—20—10 Republicans and 10 Democrats.

Nays—Anthony, Buckalew, Cameron, Cattell, Chandler, Cole, Conness, Corbett, Cragin, Drake, Edmunds, Ferry, Fessenden, Frelinghuysen, Howard, Howe, Morgan, Morrill of Maine, Nye, Patterson of New Hampshire, Pomeroy, Ramsay, Sherman, Stewart, Sumner, Thayer, Tipton, Williams, and Wilson—29—28 Republicans and 1 Democrat.

So the evidence offered by the prosecution was admitted as offered, without the enclosures referred to, the objection by the defense not being sustained. (For these rejected enclosures see appendix.)

No. 4.

The prosecution offered to prove (Mr. Geo. A. Wallace, of the Treasury Department, on the stand):

That after the President had determined on the removal of Mr. Stanton, Secretary of War, in spite of the action of the Senate, there being no vacancy in the office of Assistant Secretary of the Treasury, the President unlawfully appointed his friend and theretofore private secretary, Edmund Cooper, to that position, as one of the means by which he intended to defeat the tenure of civil office act and other laws of Congress.

After debate and Mr. Wallace's answer in explanation of the usages of the department in the disbursement of moneys, during which it was shown that no moneys could be drawn out of the treasury on the order of the assistant secretary except when authorized by the Secretary of the Treasury to draw warrants therefor, a vote was taken, and resulted as follows:

Yeas—Anthony, Cameron, Cattell, Chandler, Cole, Conkling, Corbett, Cragin, Drake, Howard, Howe, Morgan, Morrill of Vermont, Nye, Pomeroy, Ramsey, Ross, Sprague, Sumner, Thayer, Tipton and Wilson—-22—all Republicans.

Nays—Bayard, Buckalew, Conness, Davis, Dixon, Doolittle, Edmunds, Ferry, Fessenden, Fowler, Frelinghuysen, Grimes, Henderson, Hendricks, Johnson, McCreery, Morrill of Maine, Norton, Patterson of New Hampshire, Patterson of Tennessee, Sherman, Stewart, Trumbull, Van Winkle, Vickers, Willey and Williams—27—16 Republicans, 11 Democrats.

So the testimony was not received, as it was shown in the debate thereon that it would prove nothing against the President which the prosecution had expected to prove.

No. 5.

Friday April 3rd, the Prosecution offered two telegraphic messages, one from Lewis E. Parsons to Andrew Johnson, and the other Mr. Johnson's answer, as follows:

Montgomery, Ala., Jan. 17, 1867.

Legislature in session. Efforts making to reconsider vote on Constitutional Amendment. Report from Washington says it is probable an enabling act will pass. We do not know what to believe. I find nothing here.

(The State Legislature had previously rejected the Constitutional Amendment.)

The response is:

U. S. Military Telegraph. Executive Office, Washington D. C., Jan. 17, 1867.

What possible good can be obtained by reconsidering the Constitutional Amendment? I know of none in the present posture of affairs; and I do not believe that the people of the whole country will sustain any set of individuals in attempts to change the whole character of our Government by enabling acts or otherwise. I believe, on the contrary, that they will eventually uphold all who have patriotism and courage to stand by the Constitution, and who place their confidence in the people. There should be no faltering on the part of those who are honest in their determination to sustain the several co-ordinate Departments of the Government in accordance with its original design. Andrew Johnson. Hon. L. E. Parsons, Montgomery, Alabama.

The yeas and nays were demanded by Mr. Drake, and were as follows:

Yeas—Anthony, Cameron. Cattell, Chandler, Cole, Conkling, Conness, Corbett, Cragin, Drake, Henderson, Howard, Morgan, Morrill of Vermont, Nye, Patterson of New Hampshire, Pomeroy, Ramsay, Ross, Sherman, Sprague, Stewart, Sumner, Thayer, Tipton, Willey, Wilson—27—all Republicans.

Nays—Buckalew, Davis, Dixon, Doolittle, Edmunds, Ferry, Fessenden, Fowler, Frelinghuysen, McCreery, Morrill of Maine, Norton, Patterson of Tennessee, Trumbull, Van Winkle, Vickers, Williams—17—8 Democrats and 9 Republicans.

So the testimony was decided admissible, and was claimed by Mr. Manager Boutwell to be in substantiation of the charges contained in the eleventh article.

No. 6.

The prosecution offered in evidence a copy of the Cleveland Leader, a newspaper purporting to contain a speech delivered by Mr. Johnson at the City of Cleveland, Ohio, on September 30th, 1866, as evidence against the President. It was objected to by the defense, and on the call by Mr. Conness and Mr. Sumner the yeas and nays were ordered, and the vote was as follows:

Yeas—Anthony, Cameron, Cattell. Chandler, Cole, Conkling, Conness, Corbett, Cragin, Drake, Edmunds, Ferry, Fessenden, Frelinghuysen, Henderson, Howard, Johnson, Morgan, Morrill of Maine, Morrill of Vermont, Norton, Nye, Patterson of New Hampshire, Pomeroy, Ramsay, Ross, Sherman, Sprague, Stewart, Sumner, Thayer, Tipton, Van Winkle, Willey, Williams—35—33 Republicans and 2 Democrats.

Nays—Buckalew, Davis, Dixon, Doolittle, Fowler, Hendricks, Howe, McCreery, Patterson of Tennessee, Trumbull, Vickers—11—8 Democrats and 3 Republicans.

So the evidence was received. It related to the tenth article, and was based on a certain speech delivered by Mr. Johnson at Cleveland, Ohio.

No. 7.

Saturday, April 10th, 1868, General Lorenzo Thomas on the stand, called by the Defense. Mr. Stanbery asked him, with reference to certain interviews with the President: What occurred between the President and yourself at that second interview on the 21st (February)?

Mr. Drake demanded the yeas and nays, and they were ordered and were as follows:

Yeas—Anthony, Bayard, Buckalew, Cattell, Cole, Conkling, Corbett, Davis, Dixon, Doolittle, Edmunds, Ferry, Fessenden, Fowler, Frelinghuysen, Grimes, Henderson, Hendricks, Howe, Johnson, McCreery, Morgan, Morrill of Maine, Morrill of Vermont, Morton, Norton, Patterson of New Hampshire, Patterson of Tennessee, Pomeroy, Ross, Sherman, Sprague, Stewart, Sumner, Tipton, Trumbull, Van Winkle, Vickers, Willey, Williams, Wilson, Yates—42-31 Republicans and 11 Democrats.

Nays—Cameron, Chandler, Conness, Cragin, Drake, Harlan, Howard, Nye, Ramsay, Thayer—10—all Republicans.

So the testimony was received, and General Thomas' answer was:

I stated to the President that I had delivered the communication, and that Mr. Stanton gave this answer: "Do you wish me to vacate at once, or will you give me time to take away my private property?" and that I replied, "At your pleasure." I then said that after delivering the copy of the letter to him, he said: "I do not know whether I will obey your instructions or resist them." This I mentioned to the President and his answer was: "Very well, go and take charge of the office and perform the duties." * * *

Question by Mr. Stanbery: What first happened to you the next morning?

Answer: The first thing that happened to me the next morning was the appearance at my house of the marshal of the district, with an assistant marshal and a constable, and he arrested me.

Question: What time in the morning was that?

Answer: About 8 o'clock, before I had my breakfast. The command was to appear forthwith. I asked if he would permit me to see the President. * * * He went with me to the President's and went into the room where the President was. I stated that I had been arrested, at whose suit I did not know. He said, "very well, that is the place I want it in the courts." * * * I was required to give bail in $5,000. I asked the judge what it meant. He said it was simply to present myself there at half past ten the following Wednesday. I asked him if it suspended me from any of my functions. He said, "no, it has nothing to do with them." * * * I went immediately from there, first stopping at the President's on my way, and stating that I had given bail. He made the same answer, "very well, we want it in the courts."

Question: Did the President at any time prior to or including the 9th of March, authorize or direct you to use force, intimidation or threats, to get possession of the War Office?

Answer: He did not.

No. 8.

April 11, Gen. Sherman was called by the defense. In the course of his examination Mr. Stanbery asked him the following question:

In that interview, (referring to a previously mentioned interview between the General and the President in the presence of Gen. Grant) what conversation took place between the President and you in regard to the removal of Mr. Stanton?

Mr. Butler objected and the yeas and nays were ordered.

Yeas—Anthony, Bayard, Buckalew, Cole, Davis, Dixon, Doolittle, Fessenden, Fowler, Grimes, Hendricks, Johnson, McCreery, Morgan, Norton, Patterson of Tennessee, Ross, Sprague, Sumner, Trumbull, Van Winkle, Vickers, and Willey—23—22 Republicans and 11 Democrats.

Nays—Cameron, Cattell, Chandler, Conkling, Conness, Corbett, Cragin, Drake, Edmunds, Ferry, Frelinghuysen, Harlan, Henderson, Howard, Morrill of Maine, Morrill of Vermont. Morton, Nye, Patterson of New Hampshire, Pomeroy, Ramsay, Sherman, Stewart, Thayer, Tipton, Williams, Wilson and Yates—28—all Republicans.

So the proffered testimony was refused.

No. 9.

Counsel for defense put the following question to Gen. Sherman:

At the first interview at which the tender of the duties of the Secretary of War ad interim was made to you by the President, did anything further pass between you and the President in reference to the tender or your acceptance of it?

Mr. Drake demanded the yeas and nays, and they were as follows:

Yeas—Anthony, Bayard, Buckalew, Cole, Davis, Dixon, Doolittle, Fessenden, Fowler, Grimes, Hendricks, Johnson, McCreery, Morgan, Norton, Patterson of Tennessee, Ross, Sprague, Sumner, Trumbull, Van Winkle, Vickers, and Willey—23—12 Republicans and 11 Democrats.

Nays—Cameron, Cattell, Chandler, Conkling, Conness, Corbett, Cragin, Drake, Edmunds, Ferry, Frelinhuysen, Harlan, Henderson, Howard,

Howe, Morrill of Maine, Morrill of Vermont, Morton, Nye, Patterson of New Hampshire, Pomeroy, Ramsay, Sherman, Stewart, Thayer, Tipton, Williams, Wilson and Yates — 29 — all Republicans.

So the proffered testimony was refused.

No. 10.

The next question put to Gen. Sherman by the Defense was:

In either of these conversations did the President say to you that his object in appointing you was that he might thus get the question of Mr. Stanton's right to the office before the Supreme Court?

Objected to by Prosecution, and yeas and nays were taken:

Yeas — Anthony, Bayard, Fowler, McCreery, Patterson of Tennessee, Ross, and Vickers — 7 — 4 Democrats, 3 Republicans.

Nays — Buckalew, Cameron, Cattell, Chandler, Cole, Conkling, Conness, Corbett, Cragin, Davis, Dixon, Doolittle, Drake, Edmunds, Ferry, Fessenden, Frelinghuysen, Grimes, Harlan, Henderson, Hendricks, Howard, Howe, Johnson, Morgan, Morrill of Maine, Morrill of Vermont, Morton, Norton, Nye, Patterson of New Hampshire, Pomeroy, Ramsey, Sherman, Sprague, Stewart, Thayer, Tipton, Trumbull, Van Winkle, Willey, Williams, Wilson, and Yates — 44 — 37 Republicans and 7 Democrats.

So this proffered testimony was refused.

No. 11.

Mr. Stanbery, for Defense, suggested that the question had undoubtedly been overruled upon matter of form, at least, and put it again in this form.

Was anything said at either of those interviews by the President, as to any purpose of getting the question of Mr. Stanton's right to the office before the courts?

This was put and determined in the negative without a division, when Mr. Henderson offered it again in this form: Did the President, in tendering you the appointment of Secretary of War ad interim. express the object or purpose of so doing?

Prosecution again objected, and the yeas and nays were taken:

Yeas — Anthony, Bayard, Buckalew, Davis, Dixon, Doolittle, Fessenden, Fowler, Grimes, Henderson, Hendricks, Johnson, McCreery, Morrill of Maine, Morton, Norton, Patterson of Tennessee, Ross, Sherman, Sprague, Sumner, Trumbull, Van Winkle, Vickers, and Willey-25 — 14 Republicans and 11 Democrats.

Nays — Cameron, Cattell, Chandler, Cole, Conkling, Conness, Corbett, Cragin, Drake, Edmunds, Ferry, Frelinghuysen, Harlan, Howard, Howe,

Morgan, Morrill of Vermont, Nye, Patterson of New Hampshire, Pomeroy, Ramsey, Stewart, Thayer, Tipton, Williams, Wilson, and Yates — 27 — all Republicans.

So the proffered evidence was refused.

No. 12.

April 13, 1868 — General Sherman's examination continued:

Question: After the restoration of Mr. Stanton to office, did you form an opinion whether the good of the service required a Secretary of War other than Mr. Stanton; and if so, did you communicate that opinion to the President?

Mr. Conness called for the yeas and nays and they were ordered, and resulted:

Yeas — Anthony, Bayard, Buckalew, Dixon, Doolittle. Fowler, Grimes, Hendricks, Johnson, McCreery Patterson, of Tennessee, Ross, Trumbull, Van Winkle and Vickers — 15 — 6 Republicans and 9 Democrats.

Nays — Cameron, Cattell, Chandler, Cole, Conkling, Conness, Corbett, Cragin, Davis, Drake, Edmunds, Fessenden, Frelinghuysen, Harlan, Henderson, Howard, Howe, Morgan, Morrill of Maine, Morrill of Vermont, Morton, Norton, Nye, Patterson of New Hampshire, Pomeroy, Ramsay, Sherman, Stewart, Thayer, Tipton, Willey, Williams, Wilson and Yates — 35 — 33 Republicans and 2 Democrats.

So the proffered testimony was refused.

No. 13.

The next question asked of Gen. Sherman was by Senator Johnson:

Question: Did you at any time, and when, before the President gave the order for the removal of Mr. Stanton as Secretary of War, advise the President to appoint some other person than Mr. Stanton?

Mr. Drake demanded the yeas and nays, which were as following:

Yeas — Anthony, Bayard, Buckalew, Dixon, Doolittle, Edmunds, Fessenden, Fowler, Grimes, Henderson, Hendricks, Johnson, McCreery, Patterson of Tennessee, Ross, Trumbull, Van Winkle, Vickers — 18-9 — Republicans and 9 Democrats.

Nays — Cameron, Cattell, Chandler, Cole, Conkling, Conness, Corbett, Cragin, Dixon, Drake, Ferry, Frelinghuysen, Harlan, Howard, Howe, Morgan, Morrill of Maine, Morrill of Vermont, Morton, Norton, Nye, Patterson of New Hampshire, Pomeroy, Ramsay, Sherman, Stewart, Thayer, Tipton, Willey Williams, Wilson, Yates — 33 — 30 Republicans and 2 Democrats.

So the proffered testimony was refused.

No. 14.

Counsel for defense offered:

A warrant of arrest of Gen. Thomas, dated February 22, 1868, and the affidavit on which the warrant issued.

(This warrant had been issued on the affidavit of Mr. Stanton.)

The yeas and nays were as follows:

Yeas—Anthony, Bayard, Buckalew, Cattell, Cole, Corbett, Cragin, Davis, Dixon, Doolittle, Fessenden, Fowler, Frelinghuysen, Grimes, Henderson, Hendricks, Johnson, McCreery, Morrill of Maine, Morrill of Vermont, Morton, Norton, Patterson of New Hampshire, Patterson of Tennessee, Pomeroy, Ross, Sherman, Sumner, Trumbull, Van Winkle, Vickers, Willey, Williams, Yates—34—24 Republicans and 10 Democrats.

Nays—Cameron, Conkling, Chandler, Conness, Drake, Edmunds, Ferry, Harlan, Howard, Howe, Morgan, Nye, Ramsay, Stewart, Thayer, Tipton, Wilson—17—all Republicans.

So the warrant was received in evidence.

That warrant was issued by Judge Carter, Chief Justice of the Supreme Court of the District of Columbia, upon the complaint of Edwin M. Stanton, and charged Thomas with attempting forcibly to seize and take possession of the War Office, in violation of the fifth section of the Tenure-of-Office Act. The warrant was as follows:

UNITED STATES OF AMERICA, DISTRICT OF COLUMBIA.

To David S. Gooding, United States Marshal for the District of Columbia:

I, David K. Carter, Chief Justice of the Supreme Court for the District of Columbia, hereby command you to arrest Lorenzo Thomas, of said District, forthwith, and that you have the said Lorenzo before me at the chambers of the said Supreme Court in the City of Washington, forthwith, to answer to the charge of a high misdemeanor in this, that on the 21st day of February, 1868, in the District of Columbia, he did unlawfully accept the appointment of the office of Secretary of War ad interim, and did then and there unlawfully hold and exercise and attempt to hold and exercise the said office contrary to the provisions of the act entitled "An Act regulating the tenure of certain civil offices, passed March 2, 1867, and hereof fail not, but make due return.

Given under my hand and seal of said court this 22nd day of February, 1868,

D. K. Carter. Chief Justice of the Supreme Court of the District of Columbia.

Attest: R. J. Meigs, Clerk. (Marshal's Return). Washington, D. C., February 22, 1868.

The within writ came to hand at 7 o'clock a.m. and was served by me on the said Lorenzo Thomas at 8 o'clock a.m, and I now return this writ and bring him before Chief Justice Carter at 9 o'clock a. m. of to-day.

David S. Gooding, U. S. Marshal, D. C.

No. 15.

Mr. Johnson, (of the Court,) asked this question of General Sherman, witness on the stand: When the President tendered to you the office of Secretary of War, ad interim, on the 27th of January, 1868, and on the 31st of the same month and year, did he, at the very time of making such tender, state to you what his purpose in so doing was?

Counsel for Prosecution objected, and Mr. Drake called for the yeas and nays, which were taken, as follows:

Yeas—Anthony, Bayard, Buckalew, Cole, Davis, Dixon, Doolittle, Fessenden, Fowler, Frelinghuysen, Grimes, Henderson, Johnson, McCreery, Morrill of Maine, Morrill of Vermont, Morton, Norton, Patterson of Tennessee, Ross, Sherman, Sumner, Trumbull, Van Winkle, Vickers, Willey—16—16 Republicans and 10 Democrats.

Nays-Cattell, Chandler, Conkling, Conness, Corbett, Cragin, Drake, Edmunds, Ferry, Harlan, Howard, Howe, Morgan, Nye, Pomeroy, Ramsay, Stewart, Thayer, Tipton, Williams, Wilson, Yates—22—all Republicans.

The question was decided to be admissible, and the answer was "yes."

No. 16.

The next question, in immediate connection with the last, was:

If he did, state what he said his purpose was?

The yeas and nays were ordered and the vote was:

Yeas—Anthony, Bayard, Buckalew, Cole, Cobertt, Davis, Dixon, Doolittle, Fessenden, Fowler, Frelinghuysen, Grimes, Henderson, Hendricks, Johnson, McCreery, Morton, Norton, Patterson of Tennessee, Ross, Sherman, Sumner, Trumbull, Van Winkle, Vickers, Willey—26—15 Republicans and 11 Democrats.

Nays—Cameron, Cattell, Chandler, Conkling, Conness, Cragin, Drake, Edmunds, Ferry, Harlan, Howard, Howe, Morgan, Morrill of Maine, Morrill of Vermont, Nye, Patterson of New Hampshire, Pomeroy, Ramsay, Stewart, Thayer, Tipton, Williams, Wilson, Yates—25—all Republicans.

So the question was permitted to be answered, and General Sherman said:

The President told me that the relations between himself and Mr. Stanton, and between Mr. Stanton and the other members of the Cabinet, were such that he could not execute the office which he filled as President of the United States without making provision ad interim for that office; that he had the right under the law; he claimed to have the right, and his purpose was to have the office administered in the interest of the Army and of the Country; and he offered me the office in that view. He did not state to me then that his purpose was to bring it to the Courts directly; but for the purpose of having the office administered properly in the interest of the Army and the whole Country. I asked him why lawyers could not make a case, and not bring me, or any officer of the Army, into the controversy. His answer was that it was found impossible, or a case could not be made up; but, said he "if we can bring the case to the Courts, it would not stand half an hour."

Mr. Butler, of the Prosecution, objected, and after debate, General Sherman continued:

The question first asked me seemed to restrict me so close to the purpose that I endeavored to confine myself to that point alone. On the first day, or first interview, in which the President offered me the appointment ad interim, he confined himself to very general terms, and I gave him no definite answer. The second interview, which was on the afternoon of the 30th, was the interview during which he made the points which I have testified to. In speaking he referred to the constitutionality of the bill known as the civil tenure-of-office bill, I think, or the tenure of civil office bill; and it was the constitutionality of that bill which he seemed desirous of having tested, and which, he said, if it could be brought before the Supreme Court properly, would not stand half an hour. We also spoke of force. I first stated that if Mr. Stanton would simply retire, although it was against my interest, against my desire, against my personal wishes, and against my official wishes, I might be willing to undertake to administer the office ad interim. Then he supposed the point was yielded; and I made this point? "Suppose Mr. Stanton do not yield?" he answered, "Oh! he will make no objection; you present the order and he will retire." I expressed my doubt, and he remarked. "I know him better than you do: he is cowardly." I then begged to be excused from giving him an answer to give the subject more reflection, and I gave him my final answer in writing. I think that letter, if you insist on knowing my views, should come into evidence, and not parol testimony taken up; but my reasons for declining the office were mostly personal in their nature.

Mr. Henderson (of the Court) asked this question:

Did the President, on either of the occasions alluded to, express to you a fixed purpose or determination to remove Mr. Stanton from his office?

General Sherman answered:

If by removal is meant a removal by force, he never conveyed to my mind such an impression; but he did most unmistakably say that he could have no more intercourse with him in the relation of President and Secretary of War.

Mr. Howard (of the Court) asked the General:

You say the President spoke of force. What did he say about force?

General Sherman answered:

I enquired, "Suppose Mr. Stanton do not yield? What then shall be done?" "Oh," said he, "there is no necessity of considering that question. Upon the presentation of an order he will simply go away, or retire."

Mr. Henderson (of the Court) asked the question:

Did you give any opinion, or advice to the President on either of those occasions in regard to the legality or propriety of an ad interim appointment; and if so, what advice did you give, or what opinion did you express to him?

Mr. Bingham of the prosecution, objected, and the Chair put the question to the Senate whether it should be answered. The Senate, without a division, refused answer to the question, and the examination of Gen. Sherman closed for that day.

No. 17.

Wednesday, April 15th. The defense offered several extracts from records of the Navy Department, to prove the practice of the Government in cases of removal from office by different Presidents prior to Mr. Johnson, of which the following are samples:

NAVY AGENCY AT NEW YORK.

1861. June 20. Isaac Henderson was, by direction of the President, removed from the office of Navy agent at New York, and instructed to transfer to Paymaster John D. Gibson, of United States Navy, all the public funds and other property in his charge. Navy Agency at Philadelphia.

Dec. 26, 1851. James S. Chambers was removed from the office of Navy Agent at Philadelphia and instructed to transfer to Paymaster A. E. Watson, U. S. Navy, all the public funds and other property in his charge.

The prosecution objected and the yeas and nays were ordered.

Yeas—Anthony, Bayard, Buckalew, Cole, Conkling, Corbett, Davis, Dixon, Doolittle, Edmunds, Ferry, Fessenden, Fowler, Frelinghuysen, Grimes, Henderson, Hendricks, Howe, Johnson, McCreery, Morrill of Maine, Morrill of Vermont, Morton, Patterson of New Hampshire, Patterson of Tennessee, Ross, Saulsbery, Sherman, Stewart, Sumner, Trumbull, Van Winkle, Vickers, Willey, Wilson, Yates—36—25 Republicans and 11 Democrats.

Nays—Cameron, Cattell, Chandler, Conness, Cragin, Drake, Harlan, Howard, Morgan, Nye, Pomeroy, Ramsay, Thayer, Tipton, Williams—15—all Republicans.

So the evidence was admitted.

No. 18.

Thursday, April 16, Mr. Walter S. Cox on the stand. The defense offered to prove:

That Mr. Cox was employed professionally by the President, in the presence of General Thomas, to take such legal proceedings in the case that had been commenced against General Thomas as would be effectual to raise judicially the question of Mr. Stanton's legal right to continue to hold the office of Secretary for the Department of War against the authority of the President, and also in reference to obtaining a writ of quo warranto for the same purpose; and we shall expect to follow up this proof by evidence of what was done by the witness in pursuance of the above employment.

Mr. Drake demanded the yeas and nays, and they were ordered:

Yeas—Anthony, Bayard, Buckalew, Corbett, Davis, Dixon, Doolittle, Fessenden, Fowler, Frelinghuysen, Grimes, Hendricks, Howe, Johnson, McCreery, Morrill of Maine, Morton, Norton, Patterson of New Hampshire, Patterson of Tennessee, Ross, Saulsbury, Sherman, Sprague, Sumner, Trumbull, Van Winkle, Vickers, Willey—29—17 Republicans and 12 Democrats.

Nays—Cameron, Cattell, Chandler, Conkling, Cragin, Drake, Edmunds, Ferry, Harlan, Howard, Morgan, Morrill of Vermont, Nye, Pomeroy, Ramsay, Stewart, Thayer, Tipton, Williams, Wilson, Yates—21—all Republicans.

So the testimony was received, and the witness proceeded to detail the steps he had taken by direction of the President to procure a judicial determination of General Thomas' right to the office of Secretary of War and to put him in possession, till the following question was asked.

No. 19.

What did you do toward getting out a writ of habeas corpus under the employment of the President.

Prosecution objected, and the yeas and nays were ordered:

Yeas — Anthony, Bayard, Buckalew, Davis, Dixon, Doolittle, Fessenden, Fowler, Frelinghuysen, Grimes, Hendricks, Johnson, McCreery, Morrill of Maine, Morgan, Norton, Patterson of New Hampshire, Patterson of Tennessee, Ross, Saulsbury, Sherman, Sprague, Sumner, Trumbull, Van Winkle, Vickers, Willey — 27 — 15 Republicans and 12 Democrats.

Nays — Cameron, Cattell, Chandler, Conkling, Conness, Cragin, Drake, Edmunds, Ferry, Harlan, Howard, Howe, Morgan, Morrill of Vermont, Nye, Pomeroy, Ramsay, Stewart, Thayer, Tipton, Williams, Wilson, Yates — 23 — all Republicans.

The Senate having decided the evidence to be admissible,

Mr. Cox proceeded:

When the Chief Justice announced that he would proceed as an examining Judge to investigate the case of General Thomas, and not as holding Court, our first application to him was to adjourn the investigation into the Criminal Court then in session, in order to have the action of that Court. After some little discussion this request was refused. Our next effort was to have General Thomas committed to prison, in order that we might apply to that Court for a habeas corpus, and upon his being remanded by that Court; if that should be done, we might follow up the application by one to the Supreme Court of the United States. * * * The Chief Justice having indicated an intention to postpone the examination, we directed General Thomas to decline giving any bail for further appearance, and to surrender himself into custody, and announce to the Judge that he was in custody, and then present to the Criminal Court an application for a writ of habeas corpus. The Counsel on the other side objected that General Thomas could not put himself into custody, and they did not desire that he should be detained in custody. The Chief Judge also declared that he would not restrain General Thomas of his liberty, and would not hold him or allow him to be held in custody. Supposing that he must be either committed or finally discharged, we then claimed that he be discharged, not supposing that the Counsel on the other side would consent to it, and supposing that would bring about his commitment, and that we should then have an opportunity of getting a habeas corpus. They made no objection, however, to his final discharge, and accordingly the Chief Justice did discharge him.

No. 20.

The witness, Mr. Cox, was asked by counsel for defense:

After you had reported to the President the result of your efforts to obtain a writ of habeas corpus, did you do any other act in pursuance of the original instructions you had received from the President on Saturday to test the right of Mr. Stanton to continue in the office; and if so, state what the acts were?

The yeas and nays were ordered on the demand of Mr. Howard.

Yeas—Anthony, Bayard, Buckalew, Davis, Dixon, Doolittle, Fessenden, Fowler, Grimes, Hendricks, Howe, Johnson, McCreery, Morrill of Maine, Morton, Norton, Patterson of New Hampshire, Patterson of Tennessee, Ross, Saulsbery, Sherman, Sprague, Sumner, Trumbull, Van Winkle, Vickers, Willey—27—15 Republicans and 12 Democrats.

Nays—Cameron, Cattell, Chandler, Conkling, Conness, Cragin, Drake, Edmunds, Ferry, Frelinghuysen, Harlan, Howard, Morgan, Morrill of Vermont, Nye, Pomeroy, Ramsay, Stewart, Thayer, Tipton, Williams, Wilson, Yates—23—all Republicans.

So the evidence was admitted, and Mr. Cox continued.

On the same day or the next, I prepared an information in the nature of a quo warranto. I think a delay of one day occurred in the effort to procure certified copies of Gen. Thomas' commission as Secretary of War ad interim, and of the order to Mr. Stanton. I then applied to the District Attorney to sign the information in the nature of a quo warranto, and he declined to do so without instructions or a request from the President or the Attorney General. This fact was communicated to the Attorney General and the papers were sent to him. Nothing was done after this time by me.

No. 21.

The defense offered to prove:

That the President then stated that he had issued an order for the removal of Mr. Stanton and the employment of Mr. Thomas to perform the duties ad interim; that thereupon Mr. Perrin said, "Supposing Mr. Stanton should oppose the order." The President replied: "There is no danger of that, for General Thomas is already in the office." He then added: "It is only a temporary arrangement; I shall send in to the Senate at once a good name for the office."

Mr. Butler, for prosecution, objected, and the vote was:

Yeas—Bayard, Buckalew, Davis, Dixon, Doolittle, Hendricks, McCreery, Patterson of Tennessee, and Vickers—9—all Democrats.

Nays—Cameron, Cattell, Chandler, Conkling, Conness, Corbett, Cragin, Drake, Ferry, Fessenden, Fowler, Frelinghuysen, Grimes, Harlan, Howard, Howe, Johnson, Morgan, Morrill of Maine, Morrill of Vermont, Morton, Nye, Patterson of New Hampshire, Pomeroy, Ramsay, Ross, Sherman, Sprague, Stewart, Thayer, Tipton, Trumbull, Van Winkle, Willey, Williams, Wilson, and Yates—-37—36 Republicans and 1 Democrat.

So this testimony was rejected.

No. 22.

Friday, April 17. The defense offered to prove:

That on this occasion (a Cabinet meeting previously mentioned), the President communicated to Mr. Welles, and the other members of his Cabinet, before the meeting broke up, that he had removed Mr. Stanton and appointed General Thomas Secretary of War ad interim; and that, upon the inquiry by Mr. Welles whether General Thomas was in possession of the office, the President replied that he was, and on further question of Welles, whether Mr. Stanton acquiesced, the President replied that he did; all that he required was time to remove his papers.

Mr. Butler objected and the yeas and nays were ordered.

Yeas—Anthony, Bayard, Buckalew, Cole, Conkling, Corbett, Davis, Dixon, Doolittle, Fessenden, Fowler, Grimes, Hendricks, Johnson, McCreery, Morton, Patterson of Tennessee, Ross, Saulsbery, Sherman, Sprague, Sumner, Trumbull, Van Winkle, Vickers, Willey—26—15 Republicans and 11 Democrats.

Nays—Cameron, Cattell, Conness, Cragin, Drake, Edmunds, Ferry, Frelinghuysen, Harlan, Howard, Howe, Morgan, Morrill of Maine, Morrill of Vermont, Patterson of New Hampshire, Pomeroy, Ramsay, Stewart, Thayer, Tipton, Williams, Wilson, Yates—2-3-all Republicans.

So the testimony was received, and the following proceeding was had Mr. Evarts, of Counsel for the President. Mr. Welles on the stand:

Please state, Mr. Welles, what communication was made by the President to the Cabinet on the subject of the removal of Mr. Stanton and the appointment of General Thomas, and what passed at the time?

Mr. Welles: As I remarked, after the Departmental business had been disposed of, the President remarked, as usual when he had anything to communicate himself, that before they separated it would be proper for him to say that he had removed Mr. Stanton and appointed the Adjutant General Lorenzo Thomas, Secretary ad interim. I asked whether General Thomas was in possession. The President said he was; that Mr. Stanton required some little time to remove his writings, his papers; I said, perhaps, or I asked, "Mr. Stanton, then, acquiesces?" He said he did, as he considered it. * * *

Question: Now, sir, one moment to a matter which you spoke of incidentally. You were there the next morning about noon?

Answer: I was.

Question: Did you then see the appointment of Mr. Ewing?

Answer: I did.

Question: Was it made out before you came there, or after, or while you were there?

Answer: While I was there.

Question: And you then saw it?

Answer: I saw it.

Question by Mr. Johnson (of the Court): What time of the day was that?

Answer: It was about twelve.

* * * Question by Mr. Evarts: Did you become aware of the Tenure-of-office bill, as it is called, at or about the time that it passed Congress?

Answer: I was aware of it.

Question: Were you present at any Cabinet meeting at which, after the passage of that Act, it became the subject of consideration?

Answer: Yes, on two occasions. The first occasion when it was brought before the Cabinet was on the 26th of February, 1867.

Question: Who were present?

Answer: All the Cabinet were present.

Question: Was Mr. Stanton there?

Answer: Mr. Stanton was there, I think, on that occasion.

Question: This civil tenure act was the subject of consideration there?

Answer: It was submitted.

Question: As a matter of consideration in the Cabinet?

Answer: For consultation for the advice and opinion of members.

Question: How did he submit the matter to your consideration?

Mr. Butler objected and demanded that the offer be put in writing.

No. 23.

That the President at a meeting of the Cabinet, while the bill was before the President for his approval, laid before the Cabinet the tenure-of-civil-office bill for their consideration and advice to the President respecting his approval of the bill: and thereupon the members of the Cabinet then present gave their advice to the President that the bill was unconstitutional and should be returned to Congress with his objections, and that the duty of preparing a message, setting forth the objections to the constitutionality of the bill, was devolved on Mr. Seward and Mr. Stanton; to be followed by proof as to what was done by the President and Cabinet up to the time of sending in the message.

After argument the yeas and nays were taken:

Yeas—Anthony Bayard, Buckalew, Davis, Dixon, Doolittle, Fessenden, Fowler, Grimes, Henderson, Hendricks, Johnson, McCreery, Patterson of Tennessee, Ross, Saulsbury, Trumbull, Van Winkle, Vickers, and Willey—20—9 Republicans and 11 Democrats.

Nays—Cameron, Cattell, Chandler, Cole, Conkling, Conness, Corbett, Cragin, Drake, Edmunds, Ferry, Frelinghuysen, Harlan, Howard, Howe, Morgan, Morrill of Maine, Morrill of Vermont, Patterson of New Hampshire, Pomeroy, Ramsay Sherman, Sprague, Stewart, Thayer, Tipton, Williams, Wilson, and Yates—29—all Republicans.

So this testimony was rejected.

No. 21.

Counsel for Defense offered to prove:

That at the meetings of the Cabinet at which Mr. Stanton was present, held while the tenure-of-civil-office bill was before the President for approval, the advice of the Cabinet in regard to the same was asked by the President and given by the Cabinet, and thereupon the question whether Mr. Stanton and the other Secretaries who had received their appointment from Mr. Lincoln were within the restrictions upon the President's power of removal from office created by said act was considered, and the opinion expressed that the Secretaries appointed by Mr. Lincoln were not within such restrictions.

The yeas and nays were ordered, and the vote was:

Yeas—Anthony, Bayard, Buckalew, Davis, Dixon, Doolittle, Fessenden, Fowler, Grimes, Henderson, Hendricks, Johnson, McCreery, Patterson of Tennessee, Ross, Saulsbury, Sherman, Sprague, Trumbull, Van Winkle, Vickers, and Willey—22—11 Republicans and 11 Democrats.

Nays—Cameron, Cattell, Chandler, Cole. Conness. Corbett, Cragin, Drake, Edmunds, Ferry, Frelinghusen, Harlan, Howard, Howe, Morgan, Morrill of Maine, Morrill of Vermont, Patterson of New Hampshire, Pomeroy, Ramsay, Stewart, Thayer, Tipton, Williams, Wilson, and Yates—26—all Republicans.

So this testimony was rejected.

No. 25.

Counsel for defense offered to prove:

That at the Cabinet meetings between the passage of the tenure-of-civil office bill and the order of the 21st of February, 1868, for the removal of Mr. Stanton upon occasions when the condition of the public service, as affected by the operation of that bill, came up for the consideration and advice of the Cabinet, it was considered by the President and Cabinet that a proper regard to the public service made it desirable that upon some proper case a judicial determination of the constitutionality of the law should be obtained.

The question being taken by yeas and nays, resulted:

Yeas—Anthony, Bayard, Buckalew, Davis, Dixon, Doolittle, Fessenden, Fowler, Grimes, Henderson, Hendricks, Johnson, McCreery, Patterson of Tennessee, Ross, Saulsbury Trumbull, Van Winkle, and Vickers—19—8 Republicans and 11 Democrats.

Nays—Cameron, Cattell, Chandler, Cole, Conkling, Conness, Corbett, Cragin, Drake, Edmunds, Ferry, Frelinghuysen, Harlan, Howard, Howe, Morgan, Morrill of Maine, Morrill of Vermont, Patterson of New Hampshire, Pomeroy, Ramsay, Sherman, Sprague, Stewart, Thayer, Tipton, Willey, Williams, Wilson and Yates—30—all Republicans.

So the proffered testimony was rejected.

No. 26.

Counsel for defense put this question to witness, (Mr. Welles, then Secretary of the Navy.)

Was there, within the period embraced in the inquiry in the last question, and at any discussions or deliberations of the Cabinet concerning the operation of the tenure-of-civil-office act and the requirements of the public service in regard to the service, any suggestion or intimation whatever touching or looking to the vacation of any office by force or getting possession of the same by force?

Counsel for prosecution objected, and the vote was:

Yeas—Anthony, Bayard, Buckalew, Davis, Dixon, Edmunds, Fessenden, Fowler, Grimes, Hendricks, Johnson, McCreery, Patterson of Tennessee, Ross, Saulsbury, Trumbull, Van Winkle, and Vickers—18—8 Republicans and 10 Democrats.

Nays-Cattell, Chandler, Cole, Conkling, Conness, Corbett, Cragin, Ferry, Frelinghuysen, Harlan, Howard, Howe, Morgan, Morrill of Maine, Morrill of Vermont, Patterson of New Hampshire, Pomeroy, Ramsay,

Sherman, Stewart, Thayer, Tipton, Willey, Williams, Wilson, and Yates—26—all Republicans.

So the proffered testimony was rejected.

No. 27.

Defense offered to prove:

That at the meetings of the Cabinet at which Stanton was present, held while the tenure-of-civil-office bill was before the President for approval, the advice of the Cabinet in regard to the same was asked by the President, and given the Cabinet, and thereupon the question whether Mr. Stanton and the other Secretaries who had received their appointments from Mr. Lincoln were within the restrictions upon the President's power of removal from office created by said act, was considered and the opinion expressed that the Secretaries appointed by Mr. Lincoln were not within such restrictions.

Mr. Johnson: I ask that the question propounded by the Senator from Ohio (Mr. Sherman) shall now be read.

The Secretary read the question as follows:

State if, after the 2d of March, 1867, the date of the passage of the tenure-of-office act, the question whether the Secretaries appointed by President Lincoln were included within the provisions of that act came before the Cabinet for discussion; and if so, what opinion was given on this question by members of the Cabinet to the President.

The yeas and nays were ordered; and being taken resulted:

Yeas—Anthony, Bayard, Buckalew, Davis, Dixon, Doolittle, Fessenden, Fowler, Grimes, Hendricks, Johnson, McCreery, Patterson of Tennessee, Ross, Saulsbury, Sherman, Trumbull, Van Winkle, Vickers, and Willey—20—9 Republican and 11 Democrats.

Nays—Cameron, Cattell, Chandler, Cole, Conkling, Conness, Corbett, Cragin, Edmunds, Ferry, Frelinghuysen, Harlan, Howard, Howe, Morgan, Morrill of Maine, Morrill of Vermont, Patterson of New Hampshire, Pomeroy, Ramsay, Stewart, Thayer, Tipton, Williams, Wilson, and Yates—26—all Republicans.

So the proffered testimony was rejected.

No. 28.

The Prosecution proposed to put in evidence the nomination of Lieutenant General Sherman, to be General by brevet, sent to the Senate on the 13th of February, 1868, also the nomination of Major General George H.

Thomas to be Lieutenant General by brevet, and to be General by brevet, sent to the Senate on the 21st of February, 1868.

The question being taken by yeas and nays, resulted: Yeas — Anthony, Cole, Fessenden, Fowler, Grimes, Henderson, Morton, Ross, Sumner, Tipton, Trumbull, Van Winkle, Willey, and Yates — 14 — all Republicans.

Nays — Buckalew, Cameron, Cattell, Chandler, Conkling, Conness, Corbett, Cragin, Davis, Dixon, Doolittle, Drake, Edmunds, Ferry, Frelinghuysen, Harlan, Hendricks, Howard, Howe, Johnson, McCreery, Morgan, Morrill of Maine, Morrill of Vermont, Patterson of New Hampshire, Patterson of Tennessee, Pomeroy, Ramsay, Sherman, Sprague, Stewart, Thayer, Vickers, Williams, and Wilson — 35 — 26 Republicans and 9 Democrats.

So the proffered testimony was refused.

GENERAL EMORY'S TESTIMONY.

The Ninth Article of the Impeachment was based upon alleged military changes in the City of Washington whereby the number of troops on duty there was rumored to have been largely increased, with a view to their use in the controversy between the President and Congress, and more especially for the expulsion of Mr. Stanton from the War Office in case of his resistance to the order of the President for his retirement. The wildest rumors of that character prevailed — that Mr. Johnson proposed to throw off all disguise and assume direct military control and the establishment of practically a military dictatorship. Congress had some months previously enacted that all military orders from the President should be issued through the General of the Army — the Congress thereby assuming to practically abrogate a constitutional function of the Chief Executive.

There was considerable confidence among the supporters of the impeachment that they would be able to prove these allegations by General Emory, then in local command of the troops and Department of Washington. General Emory was called by the prosecution, and the following was his testimony.

Examined by Mr. Butler:

Question: Will you have the kindness to state, as nearly as you can what took place then? (Referring to an interview with the President at the Executive Mansion.)

Answer: I will try and state the substance of it, but the words I can not undertake to state exactly. The President asked me if I recollected a conversation he had had with me when I first took command of the department. I told him that I recollected the facts of the conversation distinctly. He then asked me what changes had been made. I told him no material changes, but such as had been made I could state at once. I went on to state that in the fall six companies of the 29th infantry had been brought to this City to winter; but as an offset to that, four companies of the 12th infantry had been detached to South Carolina on the request of the Commander of that District; that two companies of artillery had been detached by my predecessor, one of them for the purpose of siding in putting down the Fenian difficulties, had been returned to the command, that although the number of companies head been increased, the numerical strength of the command was very much the same, growing out of an order reducing the artillery and infantry companies from the maximum of the war establishment to the minimum of the peace establishment. The President said: "I do not refer to those changes." I replied that if he would state what changes he referred to, or who made the report of the changes, perhaps I could be more, explicit. He said, "I refer to recent changes within a day or two," or something to that effect. I told him I thought I could assure him that no changes had been made; that under a recent order issued for the government of the armies of the United States, founded upon a law of Congress, all orders had to be transmitted through General Grant to the army, and in like manner all orders coming from General Grant to any of his subordinate officers must necessarily come, if in my department, through me; that if by chance an order had been given to any junior officer of mine it was his duty at once to report that fact. The President asked me. "What order do you refer to?" I replied, "To order number 17 of the series of 1867." He said, "I would like to see the order," and a messenger was dispatched for it. At this time a gentleman came in who I supposed had business in no way connected with the business I had in hand, and I withdrew to the farther end of the room, and while there, the messenger came in with the book of orders and handed it to me. As soon as the gentleman had withdrawn, I returned to the President with the book in my hand, and said I would take it as a favor if he would permit me to call his attention to that order; that it had been passed in an appropriation bill, and I thought it not unlikely that it had escaped his attention. He took the order and read it, and observed, "This is not in conformity with the Constitution of the United States, that makes me Commander-in-Chief, or with the terns of your commission." I replied, "That is the order which you approved and issued to the army for our government," or something to that effect. I can not recollect the exact words, nor do I intend to quote the exact words of the President. He said, "Am I to understand that the President of the United States can not give an order except through the General of the Army? Or General Grant?" I said in reply, that that was my impression—that that was the opinion that the Army entertain, and I thought upon that subject they were a unit. I also said, "I think it is fair, Mr. President, to say to you that when this order came out, there was considerable discussion on the subject as to what were the obligations of an officer under that order, and some eminent lawyers were consulted. I myself consulted one—and the opinion was given to me decidedly and unequivocally that we were bound by the order, Constitutional or not Constitutional." The President observed that "the object of the law was evident."

The following is that portion of the act referred to:

"Section 2. Be it further enacted: That the headquarters of the General of the Army of the United States shall be at the City of Washington, and all orders and instructions relating to military operations issued by the President and Secretary of War shall be issued through the General of the Army, and in case of his inability, through the next in rank. The General of the Army shall not be removed, suspended, or relieved from command or assigned to duty elsewhere than at said headquarters except at his own request WITHOUT THE PREVIOUS APPROVAL OF THE SENATE; and any orders or instructions relating to Military operations issued contrary to the requirements of this section, shall be null and void. And any officer who shall issue orders or instructions, contrary to the provisions of this section, shall be deemed guilty of a misdemeanor in office; and any officer of the Army who shall transmit, convey or obey any orders or instructions so issued contrary to the provisions of this section, knowing that such orders were so issued shall be liable to imprisonment for not less than two nor more than twenty years upon conviction thereof in any Court of competent jurisdiction."

By turning to the Congressional Record of that day, it will be found that Mr. Johnson was perfectly aware of the existence of the foregoing provision of the Act of Congress in the bill referred to, at the time he returned the bill to the House with his signature. His reasons for so signing it are set out in the following communication to the House accompanying the bill.

The act entitled "An act making appropriations for the support of the Army for the year ending June 30, 1868, and for other purposes," contains provisions to which I must call attention. There are propositions contained in the second section which in certain cases deprives the President of his Constitutional functions of Commander in Chief of the Army, and in the sixth section, which denies to ten States of the Union their Constitutional right to protect themselves in any emergency, by means of their own militia. These provisions are out of place in an appropriation act, but I am compelled to defeat these necessary appropriations if I withhold my signature from the act. Pressed by these considerations, I feel constrained to return the bill with my signature, but to accompany it with my earnest protest against the section which I have indicated.

Andrew Johnson. Washington, D. C., March 2, 1868.

That Congress was to expire by limitation at 12 o'clock on the 4th, thirty-six hours later. If Mr. Johnson had vetoed the bill, as under ordinary conditions it would have been his duty to the Constitution and to himself to do, its re-passage through the two Houses in that limited time would have been impossible, and the appropriations carried by the bill for the support of the Army would have been lost. To save them Mr. Johnson submitted to the indignity put upon him by Congress in denying him a guaranteed and manifest Constitutional right and power. In that act Mr. Johnson illustrated a magnanimity and a consciousness of public responsibility that was most creditable to himself, and in marked contrast to the action of Congress toward him.

CHAPTER X — A CONFERENCE HELD AND THE FIRST VOTE TAKEN.

A few days prior to the day set for taking the vote on the several Articles of Impeachment, and after the conclusion of testimony, it was proposed that there be a private session for conference of the Senate on a day named, May 11th, to give Senators an opportunity to declare themselves on the pending impeachment.

Neither the precise object or the utility of a conference were then apparent, but the result was somewhat of a surprise to those who had, up to that time, been undoubtingly confident of the President's conviction. Comparatively few Senators had previously declared their position. Very few, if any of the Republican Senators had indicated a disposition to vote against any of the articles, but the silence of a number of them, and their refusal to commit themselves even to their associates, was a source of uneasiness in Senatorial Impeachment circles. Hence, possibly, the suggestion of a "conference."

It was taken for granted that every Democratic Senator would vote against the impeachment. But the idea was not to be entertained that the "no" votes would extend beyond the Democratic coterie of twelve. There were, however, anxious misgivings as to that. There was too much silence — too much of saying nothing when so little that might be said would go so far to relieve an oppressive anxiety.

So a session for "conference" was ordered and held, much to the surprise of gentlemen whose silence had become somewhat oppressive, and was becoming equally painful to those who wanted a conference. It savored of an attempt to "poll the Senate" in advance of judgment. It was resolved at the session of May 7th, to hold a session for deliberation on the following Monday, May 11th. The most surprising development of that session was the weakness of the bill of indictment at the very point where it was apparently strongest — the first Article. Two conspicuous and influential Senators — Messrs. Sherman of Ohio, and Howe of Wisconsin — declared, and gave convincing reasons therefor, that they would not vote for the impeachment of Mr. Johnson on that Article.

In his remarks on this occasion, after giving a history of the enactment of the Tenure-of-Office law, the first section of which specifically excepts from its operation such members of Mr. Johnson's Cabinet as had been appointed by Mr. Lincoln and still remaining, though not recommissioned by Mr. Johnson, Mr. Sherman said:

I can only say as one of the Senate conferees, under the solemn obligations that now rest upon us in construing this Act, that I did not understand it to include members of the Cabinet not appointed by the President, and that it was with extreme reluctance and only to secure the passage of the bill that, in the face of the votes of the Senate I agreed to the report LIMITING AT ALL the power of the President to remove heads of Departments. * * * I stated explicitly that the Act as reported did not protect from removal the members of the Cabinet appointed by Mr. Lincoln, that President Johnson might remove them at his pleasure; and I named the Secretary of war as one that might be removed. * * * I could not conceive a case where the Senate would require the President to perform his great executive office upon the advice and through heads of Departments personally obnoxious to him, and whom he had not appointed, and, therefore, no such case was provided for. * * * Can I pronounce the President guilty of crime, and by that vote aid to remove him from his high office for doing what I declared and still believe he had a legal right to do. God forbid: * * * What the President did do in the removal of Mr. Stanton he did under a power which you repeatedly refused to take from the office of the President—a power that has been held by that officer since the formation of the Government, and is now limited only by the words of an Act, the literal construction of which does not include Mr. Stanton. * * * It follows, that as Mr. Stanton is not protected by the Tenure-of-Civil-Office Act, his removal rests upon the Act of 1789, and he according to the terms of that Act and of the commission held by him, and in compliance with the numerous precedents cited in this cause, was lawfully removed by the President, and his removal not being contrary to the provisions of the Act of March 2nd 1867, the 1st, 4th, 5th, and 6th Articles, based upon his removal, must fail.

On this point, Mr. Howe said:

If Mr. Stanton had been appointed during the present Presidential term. I should have no doubt he was within the security of the law. But I cannot find that, either in fact or in legal intendment, he was appointed during the present Presidential term. It is urged that he was appointed by Mr. Lincoln, and such is the fact. It is said that Mr. Lincoln's term is not yet expired. Such I believe to be the fact. But the language of the proviso is, that a Secretary shall hold not during the term of MAN by whom he is appointed, but during the TERM of the PRESIDENT by whom he may be appointed. Mr. Stanton was appointed by the President in 1862. The term of that President was limited by the Constitution. It expired on the 4th of March, 1865. That the same incumbent was re-elected for the next term is conceded, but I do not comprehend how that fact extended the former term.

Entertaining these views, and because the first Article of the Impeachment charges the order of removal as a violation of the Tenure-of-Office Act, I am constrained to hold the President not guilty upon that Article.

These declarations, coming from two gentlemen of distinction and influence in the party councils, both of whom had actively participated in framing the Tenure-of-Office Act, became at once the occasion of genuine and profound surprise, and it is unnecessary to say that they tended largely to strengthen the doubts entertained by others as to the sufficiency of all the other allegations of the indictment. They naturally and logically reasoned that the removal of Mr. Stanton, set out in the first Article, constituted, in effect, the essence of the indictment, and that all that followed, save the 10th Article was more in the nature of specifications, or a bill of particulars, than otherwise — that if no impeachable offense were set out in the first Article, then none was committed, as that Article constituted the substructure of all the rest — its essence and logic running through and permeating practically all — and that without that Article, there was no coherence or force in any of them, and consequently nothing charged against the President that was impeachable, as he had not violated the Tenure-of-Office law, and was not charged with the violation of any other law.

That conference developed, further, that a large majority of the Articles of Impeachment were objectionable to and would not be supported by a number of Republican Senators.

Mr. Edmunds would not support the 4th, 8th, 9th, and 10th Articles, being "wholly unsustained by proof," but would support the 11th, though apparently doubtful of its efficiency.

Mr. Ferry could not support the 4th, 5th, 6th, 7th, 9th, or 10th Articles.

Mr. Howard declared that he would not support the 9th Article.

Mr. Morrill of Vermont, would not support the 4th, 6th, 9th, or 10th Articles, as they were unproven.

Mr. Morrill, of Maine, Mr. Yates, Mr. Harlan, and Mr. Stewart, would vote to convict on the Articles relating to the removal of Mr. Stanton — uncommitted on all others.

Mr. Fessenden, Mr. Fowler, Mr. Grimes, Mr. Henderson, Mr. Trumbull, and Mr. Van Winkle, each declared, at that conference, their opposition to the entire list of the Articles of Impeachment.

But eighteen Republicans committed themselves at that conference, for conviction, out of twenty-four who filed opinions. While it was taken for granted that the six Democrats who had failed to declare their position at that conference would oppose conviction, the position of the eighteen Republicans who had failed to declare themselves became at once a source of very grave concern in impeachment circles. Out of that list of eighteen uncommitted Republicans, but one vote was necessary to defeat the impeachment. This condition was still farther intensified by the fact that eight of the eleven Articles of Impeachment were already beaten in that conference, and practically by Republican committals, and among them the head and front and foundation of the indictment — the First Article — by Messrs. Sherman and Howe, two conspicuous Republican leaders.

A forecast of the vote based on these committals as to the several Articles, would be against the First Article, twelve Democrats and eight Republicans, one more than necessary for its defeat — the eight "not guilty" votes including Messrs. Sherman and Howe.

Against the Fourth Article — twelve Democrats and nine Republicans — including Messrs. Edmunds, Ferry, and Morrill of Vermont.

Against the Fifth Article — twelve Democrats and eight Republicans- including Messrs. Edmunds and Ferry.

Against the Sixth Article — twelve Democrats and nine Republicans- including Messrs. Ferry, Howe, and Morrill of Vermont.

Against the Seventh — Article-twelve Democrats and seven Republicans — including Mr. Ferry.

Against the Eighth Article — twelve Democrats and seven Republicans — including Mr. Edmunds.

Against the Ninth Article — twelve Democrats and twelve Republicans — including Messrs. Sherman, Edmunds, Ferry, Howe, Howard, and Morrill of Vermont.

Against the Tenth Article — twelve Democrats and ten Republicans — including Messrs. Edmunds, Sherman, Ferry, and Morrill of Vermont.

It is somewhat conspicuous that but three gentlemen — Messrs. Sumner, Pomeroy, and Tipton, in their arguments in the Conference, pronounced the President guilty on all the charges — though five others, Messrs. Wilson, Patterson of New Hampshire, Frelinghuysen, Cattell, and Williams, pronounced the President guilty on general principles, without specification; and Messrs. Morrill of Maine, Yates and Stewart, guilty in the removal of Mr. Stanton, without further specification of charges.

As but one vote, in addition to the twelve Democratic and the six Republican votes pledged against conviction at the Conference, was necessary to defeat impeachment on the three remaining Articles—the 2nd, 3rd, and 11th—and as nearly a half of the Republicans of the Senate had failed to commit themselves, at least in any public way, the anxiety of the advocates of Impeachment became at once, and naturally, very grave. How many of the eighteen Republicans who had failed to declare themselves at that Conference might fail to sustain the Impeachment, became, therefore, a matter of active solicitude on all sides, especially in impeachment circles in and out of the Senate. Republican committals in the Conference had rendered absolutely certain the defeat of every Article of the Impeachment except the Second, Third, and Eleventh, and the addition of but a single vote from the eighteen uncommitted Republicans to the "No" side, would defeat them.

It was under this unfavorable condition of the Impeachment cause, that the Senate assembled on May 16th, 1868, for the purpose of taking final action on the indictment brought by the House of Representatives, the trial of which had occupied the most of the time of the Senate for the previous three months, and which had to a large degree engrossed the attention of the general public, to the interruption of legislation pending in the two Houses of Congress, and more or less to the embarrassment of the commercial activities of the country.

For the first time in the history of the government, practically eighty years, the President of the United States was at the bar of the Senate, by virtue of a constitutional warrant, on an accusation of the House of Representatives of high crimes and misdemeanors in office, and his conviction and expulsion from office demanded in the name of all the people. No event in the civil history of the country had ever before occurred to so arouse public antipathies and public indignation against any man-and these conditions found special vent in the City of Washington, as the Capitol of the Nation, as it had become during the trial the focal point of the politically dissatisfied element of the entire country. Its streets and all its places of gathering had swarmed for many weeks with representatives of every State of the Union, demanding in a practically united voice the deposition of the President.

On numbers of occasions during the previous history of the Government there had been heated controversies between the Congress and the Executive, but never before characterized by the intensity, not infrequently malevolence, that had come to mark this and never before had a division between the Executive and the Congress reached a point at which a suggestion of his constitutional ostracism from office had been seriously entertained, much less attempted.

But it had now come. The active, intense interest of the country was aroused, and everywhere the division among the people was sharply defined and keen, though the numerical preponderance, it cannot be denied, was largely against the President and insistent upon his removal.

The dominant party of the country was aroused and active for the deposition of the President. Public meetings were held throughout the North and resolutions adopted and forwarded to Senators demanding that Mr. Johnson be promptly expelled from office by the Senate—and it had become apparent, long before the taking of the vote, that absolute, swift, and ignominious expulsion from office awaited every Republican Senator who should dare to disregard that demand.

Under these conditions it was but natural that during the trial, and especially as the close approached, the streets of Washington and the lobbies of the Capitol were thronged from day to day with interested spectators from every section of the Union, or that Senators were beleaguered day and night, by interested constituents, for some word of encouragement that a change was about to come of that day's proceeding, and with threats of popular vengeance upon the failure of any Republican Senator to second that demand.

In view of this intensity of public interest it was as a matter of course that the coming of the day when the great controversy was expected to be brought to a close by the deposition of Mr. Johnson and the seating of a new incumbent in the Presidential chair, brought to the Capitol an additional throng which long before the hour for the assembling of the Senate filled all the available space in the vast building, to witness the culmination of the great political trial of the age.

Upon the closing of the hearing—even prior thereto, and again during the few days of recess that followed, the Senate had been carefully polled, and the prospective vote of every member from whom it was possible to procure a committal, ascertained and registered in many a private memoranda. There were fifty-four members—all present. According to these memoranda, the vote would stand eighteen for acquittal, thirty-five for conviction—one less than the number required by the Constitution to convict. What that one vote would be, and could it be had, were anxious queries, of one to another, especially among those who had set on foot the impeachment enterprise and staked their future control of the government upon its success. Given for conviction and upon sufficient proofs, the President MUST step down and out of his place, the highest and most honorable and honoring in dignity and sacredness of trust in the constitution of human government, a disgraced man and a political pariah. If so cast upon insufficient proofs or from partisan considerations, the office of President of the United States would be degraded—cease to be a coordinate branch of the Government, and ever after subordinated to the legislative will. It would have practically revolutionized our splendid political fabric into a partisan Congressional autocracy. A political tragedy was imminent.

On the other hand, that vote properly given for acquittal, would at once free the Presidential office from imputed dishonor and strengthen our triple organization and distribution of powers and responsibilities. It would preserve the even tenor and courses of administration, and effectively impress upon the world a conviction of the strength and grandeur of Republican institutions in the hands of a free and enlightened people.

The occasion was sublimely and intensely dramatic. The President of the United States was on trial. The Chief Justice of the Supreme Court was presiding over the deliberations of the Senate sitting for the trial of the great cause. The board of management conducting the prosecution brought by the House of Representatives was a body of able and illustrious politicians and statesmen. The President's counsel, comprising jurists among the most eminent of the country, had summed up for the defense and were awaiting final judgment. The Senate, transformed for the occasion into an extraordinary judicial tribunal, the highest known to our laws, the Senators at once judges and jurors with power to enforce testimony and sworn to hear all the facts bearing upon the case, was about to pronounce that judgment.

The organization of the court had been severely Democratic. There were none of the usual accompaniments of royalty or exclusivism considered essential under aristocratic forms to impress the people with the dignity and gravity of a great occasion. None of these were necessary, for every spectator was an intensely interested witness to the proceeding, who must bear each for himself, the public consequences of the verdict, whatever they might be, equally with every member of the court.

The venerable Chief Justice, who had so ably and impartially presided through the many tedious weeks of the trial now about to close, was in his place and called the Senate to order.

The impressive dignity of the occasion was such that there was little need of the admonition of the Chief Justice to abstention from conversation on the part of the audience during the proceeding. No one there present, whether friend or opponent of the President, could have failed to be impressed with the tremendous consequences of the possible result of the prosecution about to be reached. The balances were apparently at a poise. It was plain that a single vote would be sufficient to turn the scales either way—to evict the President from his great office to go the balance of his life's journey with the brand of infamy upon his brow, or be relieved at once from the obloquy the inquisitors had sought to put upon him—and more than all else, to keep the honorable roll of American Presidents unsmirched before the world, despite the action of the House.

The first vote was on the Eleventh and last Article of the Impeachment. Senators voted in alphabetical order, and each arose and stood at his desk as his name was called by the Chief Clerk. To each the Chief Justice propounded the solemn interrogatory—"Mr. Senator—, how say you—is the respondent, Andrew Johnson, President of the United States, guilty or not guilty of a high misdemeanor as charged in this Article?"

Mr. Fessenden, of Maine, was the first of Republican Senators to vote "Not Guilty." He had long been a safe and trusted leader in the Senate, and had the unquestioning confidence of his partisan colleagues, while his long experience in public life, and his great ability as a legislator, and more especially his exalted personal character, had won for him the admiration of all his associates regardless of political affiliations. Being the first of the dissenting Republicans to vote, the influence of his action was feared by the impeachers, and most strenuous efforts had been made to induce him to retract the position he had taken to vote against conviction. But being moved on this occasion, as he had always been on others, to act upon his own judgment and conviction, though foreseeing that this vote would probably end a long career of conspicuous public usefulness, there was no sign of hesitancy or weakness as he pronounced his verdict.

Mr. Fowler, of Tennessee, was the next Republican to vote "Not Guilty." He had entered the Senate but two years before, and was therefore one of the youngest Senators, with the promise of a life of political usefulness before him. Though from the same State as the President, they were at political variance, and there was but little in common between them in other respects. A radical partisan in all measures where radical action seemed to be called for, he was for the time being sitting in a judicial capacity and under an oath to do justice to the accused according to the law and the evidence. As in his judgment the evidence did not sustain the charge against the President such was his verdict.

Mr. Grimes, of Iowa, was the third anti-impeaching Republican to vote. He had for many years been a conspicuous and deservedly influential member of the Senate. For some days prior to the taking of the vote he had been stricken with what afterwards proved a fatal illness. The scene presented as he rose to his feet supported on the arms of his colleagues, was grandly heroic, and one never before witnessed in a legislative chamber. Though realizing the danger he thus incurred, and conscious of the political doom that would follow his vote, and having little sympathy with the policies pursued by the President, he had permitted himself to be borne to the Senate chamber that he might contribute to save his country from what he deemed the stain of a partisan and unsustained impeachment of its Chief Magistrate. Men often perform, in the excitement and glamour of battle, great deeds of valor and self sacrifice that live after them and link their names with the honorable history of great events, but to deliberately face at once inevitable political as well as physical death in the council hall, and in the absence of charging squadrons; and shot and shell, and of the glamor of military heroism, is to illustrate the grandest phase of human courage and devotion to convictions. That was the part performed by Mr. Grimes on that occasion. His vote of "Not Guilty" was the last, the bravest, the grandest, and the most patriotic public act of his life.

Mr. Henderson of Missouri, was the fourth Republican Senator to vote against the impeachment. A gentleman of rare industry and ability, and a careful, conscientious legislator, he had been identified with the legislation of the time and had reached a position of deserved prominence and influence. But he was learned in the law, and regardful of his position as a just and discriminating judge. Though then a young man with a brilliant future before him, he had sworn to do justice to Andrew Johnson "according to the Constitution and law," and his verdict of "Not Guilty" was given with the same deliberate emphasis that characterized all his utterances on the floor of the Senate.

Mr. Ross, of Kansas, was the fifth Republican Senator to vote "Not Guilty." Representing an intensely Radical constituency—entering the Senate but a few months after the close of a three years enlistment in the Union Army and not unnaturally imbued with the extreme partisan views and prejudices against Mr. Johnson then prevailing—his predilections were sharply against the President, and his vote was counted upon accordingly. But he had sworn to judge the defendant not by his political or personal prejudices, but by the facts elicited in the investigation. In his judgment those facts did not sustain the charge.

Mr. Trumbull, of Illinois, was the sixth Republican Senator to vote against the Impeachment. He had been many years in the Senate. In all ways a safe legislator and counsellor, he had attained a position of conspicuous usefulness. But he did not belong to the legislative autocracy which then assumed to rule the two Houses of Congress. To him the Impeachment was a question of proof of charges brought, and not of party politics or policies. He was one of the great lawyers of the body, and believed that law was the essence of justice and not an engine of wrong, or an instrumentality for the satisfaction of partisan vengeance. He had no especial friendship for Mr. Johnson, but to him the differences between the President and Congress did not comprise an impeachable offense. A profound lawyer and clear headed politician and statesman, his known opposition naturally tended to strengthen his colleagues in that behalf.

Mr. Van Winkle, of West Virginia, was the seventh and last Republican Senator to vote against the Impeachment. Methodical and deliberate, he was not hasty in reaching the conclusion he did, but after giving the subject and the testimony most careful and thorough investigation, he was forced to the conclusion that the accusation brought by the House of Representatives had not been sustained, and had the courage of an American Senator to vote according to his conclusions.

The responses were as follows:

Guilty—Anthony, Cameron, Cattell, Cole, Chandler, Conkling, Conness, Corbett, Cragin, Drake, Edmunds, Ferry, Frelinghuysen, Harlan, Howard, Howe, Morgan, Morton, Morrill of Maine, Morrill of Vermont, Nye, Patterson of New Hampshire, Pomeroy, Ramsay, Sherman, Sprague, Stewart, Sumner, Tipton, Thayer, Wade, Williams, Wilson, Willey, Yates.

Not Guilty—Bayard, Buckalew, Davis, Dixon, Doolittle, Fessenden, Fowler, Grimes, Henderson, Hendricks, Johnson, McCreery, Norton, Patterson of Tennessee, Ross, Saulsbury, Trumbull, Van Winkle, Vickers.

Not Guilty—19. Guilty—35—one vote less than a Constitutional majority.

CHAPTER XI — THE IMPEACHERS IN A MAZE. A RECESS ORDERED.

THE FINAL VOTE TAKEN.

The defeat of the Eleventh Article was the second official set-back to the Impeachment movement—the first being the practical abandonment of the First Article by the change in the order of voting.

The vote had been taken on what its friends seemed to consider its strongest proposition; the Eleventh Article having been so framed as to group the substance, practically, of all the pending ten Articles. The impeachers had staked their cause upon that Article, and lost. They seemed not to have contemplated the possibility of its defeat. So confident were they of its success, in which event it would be immaterial what became of the other Articles, that they apparently had agreed upon no order of procedure after that should have been defeated. They were in the condition of a flock of game into which the sportsman had fired a shot and broken its ranks. They were dazed, and for a moment seemed not to know what next to do, or which way to turn. They did not dare now go back to the fated First Article, according to the program agreed upon, as Mr. Sherman and Mr. Howe had demonstrated its weakness, and they were fearful of going to the Second or Third, as in the then temper of the anti-impeachers it was manifest there would be little hope for either of them, and the other eight had been already beaten without a vote, at the conference previously held, and by Republican commitals.

The Chief Justice ordered the reading of the First Article, according to the order agreed upon, but before that could begin, apparently to gain time for recovery, Mr. Williams moved that the Senate take a recess of fifteen minutes, but the motion was not agreed to.

The Chief Justice again ordered the reading of the First Article, but again, before the clerk could begin the reading, Mr. Williams intervened to move an adjournment to Tuesday, the 26th day of the month.

After numerous conflicting motions relating to the date of the proposed reassembling, and several roll calls thereon, the anti-impeachers generally insisting on proceeding at once to vote on the other articles of impeachment, the motion of Mr. Williams to adjourn to June 26th, prevailed.

Of course the purpose, and the only purpose then apparent, of that adjournment, was to gain time, apparently in the hope of more favorable developments in the next ten days.

The supposably strongest count of the indictment having been beaten, it was apparent that it would be folly to hazard a vote on any other at that time. There was a possibility that changes might occur in the personnel of the Senate in the interim. As but one article had been put to vote, and as that was beaten by the lack of a single vote, there seemed a further possibility that influences could be brought to bear, through the industry of the House, as was very soon after developed, to secure the support of an anti-impeaching Senator on at least one of the articles of impeachment yet to be voted upon. A vacancy in the ranks of the anti-impeaching Republicans to be filled by an impeaching appointee might happen. Many contingencies were possible during the next ten days for a reversal of the action of the Senate just had. At all events, everything would be hazarded by permitting further immediate action, while the situation could be rendered no worse by delay, and time and other mollifying conditions and influences might bring changes more promising of success.

The anti-impeachment Republicans had not long to wait for the development of the purpose of the recess, at least so far its supporters in the House were concerned. Immediately upon the adjournment of the Senate, the House re-assembled, and the following proceeding was had:

Mr. Bingham: I have been directed by the Managers on the part of the House of Representatives, in the matter of the Impeachment of Andrew Johnson, to report the following preamble and resolutions for consideration at this time:

Whereas, information has come to the Managers which seems to them to furnish probable cause to believe that improper or corrupt means have been used to influence the determination of the Senate upon the Articles of Impeachment submitted to the Senate by the House of Representatives against the President of the United States; therefore.

Be it Resolved, That for the further and more efficient prosecution of the Impeachment of the President, the Managers be directed and instructed to summon and examine witnesses under oath, to send for persons and papers, and employ a stenographer, and appoint sub-committee to take testimony; the expense thereof to be paid from the Contingent Fund of the House.

This resolution was immediately and without debate adopted by a vote of 88 to 14. It would be stating it mildly to say that the House was in a tumult. The Republican leaders were wild with rage. They had selected for the first vote what they deemed the strongest point in their indictment, and lost; and their vengeance now turned upon those Republican Senators who had failed to support them. Hence the adjournment of the Senate for ten days to afford them time to discipline the recusants and force an additional vote for conviction on the next ballot.

The conspicuous indelicacy of this move was two-fold: 1st, in that the House proposed to investigate the action of a co-ordinate branch of Congress: and 2nd, that the trial not being concluded, it had to a pointed degree the appearance of an attempt to intimidate Senators who had voted against conviction into changing their votes at the next ballot in fear of an inquisition for alleged corruption. In that sense it was an act of intimidation—a warning. It was an ill-disguised threat and a most unseemly proceeding—yet there was not one among the supporters of the Impeachment to condemn it, and few who failed openly to justify it. Partisan rancor and personal and political hostility to the President had reached a point that condoned this indelicacy of the House towards the Senate, and justified the public assault upon the dissenting Republican Senators, and the insult to the Senate itself.

The demand for adjournment and delay seemed to have been understood by the impeaching majority of the Senate, and was of course promptly granted and further voting postponed, and the Senate adjourned to May 26th.

The next ten day were days of unrest—of anxiety to all who were involved or in any way interested in the impeachment proceeding. While the result of the 16th gave hope and comfort to the opponents of impeachment, it caused little or no perceptible discouragement to its more radical friends. They were more active and persistent than ever. The footsteps of the anti-impeaching Republicans were dogged from the day's beginning to its end and far into the night, with entreaties, considerations and threats, in the hope of securing a reversal of the result of the 16th. The partisan press of the States represented by the anti-impeaching Republicans came daily filled with vigorous animadversions upon their action, and not a few threats of violence upon their return to their constituents. But it was in vain.

The Senate reassembled on the 26th of May to complete the vote on the articles of impeachment. After the usual preliminary proceedings, Mr. Williams moved to begin the voting on the Second Article, which was had with the same result as on the 11th—and then the Third, and still with the same result. It then became manifest that it was useless to go farther, as all the balance had been rendered certain of defeat, and by still more decisive votes—a considerable number of those so far voting for impeachment having committed themselves in the previous conference against all the balance. So, to save themselves from being forced to vote against impeachment on any of the articles, there was a unanimous vote of the impeachers to abandon the case and adjourn—and with it went glimmering the visions of office, and spoils, and the riotous assaults on the public treasury that had for months been organizing for the day when Mr. Johnson should be put out and Mr. Wade put in, with the political board clear for a NEW DEAL.

An analysis of the Eleventh, Article shows that it comprised four distinct counts, or accusations.

First—That Mr. Johnson had said that the Thirty-Ninth Congress was not a Congress of the United States, but a Congress of only part of the States, and therefore had no power to propose amendments the Constitution.

The latter clause of this accusation was the only portion of the first count that received any consideration during the trial, and the only testimony brought in its support was the Parsons-Johnson telegraphic correspondence set out in Interrogatory No. 5.

In that dispatch, referring to then pending Constitutional amendment (the 14th) Mr. Johnson referred to Congress as "a set of individuals." Mr. Manager Boutwell declared this expression to be "the gist of the offense of this particular telegraphic dispatch."

Counsel for defense objected to this testimony, but it was received by a vote of yeas twenty-seven, nays seventeen.

As the Fourteenth Amendment was not declared adopted or a part of the Constitution for more than a year after the transmission of that dispatch, and as the Constitution of the United States prohibits any abridgment of the freedom of speech, and as this remark was unaccompanied by any act in violation of law, it is difficult to see how it could be construed into an impeachable offense. Moreover, saying nothing of the good taste or propriety of that dispatch, Mr. Johnson was opposed to the proposed amendment, and had the same right to oppose it, or to characterize it or the members of Congress favoring it, as had any private citizen, or as had the members of Congress to characterize his action in the premises, without being called to account therefor.

The second count of that article was:

Violation of the Tenure-of-Office Act of March 2nd, 1867, in seeking to prevent the resumption by Mr. Stanton of the office of Secretary of War.

This clause had been very effectually disposed of by Messrs. Sherman and Howe several days before the vote was taken on the Eleventh Article, when they pointed out the fact that the language cage of the first section of the Tenure-of-Office Act clearly excepted, and was intended by the Senate, to except Mr. Stanton and all other persons then in Mr. Johnson's Cabinet who had been originally appointed by Mr. Lincoln and were still holding over under Mr. Johnson without having been recommissioned by him; and that Mr. Johnson had therefore the legal right and power to remove them at his pleasure.

And so convincing had been the argument of those gentlemen at that time, that there was unanimous consent on the pro-impeachment side of the Senate, on two different occasions, to set aside the First Article, of which the alleged unlawful attempt to remove Mr. Stanton was practically the principal accusation. Not illogically, that unanimous consent to abandon the First article by thus setting it aside, and afterwards refusing to put it to a vote, may be said to have been equivalent to a vote of its insufficiency.

It is pertinent to suggest here that the President believed the Tenure-of-Office Act to be unconstitutional, as it was clearly an attempted abridgment of his power over his Cabinet which had never before been questioned by Congress. The only method left him for the determination of that question was in the course he took, except by an agreed case, but it is manifest from the record that no such agreement could be had, as an effort thereto was made in the Thomas case in the District Court, but failed, the prosecution withdrawing the case at the point where that purpose of the President became manifest.

The third count was:

Attempting to prevent the execution of the Army appropriation Act of March 2nd, 1867.

The means specified in this alleged attempt was the appointment of Mr. Edward Cooper to be Assistant Secretary of the Treasury, with power to draw warrants on the Treasury without the consent of the Secretary — the purpose being to show that, with General Thomas acting as Secretary of War, and Mr. Cooper as Assistant Secretary of the Treasury to honor General Thomas' drafts, and thus, in control of expenditures for the support of the Army, a conspiracy was sought to be proven whereby the President intended and expected to defeat the Reconstruction Acts of Congress by preventing the use of the Army for its enforcement.

Mr. Johnson, of the Court, asked this question:

The Managers are requested to say whether they propose to show whether Mr. Cooper was appointed by the President in November, 1867, as a means to obtain unlawful possession of the public money, other than by the fact of the appointment itself?

Mr. Manager Butler answered:

We certainly do.

Mr. Butler read the law on this subject, passed March 2nd, 1867, as follows:

That the Secretary of the Treasury shall have power, by appointment under his hand and official seal, to delegate to one of the Assistant Secretaries of the Treasury authority to sign in his stead all warrants for the payment of money into the public Treasury and all warrants for the disbursments from the public Treasury of money certified by the accounting officers of the Treasury to be due upon accounts duly audited and settle by them; and such warrants signed shall be in all cases of the same validity as if they had been signed by the Secretary of the Treasury himself.

Mr. William E. Chandler, who had been Assistant Secretary of the Treasury, was on the witness stand, called by the prosecution. Mr. Butler asked whether it was the practice of the Assistant Secretary to act as Secretary in case of removal of the Secretary.

Answer: I am not certain that it is, without his appointment as Acting Secretary by the President.

Mr. Fessenden, of the Court, propounded this interrogatory?

1st—Has it been the practice, since the passage of the law, for an Assistant Secretary to sign warrants unless especially appointed and authorized by the Secretary of the Treasury?

2nd—Has any Assistant Secretary been authorized to sign any warrants except such as are specified in the Act?

The witness answered as to the first:

It has not been the practice for any Assistant Secretary since the passage of the Act to sign warrants except upon an appointment by the Secretary for that purpose in accordance with the provisions of the Act. Immediately upon the passage of the Act, the Secretary authorized one of his Assistant Secretaries to sign warrants of the character described in the Act, and they have been customarily signed by that Assistant Secretary in all cases since that time.

As to the second question the answer was:

No Assistant Secretary has been authorized to sign warrants except such as are specified in this Act, unless when acting as Secretary.

That disposed of the third count in the Eleventh Article, and the testimony was rejected by a vote of yeas 22, nays 27.

These answers to tire interrogatories seemed to prove the reverse of what the Prosecution had expected. The accusation of the Third count was not sustained.

As to the Fourth count of the Eleventh Article, that Mr. Johnson sought to prevent the execution of the "Act to provide for the more efficient government of the rebel States," passed March 2nd, 1867, by the removal of Mr. Stanton from the War Office, the proceedings of the trial disclose no testimony of a sufficiently direct character for specification, except, possibly, a number of speeches delivered at different points by Mr. Johnson, which are set out in the Tenth Article of the Impeachment. As that Article was by unanimous consent abandoned and never put to vote, all its allegations logically fell as unproven.

There was, therefore, no force and little coherency in the Eleventh Article. It fell of its own weight. Every one of its several averments had been disproven, or at least not proven. It was to a good degree a summing up — an aggregation, of the entire bill of indictment on the several distinct forms of offenses charged — a crystallization of the whole.

The entire impeachment scheme was in reality beaten by the vote on that Article, and the adjournment of ten days then taken could have been only in the hope on the part of the majority that ultimate success on some one of the remaining Articles could be made possible, in some way, legitimate or otherwise, in part by the importunate throng of visitors to the Capitol who were vociferously and vindictively urging Mr. Johnson's removal largely for reasons personal to themselves — but more especially through the efforts of the House of Representatives to discipline one or more of the anti-impeaching Republicans of the Senate.

The allegation of the Second Article, put to vote on the 26th, and beaten by the same vote as was the Eleventh, was a corollary of the First-violation of the Tenure-of-Office Act in the appointment of General Thomas as Secretary of War ad interim, WITHOUT THE ADVICE AND CONSENT OF THE SENATE. This was the first declaration ever made in the Senate that an ad interim or merely temporary appointment to fill a vacancy, required confirmation by that body. The power to make such an appointment is so clearly possessed by the President without consultation of the Senate-had been so uniformly exercised by every preceding President without question, that argument on that point would be superfluous.

In reality the essence of the Second Article, as of the First, was the removal of Mr. Stanton. If the President could remove him without the consent of the Senate, which was clearly established in the debate in the conference by Messrs. Sherman and Howe, the way was clear for the appointment of an act interim Secretary, to the end that the office be filled until such time as the President would be prepared to refill the place with a Secretary on consultation with the Senate. That was the very thing he attempted to do on the 22nd of February, the day after Mr. Stanton's removal, when he sent to the Senate the nomination of Thomas Ewing, Senior, to be Secretary of War, for the action of that body.

The Third Article was so closely analagous to the Second, that an analysis of it would be in the nature of repetition. If there were any distinctions between them, they were so finely drawn that they amounted simply to a distinction without a difference—a characteristic, indeed, of a large part of the eleven Articles of Impeachment—a characteristic so conspicuous that it was not deemed worth while by the majority to go further in their submission to the Court.

These three Articles—the Second, Third and Eleventh—being the only Articles of the entire list of eleven put to a vote, and having been taken up and passed upon out of their numerical but in the order of their supposed availability—must therefore be regarded as confessedly the strongest and most likely of the entire list to command the support of the Senate. They were selected and set out for the test. That selection was equivalent to saying, "we put the Impeachment cause to test on these three Articles. If they fail, we have nothing more to offer."

They were put to test and failed. They failed because of their innate weakness. Failed because they proved nothing. Failed because not a single allegation of the entire indictment was or could be proven or tortured into all impeachable offense. Not a remark made by the President or an act performed in all the long and bitter controversy that had subsisted between himself and Congress could be brought nearer to the impeachment mark, in fact, few if any of them so near, as had been the every day rule in the House of Representatives during the previous two years in their treatment of the President. Yet nobody thought of impeaching members of the House for their every day personal vituperations against him.

Bill after bill had been offered in Congress, and law after law enacted, with apparently the sole purpose of hampering the Constitutional authority apparently functions of the President—even the assumption of Executive powers and judicial functions by Congress—the not remote purpose of which seemed to be his entrapment into some measure of resistance upon which could be based an indictment. The House seemed to be literally "lying in wait" for him, with traps set on every side for his ensnarement.

At last, after two years of this sort of scheming and impatient and anxious waiting, the opportunity seemed to have offered in the alleged violation of the Tenure-of-Office Act. The fosterers of the impeachment crusade, weary with their long vigil and growing desperate with every additional day's delay, clutched at the new turn of affairs like a drowning man at a floating straw, and with the avidity of a starved gudgeon at a painted fly.

It was not strange that this sort of diplomacy, developed and exposed as it was in the Senate, in spite of the unfair and partisan maneuvering of the prosecution to prevent it, should have reacted, and contributed to turn against the impeachment movement gentlemen who entered upon the investigation under oath to give Mr. Johnson a fair, non-partisan trial. The only surprise was that, after the exposure of the malignant partisan spirit that sat in judgment upon Mr. Johnson, and the utter and absolute failure to prove any violation of law on his part, but on the contrary, a determination to preserve from infringement the functions of his office and prevent a revolution from fundamental political forms by the absorption of the Executive authority by the legislative branch of the government—that even a majority, and more especially, that nearly two-thirds of the Senate, could have been found at the close in support of the Impeachment.

This record will serve to explain the omission to vote on the First Article—Messrs. Sherman and Howe being precluded from supporting it in consequence of the position taken by them in the controversy between the two Houses of Congress over the first section of the Tenure-of-Office Bill while that bill was pending, and to avoid defeat on the first vote taken, which was inevitable on that Article—and also to explain, so far as any explanation is possible, the zig-zag method of conducting the ballot—skipping all the first ten Articles and going down to the bottom of the list for the first vote, with the promise of then going back to the first Article and continuing to the end, but instead, skipping that for the second time, and starting in again on the Second and then the Third.

Of course, the natural effect of this battle-dore and shuttle-cock method of treating so grave a matter as an impeachment of the President of the United States, added to the effect of the manifest unfairness of the majority in their treatment of testimony offered in the President's defense—was to disgust some who doubtless entered upon the trial honestly inclined to vote for Andrew Johnson's impeachment, but wanted it done fairly and openly, without any suppression of pertinent testimony or juggling for a verdict—and amusing to others, who viewed it as proof of weakness in the indictment, and of misgiving as to the result on the part of its supporters.

To still others it was more than that. It was not only an indication of weakness, but of a determination to take every possible advantage, fair and unfair, to save votes for conviction. The impeachers not unnaturally feared the effect of the defeat of the First Article by the nay votes of Messrs. Sherman and Howe, and probably other Republicans, which was certain to follow the submission of that Article to a vote. Its only allegation was the unlawful removal of Mr. Stanton from the office of Secretary of War in violation of the Tenure-of-Office Act. That alleged offense was repeated in varied but more or less specific forms, in every succeeding Article of the Impeachment except the Tenth, and constituted the sum and substance — the gravamen — of the entire indictment. It was the basis upon which the impeachment super-structure had been erected. Without that Article there was not only no foundation, but no coherence in the recital of Mr. Johnson's alleged offenses, and when that fell by its abandonment, the entire impeachment scheme fell with it — as, if there were nothing in the First Article on which to hang an impeachment, there could be nothing in those that followed and were but an amplification — a mere exploitation — of the First.

In substantiation of this view of the First Article, the declaration of Mr. Boutwell to that effect is here inserted. Mr. Boutwell was chairman of the committee of the House appointed to prepare the Articles of Impeachment upon which Mr. Johnson was tried. On his report of these Articles to the House he said, after speaking particularly of the Tenth Article:

The other Articles are based upon facts which are of public knowledge, growing out of the attempt of the President to remove Secretary Stanton from the office of Secretary for the Department of War.

That is, that the basis of the entire accusation was the alleged violation of the Tenure-of-Office Act in the removal of Mr. Stanton, as recited in the First Article.

So, after taking the vote on the Second and Third Articles and their defeat by the same vote as that on the Eleventh, it became manifest that further effort to the impeachment of the president on any of the remaining eight Articles would be useless, and Mr. Williams moved that the Senate, sitting as a Court of Impeachment, adjourn sine die, which motion was carried by the following vote:

Yeas — Anthony, Cameron, Cattell, Chandler, Cole, Conkling Corbett, Cragin, Drake, Edmunds, Ferry, Frelinghuysen, Harlan, Howard, Morgan, Morrill of Maine, Morrill of Vermont, Morton, Nye, Patterson of New Hampshire, Pomeroy, Ramsay, Sherman, Sprague, Stewart, Sumner, Thayer, Tipton, Van Winkle, Wade. Willey, Williams, Wilson, Yates — 34.

Nays — Bayard, Buckalew, Davis, Dixon, Doolittle, Fowler, Henderson, Hendricks, Johnson, McCreery, Norton, Patterson of Tennessee, Ross, Saulsbury, Trumbull, Vickers — 16.

Every Senator present who had voted for conviction voted to abandon the prosecution and end the trial, and every Senator present who had voted against conviction, voted to continue and go through the indictment.

Of course, it was useless to go farther with any hope of success, as, it will be seen by this record, all the remaining Articles were dead, beaten in caucus before the voting commenced, and by the professed friends and leaders of the movement.

Possibly it was the anticipation of this effect of the abandonment of the First Article, that was the "sickness" to which Mr. Edmunds, at the outset of the voting, ten days before, ascribed the peculiar order of taking the vote.

It is not intended to aver that there was any privity or concert in this particular manipulation—yet it is suggestive. The Impeachment had been dragging since the 22nd of February, to May 26th—more than three months,—and had been everywhere the engrossing topic of the time. It was becoming tiresome-not only to the Senate, but to the general public.

Notwithstanding the City of Washington was still filled with people who had been waiting weary weeks and months for the deposition of Mr. Johnson and the accession of Mr. Wade to the Presidency, for the fulfillment of pledges of appointment based thereon, and who were still importunate for impeachment, the business element of the country at large was tiring of it and its depressing effect upon the commercial activities. Even Senators and Congressmen were being moved to a sense of the obstructive and somewhat ridiculous phases the impeachment movement was beginning to take on—and not a few of those who in its earlier stages had honestly favored the movement, inside as well as outside the membership of both Houses of Congress, had begun to realize the actual nature and purposes, as also the shallowness of the impeachment movement that from whatever motives it had originated, it had degenerated very much into a game of personal ambition—of vindictiveness—and office getting and spoils—and practically nothing higher.

While some of its supporters who had manifestly entered upon the trial with a determination to convict, were still insistent for further prosecution had there been a shadow of ultimate success, there were others who had begun to realize, weeks before the end came, the awkwardness of the predicament in which they had allowed themselves and their party to be placed, and desired to abandon the enterprise.

The strain was becoming too great—there was certain to be a recoil sooner or later. The foundations of the Impeachment were shown to be too slender. There was a future ahead that must be faced, but Senators must preserve their consistency. They could not go before their pro-impeachment constituencies with a record indicating any degree of weakening in the impeachment crusade. They had insisted for months that Mr. Johnson must be removed, and it would be politically inexpedient to retract.

But they wanted somebody to "help them let go."

So the plan of "desultory" procedure herein outlined seems to have "happened" — whether by design or otherwise, is immaterial — and that plan was made easy by the concerted abandonment of the head and front of the indictment — the First Article — which was side-tracked and logically carried with it all that followed, as would manifestly have been the result if the voting had begun on that Article.

While, to degree, the turmoils and bitterness of that time have passed out of public mind, there are still many living who retain a keen remembrance of the struggle and the enmities it produced. There were during the trial many thousands of men in the City of Washington awaiting the Impeachment and removal of the President for the fulfillment of pledges of official appointment based thereon, and their numbers increased as the trial progressed.

These anticipated beneficiaries were naturally not idle in efforts to the stimulation of zeal in the cause of Impeachment, and Senators were importuned at all seasonable and unseasonable hours in behalf of immediate and positive action. The lively anxiety, even anxious haste, of these patriots for their earliest possible entry upon the service of the Government, was emphasized on every corner and at every place of gathering, day and night, and the lobbies of the Capitol were thronged by them during the sessions of the Senate. No opportunity for a word with a Senator in behalf of the immediate deposition of the President, nor any appliance that seemed to promise a successful overture, was overlooked or forgotten.

When these seemed to fail of the desired effect, more direct and, it was hoped, more effective methods were resorted to. The beleaguered Senator was reminded that the applicant represented the united sentiment of the people of the State from which he held his Senatorial seat — that they demanded Mr. Johnson's conviction and removal — that that demand could not be safely denied, trifled with, or delayed; and that if money was wanted, to use the language of a notorious inquisitor of the House, Mr. Butler, speaking of the possibility of securing a designated vote for Impeachment "tell the d — — d scoundrel that if he wants money, there is a bushel of it here to be had!" Mr. Butler's message was delivered.

So desperate were the inquisitors, and so close the certainty of the vote, that even a project of kidnapping a Senator under the pretense of taking a trip to Baltimore for much needed rest, where, if the terms to be there proffered were refused, a vacancy was to be created — by assassination, if necessary — then a recess of the Senate to afford time for the appointment by the Governor of that Senator's State of a successor who would vote for the Impeachment, of the President—was entered upon and its execution attempted. But the trip to Baltimore for "rest" was not taken.

These are not pleasant facts to contemplate, but they somewhat conspicuously characterized the conditions of that time, and illustrate the real nature of the impeachment scheme. They boded the control of the Government by the worst element of American politics. It is unnecessary to say here what that control would have involved. During all the previous history of the Government—its wars and political turmoils—the Democratic-Republican forms that characterize its administrations have never faced so insidious or threatening a danger as during that hour. It was a crucial test, and the result a magnificent vindication of the wisdom and patriotism of the founders of our composite form of Government. Its results have but strengthened those forms and broadened the scope of the beneficent political institutions that have grown up under and characterize its operation.

It was a test such as probably no other form of Government on earth could have successfully passed, and it is to be hoped that its like may never return.

CHAPTER XII — WAS IT A PARTISAN PROSECUTION?

The weakest point in the entire record of the Prosecution of President Johnson, from the indictment by the House of Representatives to the finish in the Senate, except the Bill of Impeachment itself, was the refusal of the more than three-fourths Republican majority of the Senate to permit the reception of testimony in his behalf. That majority naturally gave them absolute control of the proceedings, and they should have realized from the outset that they could not afford to give it the least tinge of partisan bias.

It is therefore not material to discuss in detail the instances of the two interrogatories put by counsel for the Prosecution and rejected, Nos. 4 and 28, because it was shown that their answer would prove nothing against the President, but rather to his vindication, and their rejection could not have occurred but for the intervention of many more nay Republican than Democratic votes—but will pass to the analyzation of the votes on the twelve interrogatories propounded by counsel for Defense and rejected, which rejections could not have occurred but by the intervention of a large preponderance, in every instance, of the Republican votes cast thereon, and many of them by a unanimous Republican vote.

Without doubt, many of these votes on the admissibility of testimony were governed by, the usual rules prevailing in the courts, but it was deemed by others that every question not manifestly frivolous, or not pertinent, should be permitted answer without objection, regardless of such rules—that the Senate sitting for the trial of an Impeachment of the President of the United States—the occasion a great State Trial—should not be trammeled or belittled by the technicalities common to ordinary court practice—that the Senate was composed supposedly of gentlemen and lawyers of high standing in their profession and familiar with public affairs and public law—that they were sitting in a semi-judicial capacity—not merely as Senators or jurors, but, judges also—judges of fact as well as of law—and constituted the highest trial body known to our laws—a tribunal from which there was no appeal—that each of its members had taken a solemn oath to "do impartial justice" in this cause, absolutely unswerved by partisan or personal considerations, and that as such each member had not only the right, but it was his duty under his oath, as well, to hermit no obstacle or condition to unnecessarily keep from him a knowledge of all available facts pertinent to the cause, no matter on which side they might weigh — to help or to hurt. That the body, each member for himself, was the proper party to determine the admissibility of testimony, as Mr. Manager Boutwell had declared in his opening argument, "AFTER HE HAD HEARD IT," and knew its trend an purport. Every member of that body had the right to know all the witness knew about the case, and, moreover, the witnesses were brought for the purpose, and for the sole purpose, of telling what they knew.

The same assurance of absolute fairness as that of Mr. Boutwell, was also given by Mr. Bingham, another of the Managers of the Prosecution on the part of the House, in his opening plea before the Senate: "It is," said he, "certainly very competent for the Senate, as it is competent for any court of justice in the trial of cases where questions of doubt arise, to HEAR THE EVIDENCE, and, where they themselves are the judges of both the law and the fact, to DISMISS SO MUCH OF IT AS THEY MAY FIND INCOMPETENT, if any of it be incompetent. * * * Under the Plea of Not Guilty, as provided in the rules, every conceivable defense that the accused party could make to the Articles here preferred, can be admitted."

Mr. Manager Butler also said, on the same occasion: "Upon this so great trial, I pray let us not belittle ourselves with the analyses of the common law courts, or the criminal courts, because nothing is so dangerous to mislead us."

These and other like assurances were given of the widest reasonable latitude in the reception of testimony in the trial then opening. There was thus every reason to expect that Mr. Johnson would have a fair trial. But no sooner had the Prosecution completed its examination of witnesses, in which but seven interrogatories had been objected to of the long list proffered by the Prosecution, than a different rule seemed to have been established for the treatment of proffered testimony, and a large mass of relevant and valuable testimony in behalf of the President was ruled out on objection of the Prosecution, as inadmissible, and, as a rule that, had very few exceptions, on partisan divisions of the Senate.

Of course it will not be admitted, nor is it here charged, that these refusals to hear testimony were because of any fear that the answers would have any improper force or effect upon the Senate. Nor will it signify to say that the President's attorneys could not have proved what they offered to prove. They hail the right to an opportunity to so prove, and the denial of that right and opportunity was not only a denial of a manifest right of the attorneys, but especially in this case, a more flagrant denial of the rights of the accused, and not only that, but they amounted to an impugnment of the discretion of the Senate.

It is conspicuous, too, that while the defense objected to but seven of the interrogatories submitted by the Prosecution, and five of them were permitted answer by the vote of the Senate; twenty-one of the proffers of testimony by the defense were objected to by the prosecution and but nine of them permitted answer: and that condition was aggravated by the fact that the numerical strength of the majority party in the Senate was sufficient to determine absolutely the disposition of every question, and they could therefore afford to be strictly fair to the accused, and by the further fact that the objections to testimony offered in behalf of the defense were as three to one of the objections to testimony offered in behalf of the prosecution.

These denials of testimony in behalf of the defense were unfortunate. That practice lowered the dignity of the occasion and of the proceeding, as they could but have given ground for criticism of partisan bias and a vindictive judgment in case of successful impeachment. Most, if not all these rejected interrogatories implied important information in possession of the witnesses which the Senate had a right to, and which the party offering had the right to have produced. Moreover, it was the right and the duty of the Senate to know what the witness was presumed to know, and then to judge, each Senator for himself, of the relevancy of the testimony.

As stated, the principal averment against the President, was his alleged violation of the Tenure-of-Office Act in the removal of Mr. Stanton from the office of Secretary of War, presented in various phases throughout the Articles of Impeachment.

In illustration of the treatment of testimony offered in the President's behalf by a majority of the Republican Senators, the record shows that on the eighth disputed interrogatory, the second put by the defense, General Sherman being on the witness stand:—Defense asked as to a certain conversation relating to that removal, had between the General and the President at an interview specified. The prosecution objected to the question being answered, and a vote of the Senate was demanded. The vote was—for receiving the testimony, 23; against receiving it, 28. Of the latter number, twenty-seven, all Republicans, voted at the close of the trial to convict the President of violating the Tenure-of-Office Act, in the removal of Mr. Stanton, after refusing to hear testimony in his behalf on that charge.

The next interrogatory, No. 9, was "when the President asked the witness (Gen. Sherman,) to accept the War Office, was anything further said in reference to it?" This was objected to by the prosecution, and the vote thereon was 23 to 29. Twenty-eight of the twenty-nine gentlemen thus refusing answer to this question, afterwards voting to convict the President, after refusing to bear the testimony of a very important witness in his behalf, which his counsel proposed to produce and tried in vain to get before the Senate.

On the tenth interrogatory, by Defense, "whether the President had stated to the witness, (General Sherman), his object in asking him to accept the War Office," the vote was 7 to 44 against receiving it, and thirty-one of the gentlemen voting not to hear this testimony, at the close of the hearing voted to convict Mr. Johnson of a high misdemeanor in office in the removal of Mr. Stanton, after refusing to hear his defense.

The next, No. 11, was as to the President's attempt to get a case before the Supreme Court for a judicial determination of Mr. Stanton's right to retain the War Office against the President's wish. This testimony was refused by a vote of 25 to 27—every nay vote being cast by a Republican, every one of whom at the close of the trial, voting in effect to convict Mr. Johnson of a high misdemeanor in office in seeking resort to the courts to test the legality of an act of Congress passed for the practically sole purpose of restricting an executive function never before questioned.

The next interrogatory, No. 12, was whether the witness, (General Sherman), had formed an opinion whether the good of the service required a Secretary of War other than Mr. Stanton. It was well understood that General Sherman believed that for the good of the service Mr. Stanton ought to retire, and as the Chief Officer of the Army his opinion was certainly entitled to weight, and the President had a right to the benefit of his judgment. This interrogatory was objected to by the Prosecution, and was rejected by a vote of 18 to 35—thirty-one of the thirty-five being Republicans, who at the close of the trial voted to convict Mr. Johnson of a high misdemeanor in the removal of Mr. Stanton, after refusing him the benefit of the opinion of the Chief Officer of the Army on a question affecting the military service, and to which he was in all fairness clearly entitled.

No. 13, General Sherman was asked whether he had advised, the President to appoint a successor to Mr. Stanton. (It was well understood that he had.) Answer to this was refused, 18 to 32—thirty of the latter, all Republicans, voting at the close of the trial to convict Mr. Johnson, after refusing to hear this important testimony in his behalf. No. 16. The answer to the last interrogatory, ("if he did, state what his purpose was,") was received by a majority of one, 26 to 25—every nay vote being a Republican, and constituting a majority of the Republicans of the Senate.

No. 21. Mr. O. E. Perrin on the stand, was asked as to the President's statement that Mr. Stanton would relinquish the office at once to General Thomas—"that it was only a temporary arrangement"—that he would "send to the Senate at once the name of a good man," (which he did). This testimony was rejected by a vote of 9 to 37—thirty of the latter number being Republicans who at the close of the trial voted to convict Mr. Johnson of a high misdemeanor in sending to the Senate the name of Thomas Ewing, Senior, for appointment as Secretary of War, vice Stanton removed in assumed violation of the Tenure-of-Office Act.

The next offer of testimony to be rejected was No. 23—Mr. Gideon Welles, Secretary of the Navy, on the stand, to prove that the Cabinet had advised the President to veto the Tenure-of-Office Bill as unconstitutional. The Chief Justice ruled the testimony admissible for the purpose of showing the intent with which the President had acted in the transaction. Prosecution objected, and by a vote of 20 to 29, the decision of the Chief Justice was overruled. No answer to this interrogatory was permitted, every vote to refuse this testimony being cast by a Republican, every one of whom, at the close of the trial, voting to convict and remove Mr. Johnson for alleged violation of a law which he believed to be unconstitutional—which he was advised by the head of the Law Department of the Government was unconstitutional and therefore not a law which he had sworn to execute, and the constitutionality of which he had endeavored to get before the courts for adjudication—those 29 Republicans so voting after having refused to hear testimony in his defense on these identical points.

The next disputed interrogatory was No. 24—that Mr. Johnson's Cabinet had advised him that the Secretaries who had been appointed by Mr. Lincoln and still holding, (Mr. Stanton, Mr. Seward, and Mr. Welles,) were removable by the President, notwithstanding the assumed restriction of the Tenure-of-Office Act. The Chief Justice ruled this testimony to be admissible. Objection was made by the Prosecution, and a vote taken, and the interrogatory was rejected—22 to 26—every nay vote being a Republican, every one of whom at the close of the trial, voting to convict and remove Mr. Johnson from office, after having refused to hear this very important testimony in his behalf.

Defense next offered to prove (No. 25) that it was determined by the President, with the concurrence of the Cabinet, that an agreed case for the determination of the constitutionality of the Tenure-of-Office Act should be made. This testimony was objected to, and a vote taken, which was 19 to 30. Every one of the gentlemen voting to reject this testimony, Mr. Johnson's right to which cannot with any possible showing of fairness be successfully disputed, were Republicans, and after so voting, at the close of the trial, declared by their several verdicts that he had been fairly proven guilty of a high misdemeanor in office, by violation of the Tenure-of-Office Act in seeking a judicial determination of the validity of a disputed Act of Congress, and should be expelled from office.

No. 26, was as to any suggestion by the President of the employment of force for the vacation of any office, (relating of course, to the War Office.) Mr. Johnson had been charged with seeking the removal of Mr. Stanton by force, should he resist. Knowing perfectly that the answer would be in the negative, the Senate refused to permit answer to this interrogatory, by a vote of 18 to 26, every one of the twenty-six gentlemen at the close of the trial in effect voting that the President was guilty as charged, of seeking to remove Mr. Stanton by violence, after refusing to hear either his denial or witnesses in his behalf on that point.

No. 27. Defense proposed to prove that the Cabinet had advised the President that the Tenure-of-Office Act did not prevent the removal of those members who had been originally appointed by Mr. Lincoln. This testimony, which, if permitted answer, would, in the minds of unprejudiced people, have at once set aside the entire impeachment scheme, was not permitted answer. The vote was 20 to 26—every one of the twenty-six gentlemen who voted to reject that most important and conclusive testimony in Mr. Johnson's behalf, at the close of the examination voting to convict him of a high misdemeanor in office by violating the Tenure-of-Office Act in removing Mr. Stanton from the office of Secretary of War—after refusing this offer to prove by his Cabinet advisers; the witness himself, (Mr. Welles, and his testimony, if received, was to be followed by that of Mr. Seward and Mr. Stanton, all of whom had been appointed by Mr. Lincoln and not re-appointed by Mr. Johnson,) that that act did not apply to or protect them against removal at the pleasure of the President. So that on eighteen of these twenty-one disputed interrogatories put in behalf of the Defense, a majority of the Republicans of the Senate refused in every instance to hear testimony, after having sworn to give Mr. Johnson a fair and impartial trial.

But the most flagrant case of unfairness to the defendant in this examination of witnesses occurred in the treatment of interrogatory No. 3, put by the prosecution, in their introduction of a letter from the President to General Grant, purporting to enclose letters from different members of the Cabinet in substantiation of the position of the President in the controversy then pending between Gen. Grant and himself. These letters were enclosed with, and specifically referred to and made a part of the President's communication, and were necessary to a correct apprehension of the controversy, from the President's or any other standpoint.

Being so enclosed and referred to in the letter transmitting and enclosing them, they became quite as much a part of the President's communication as his own letter which enclosed them. Counsel for Defense objected to the introduction of the President's letter without the enclosures, but the objection was not sustained and the letters were not permitted to be introduced, but the letter enclosing and referring to them was. The vote on the production of the enclosures was, yeas 20, nays 29 — twenty-eight of the thirty-eight Republicans present, voting to exclude this essential testimony in the President's behalf, and twenty-seven of the number afterwards voted to convict him of a high misdemeanor in office in removing Mr. Stanton from the War Office, after refusing him the benefit of the testimony of his Constitutional Cabinet advisers in this important matter.

It is possible that under other conditions this proceeding might have been legitimate and proper; but Mr. Johnson was on trial under grave charges, before the highest, and supposably fairest tribunal on earth, and had a right to the benefit of the testimony of his cabinet, in full, and more especially when that testimony was presented in a distorted and garbled shape by his accusers. Moreover, every member of the Court had the right to know what was in those letters, if any part of the correspondence was to be received. But whether or not Mr. Johnson had the right to the testimony in his behalf which it was claimed these enclosures contained, he certainly had the right to resist the introduction of mutilated testimony against him. The purpose of the trial was to ascertain the facts in the case — all the facts bearing on either side. The Court was sitting and the witnesses were called for that purpose, and no other.

This record shows, that in but three instances out of twenty-one, did a majority of the Republicans of the Senate vote to receive testimony offered in the President's behalf—that on one interrogatory there was an equal division—that on seventeen of the twenty-one interrogatories put by the Defense, a majority of the Republicans voted to exclude testimony, in several cases by a two-thirds vote—and that but nine of the twenty-one interrogatories put in behalf of the President were by Republican votes permitted to be answered—also that, as a rule which had very rare exceptions, such interrogatories in behalf of the President as were permitted answer, were so permitted by very close majorities.

It is undoubted that every Republican member of the Senate entered upon that trial in the expectation that the allegations of the Prosecution would be sustained, but it was also expected that a fair, free, full, open investigation of all the charges preferred would be had, and that all the information possible to be obtained bearing upon the case, pro and con, would be admitted to testimony—but that expectation was not realized.

To sum up this feature of the proceeding—the Republican majority of the Senate placed themselves and their party in the attitude of prosecutors in the case—instead of judges sworn to give the President an impartial trial and judgment that their course had the appearance, at least, of a conspiracy to evict the President for purely partisan purposes, regardless of testimony or the facts of the case-that public animosity against Mr. Johnson had been manufactured throughout the North by wild and vicious misrepresentations for partisan effect—that practically the entire Republican Party machinery throughout the country was bent to the work of prosecution. The party cry was "Crucify him!" "Convict him anyway, and try him afterwards!" With rare exceptions, the Republican Party of the country, press and people, were a unit in this insensate cry.

They were ready to strike, but not to hear.

There can be but one conclusion from these premises, established by the record of the trial—that the entire proceeding, from its inception in the House of Representatives to its conclusion in the Senate, was a thoroughly partisan prosecution on the part of the majority in both Houses, and that the country was saved from the shameful spectacle, and the dangerous consequences of such a proceeding, by the intervention and self-sacrifice of a few gentlemen who proposed to respect the obligation of their oath, and give Mr. Johnson, so far as in their power, a fair trial and judgment—and not having had such a trial—to give him the benefit of what he claimed he could prove in his own behalf and was not permitted to—and a verdict of "Not Guilty," regardless of consequences to themselves.

What every member of the Court had sworn to do was "impartial justice" to Andrew Johnson, and nothing less. The Counsel on neither side had taken that oath, but the Court had; and its performance of that oath was impossible without possession of all the information relating to and bearing upon the case that it was reasonably possible to obtain. That is the essential ingredient and characteristic of a fair trial.

THAT ESSENTIAL INGREDIENT OF JUDICIAL FAIRNESS WAS NOT SHOWN TO MR. JOHNSON IN THIS CASE BY THE REPUBLICAN MAJORITY OF THE SENATE, as the official record of the trial clearly establishes. It was an ill-disguised and malevolent partisan prosecution.

CHAPTER XIII — THE CONSTITUTIONAL POWER OF IMPEACHMENT.

The power conferred by the Constitution upon Congress to impeach and remove the President for cause, is unquestionably a wise provision. The natural tendency of the most patriotic of men, in the exercise of power in great public emergencies, is to overstep the line of absolute safety, in the conscientious conviction that a departure from strict constitutional or legal limitations is demanded by the public welfare.

The danger in such departures, even upon apparent necessity, if condoned or permitted by public judgment is in the establishment of precedents whereby greater and more dangerous infractions of organic law may be invited, tolerated, and justified, till government takes on a form of absolutism in one form or another, fatal to free institutions, fatal to a government of law, and fatal to popular liberty.

On the other hand, a too ready resort to the power of impeachment as a remedial agent—the deposition of a public officer in the absence of proof of the most positive and convincing character of the impeachability of the offense alleged, naturally tends to the other extreme, till public officers may become by common consent removable by impeachment upon insufficient though popular charges—even upon partisan differences and on sharply contested questions of public administration.

The power of impeachment and removal becomes, therefore, a two-edged sword, which must be handled with consummate judgment and skill, and resort thereto had only in the gravest emergencies and for causes so clearly manifest as to preclude the possibility of partisan divisions or partisan judgments thereon. Otherwise, too ready resort to impeachment must inevitably establish and bring into common use a new and dangerous remedy for the cure of assumed political ills which have their origin only in partisan differences as to methods of administration. It would become an engine of partisan intolerance for the punishment and ostracism of political opponents, under the operation of which the great office of Chief Magistrate must inevitably lose its dignity, and decline from its Constitutional rank as a co-ordinate department of the Government, and its occupant no longer the political head and Chief Executive of the Nation, except in name.

It was in that sense, and to a pointed degree, that in the impeachment and trial of Andrew Johnson the quality of coordination of the three great Departments of Government—the Executive, Legislative, and Judicial—was directly involved—the House of Representatives as prosecutor—the President as defendant—the Senate sitting as the trial court in which the Chief Justice represented the judicial department as presiding officer.

The anomaly of the situation was increased and its gravity intensified, by the fact that the President pro tempore of the Senate, who stood first in the line of succession to the Presidency in case of conviction, was permitted, in a measure, indeed, forced by his pro-impeachment colleagues, on a partisan division of the Senate, to sit and vote as such President pro tempore for the impeachment and removal of the President whom he was to succeed.

These facts of condition attending and characterizing the trial of President Johnson, pointedly accentuate the danger to our composite form of government which the country then faced. That danger, as it had found frequent illustration in the debates in the House of Representatives on the several propositions for the President's impeachment preceding the bringing of the indictment, lay in the claim of superiority of political function for the Legislative branch over the Executive. The quality of co-ordination of these departments was repeatedly and emphatically denied by conspicuous and influential members of that body during the initial proceedings of the impeachment movement, and even on the floor of the Senate by the managers of the impeachment. To illustrate:

Mr. Bingham, in the House, Feb. 22nd, 1868, announced the extraordinary doctrine that "there is no power to review the action of Congress." Again, speaking of the action of the Senate on the 21st of February, on the President's message announcing the removal of Mr. Stanton, he said: "Neither the Supreme Court nor any other Court can question or review this judgment of the Senate."

The declaration was made by Messrs. Stevens and Boutwell in the House, that the Senate was its own judge of the validity of its own acts.

Mr. Butler, in his opening speech to the Senate, at the beginning of the trial, used this language:

A Constitutional tribunal solely, you are bound by no law, either Statute or Common, which may limit your constitutional prerogative. You consult no precedents save those of the law and custom of parliamentary bodies. You are a law unto yourselves, bound only by the natural principles of equity and justice, and salus populi suprema est lex.

Feb. 24, 1868, Mr. Stevens said in the House:

Neither the Executive nor the Judiciary had any right to interfere with it (Reconstruction) except so far as was necessary to control it by military rule until the sovereign power of the Nation had provided for its civil administration. NO POWER BUT CONGRESS HAD ANY RIGHT TO SAY WHETHER EVER, OR WHEN, they (the rebel States), should be admitted to the Union as States and entitled to the privileges of the Constitution of the United States. * * * I trust that when we come to vote upon this question we shall remember that although it is the duty of the President to see that the laws be executed, THE SOVEREIGN POWER OF THE NATION RESTS IN CONGRESS.

Mr. Butler, the leading spirit of the impeachment enterprise, went so far as to make the revolutionary suggestion of the abrogation of the Presidential office in the event of final failure to convict the President—set out in the 8th Chapter.

Mr. Sumner insisted that in no judicial sense was the Senate a Court, and therefore not bound by the rules of judicial procedure:

If the Senate is a Court bound to judicial forms on the expulsion of the President, must it not be the same in the expulsion of a Senator? But nobody attributes to it any such strictures in the latter case. * * In the case of Blount, which is the first in our history, the expulsion was on the report of a committee declaring him guilty of a high misdemeanor. At least one Senator has been expelled on simple formal motion. Others have been expelled without any formal allegations or formal proofs. * * * The Constitution provides that "Each House shall determine its rules of proceeding." The Senate on the expulsion of its own members has already done this practically and set an example of simplicity. But it has the same power over its rules of proceeding on the expulsion of the President, and there can be no reason for simplicity in the one case not equally applicable in the other. Technicality is as little consonant with the one as with the other. Each has for its object the PUBLIC SAFETY. For this a Senator is expelled; for this, also, the President is expelled. Salus Populi Suprema Lex. The proceedings in each case must be in subordination to this rule."

Thus, Mr. Sumner would have removed the President by an ordinary concurrent resolution of Congress.

The purpose of all this was apparent—that the President was in effect, to be tried and judged before a Court of Public Opinion, and not before the Senate sitting as a High Court of Impeachment, but BY the Senate sitting in its legislative capacity—to create the impression in the minds of Senators that in this high judicial procedure they were still acting as a legislative body— simply as Senators, and not in a judicial capacity, as judges and jurors, and therefore not bound specifically by their oaths as such, to convict only for crime denounced by the law, or for manifest high political misdemeanors, but could take cognizance of and convict on alleged partisan offenses and allegations based on differences of opinion and partisan prejudices and partisan predilections—that it was not essential that the judgment of Senators should be confined to the specific allegations of the indictment, but that the whole range of alleged political and partisan misdemeanors and delinquencies could be taken into account in seeking a pretext for Mr. Johnson's conviction.

The superiority of the Legislative branch was thus openly advocated and insisted, and uncontroverted by any Republican supporting the impeachment. Mr. Johnson, according to these oft repeated declarations, was to be tried and convicted, not necessarily for any specific violation of law, or of the Constitution, but by prevailing public opinion—public clamor-in a word, on administrative differences subsisting between the President and the leaders of the dominant party in and out of Congress, and that public opinion, as concurrent developments fully establish, was industriously manufactured throughout the North, on the demand of leaders of the impeachment movement in the House, through the instrumentality of a partisan press and partisan public meetings, and in turn reflected back upon the Senate, in the form of resolutions denunciatory of the President and demanding his impeachment and removal.

That was in fact, and in a large sense, the incentive to the impeachment movement, and it was—not confined to a faction, but characterized the dominant portion of the political party then in the ascendancy in and out of Congress.

In this state of facts lay largely the vice of the impeachment movement, and it illustrated to a startling degree the danger in the departure from established forms of judicial procedure in such cases.

It became apparent, long before the close, that it was but little if anything more than a partisan prosecution—and that fact became more generally and firmly fixed, from day to day, as the trial approached conclusion.

In that state of facts, again, and in that sense, the impeachment of the President, was an assault upon the principle of coordination that underlies our political system and thus a menace to our established political forms, as, if successful, it would, logically, have been the practical destruction of the Executive Department—and, in view of previous legislation out of which the impeachment movement had to a degree arisen, and of declarations in the House and Senate quoted in this connection, the final and logical result of conviction would have been the absorption of the Executive functions of the Government by the Legislative Department, and the consequent declension of that Department to a mere bureau for the registration of the decrees of the Legislature.

Conscious of the natural tendency to infringement by a given Department of the Government upon the functions of its coordinates, the framers of the Constitution wisely defined the respective spheres of the several departments, and those definitions constitute unmistakable admonition to each as to trespass by either upon the political territory of its coordinates.

As John C. Calhoun wrote, in the early days of the Republic:

"The Constitution has not only made a general delegation of the legislative power to one branch of the Government, of the executive to another, and of the judicial to the third, but it has specifically defined the general powers and duties of each of those departments. This is essential to peace and safety in any Government, and especially in one clothed only with specific power for national purposes and erected in the midst of numerous State Governments retaining exclusive control of their local concerns.* * * Were there no power to interpret, pronounce and execute the law, the Government would perish through its own imbecility, as was the case with the Articles of Confederation; or other powers must be assumed by the legislative body, to the destruction of liberty." Again, as was eloquently and forcefully said by Daniel Webster in the U. S. Senate in 1834:

"The first object of a free people is the preservation of their liberty, and liberty is only to be preserved by maintaining constitutional restraints and just division of political power. Nothing is more deceptive or more dangerous than the pretense of a desire to simplify government. The simplest governments are despotisms; the next simplest, limited monarchies; but all republics, all governments of law, must impose numerous limitations and qualifications of authority and give many positive and many qualified rights. In other words, they must be subject to rule and regulation. This is the very essence of free political institutions. The spirit of liberty is, indeed, a bold and fearless spirit; but it is also a sharp-sighted spirit: it is a cautious, sagacious, discriminating, far-seeing intelligence; it is jealous of encroachment, jealous of power, jealous of man. It demands checks; it seeks for guards; it insists on securities; it entrenches itself behind strong defenses, and fortifies itself with all possible care against the assaults of ambition and passion. It does not trust the amiable weaknesses of human nature, and, therefore, it will not permit power to overstep its prescribed limits, though benevolence, good intent, and patriotic purpose come along with it. Neither does it satisfy itself with flashy and temporary resistance to illegal authority. Far otherwise. It seeks for duration and permanence; it looks before and after; and, building on the experience of ages which are past, it labors diligently for the benefit of ages to come. This is the nature of constitutional liberty; and this is our liberty, if we will rightly understand and preserve it. Every free government is necessarily complicated, because all such governments establish restraints, as well on the power of government itself as on that of individuals. If we will abolish the distinction of branches, and have but one branch; if we will abolish jury trials, and leave all to the judge; if we will then ordain that the legislator shall himself be that judge; and if we will place the executive power in the same hands, we may readily simplify government. We may easily bring it to the simplest of all possible forms, a pure despotism. But a separation of departments, so far as practicable, and the preservation of clear lines of division between them, is the fundamental idea in the creation of all our constitutions; and, doubtless, the continuance of regulated liberty depends on maintaining these boundaries."

Each department is supreme within its own constitutionally prescribed limits, and the Supreme Court is made the umpire for the definition of the limits and the protection of the rights of all. Neither Congress, nor the Executive, are authorized to determine the constitutionality and therefore the validity of their acts, or the limits of their jurisdiction under the Constitution, but the Supreme Court is so authorized, and it is the umpire before which all differences in that regard must be determined. It is the tribunal of last resort, save the people themselves, before whom both Senate and House, and the Executive, must bow, and its decision is final in the interpretation of the Constitution.

A due regard, therefore, for the interpretation of law and the division of powers thus established, constitutes the great safeguard upon which the harmonious and successful operation of our political system depends. On its religious observance rests, primarily, the preservation of our free institutions and the perpetuation of our peculiar system of popular government. That quality of co-ordination—of the equality of the several Departments as adjusted by the Organic Act—constitutes the balance wheel of our political system.

The logical effect of the doctrines promulgated by the House of Representatives in that regard, and re-echoed on the floor of the Senate, in the press and on the stump throughout the North, were therefore not only revolutionary, but destructive. To have removed the President upon accusations in reality based upon partisan and personal—not amounting even to substantial political differences—would have been the establishment of a precedent of the most dangerous character.

In a large sense, the American system of politics and of government was on trial, quite as much as was Andrew Johnson. The extreme element of American politics was in absolute control in the House of Representatives, and practically so, in the Senate. The impeachment and removal of the President on unsubstantiated, or even remotely doubtful charges, simply: because of a disagreement between himself and Congress as to the method of treating a great public emergency, would have introduced a new and destructive practice into our political system.

Logically, the introduction of such a practice on that occasion would have been construed as a precedent for the treatment of future public emergencies. Thus, it would have tended to disturb the now perfect adjustment of the balance of powers between the co-ordinate branches. That quality of absolute supremacy of the several departments in their respective spheres, or functions, and of co-ordination or equality in their relations to each other, established by the Constitution as a guarantee of the perpetuity of our political system, would have been endangered, and the result could not have been otherwise than disaster in the future.

Logically, the Presidency would in time have been degraded to the position of a mere department for the execution of the decrees of the legislative branch. Not illogically, the Supreme Court would have been the next object of attack, and the legislature have become, by this unconstitutional absorption of the powers of Government, the sole, controlling force—in short the Government.

That would, in time, by equally logical sequence, have been the natural, inevitable result—and the end. The wreckage of the Great Republic of the age would have been strown upon the sands of the political seashore—relics of the disregard of the checks and balances established by the wisdom of its framers, in the fundamental law—and all for the satisfaction of personal ambitions and the hates of factional animosities.

History affords too many illustrations of that tendency to decadence and disruption from disregard of the proper and necessary checks and balances in the distribution and equalization of the powers of government, to permit us to doubt what the final end would have been had the President been removed on the unsubstantiated accusation preferred by the House of Representatives, Our peculiar system of political government—a Democratic Republic—passed the danger point of its history in that hour.

It was indeed a narrow escape. The history of civilization records no precisely similar condition. The country then passed the most threatening period of its history—but passed it safely. The result was the highest possible testimonial to the strength and endurance of properly adjusted Democratic institutions that history records.

It emphasized not only the capacity of the American people for intelligent and orderly self-government, but also the strength and endurance of our popular forms. It was a profound surprise to those habituated to different political conditions. They had witnessed with astonishment the quiet disbandment of millions of men but as yesterday engaged in mortal strife—the vast armies as peacefully returning to former vocations as though from a great parade—and now, from a state of civil convulsion that in many another nation would have produced armed collision and public disorder, they saw an entire people quietly accepting the verdict of the highest authoritive body of the land, and practically dismissing the subject from thought. It was a splendid world-wide tribute to the strength and endurance of our system of popular government.

Yet the conclusion must not be deduced that the power of impeachment is not a wise provision of our Constitution, nor in any sense inconsistent with our popular forms. Conditions may, and are not unlikely to arise, some day, when the exercise of the power to impeach and remove the President may be quite as essential to the preservation of our political system as it threatened to become in this instance destructive of that system. Should that day ever come, it is to be hoped that the remedy of impeachment, as established by the Constitution, may be as patriotically, as fearlessly, and as unselfishly applied as it was on this occasion rejected.

SUPPLEMENT.

Copy of letter addressed to each of the members of the Cabinet present at the conversation between the President and General Grant on the 14th of January, 1868, and the answers thereto:

Executive Mansion, Washington, D. C., February 5, 1868. Sir:—The Chronicle of this morning contains a correspondence between the President and General Grant, reported from the War Department, in answer to a resolution of the House of Representatives. I beg to call your attention to that correspondence, and especially to that part of it which refers to the conversation between the President and General Grant, at the Cabinet meeting on Tuesday, the 14th of January, and to request you to state what was said in that conversation.

Very respectfully yours, Andrew Johnson.

Washington, D. C., February 5, 1868.

Sir:—-Your note of this date was handed to me this evening. My recollection of the conversation at the Cabinet meeting on Tuesday, the 14th of January, corresponds with your statement of it in the letter of the 31st ultimo, in the published correspondence. The three points specified in that letter, giving your recollection of the conversation, are correctly stated.

Very respectfully, Gideon Welles.

To the President.

Treasury Department, February 6, 1868.

Sir:—I have received your note of the 5th instant, calling my attention to the correspondence between yourself and General Grant, as published in the Chronicle of yesterday, especially to that part of it which relates to what occurred at the Cabinet meeting on Tuesday the 14th ultimo, and requesting me to state what was said in the conversation referred to.

I cannot undertake to state the precise language used, but I have no hesitation in saying that your account of that conversation, as given in your letter to General Grant under date of the 31st ultimo substantially and in all important particulars accords with my recollection of it.

With great respect, your obedient servant. Hugh McCulloch. To the President.

Post Office Department Washington, February 6, 1868.

Sir:—I am in receipt of your letter of the 5th of February, calling my attention to the correspondence published in the Chronicle between the President and General Grant, and especially to that part of it which refers to the conversation between the President and General Grant at the Cabinet meeting on Tuesday, the 14th of January, with a request that I state what was said in that conversation. In reply, I have the honor to state that I have read carefully the correspondence in question, and particularly the letter of the President to General Grant, dated January 31, 1868. The following extract from your letter of the 31st January to General Grant is, according to my recollection, a correct statement of the conversation that took place between the President and General Grant at the Cabinet meeting on the 14th of January last. In the presence of the Cabinet the President asked General

Grant whether, "in conversation which took place after his appointment as Secretary of War ad interim, he did not agree either to remain at the head of the War Department and abide any judicial proceedings that might follow the non-concurrence by the Senate in Mr. Stanton's suspension, or, should he wish not to become involved in such a controversy, to put the President in the same position with respect to the office as he occupied previous to General Grant's appointment by returning it to the President in time to anticipate such action by the Senate." This General Grant admitted.

The President then asked General Grant if, at the conference on the preceding Saturday, he had not, to avoid misunderstanding, requested General Grant to state what he intended to do; and further, if in reply to that inquiry he (General Grant) had not referred to their former conversations, saying that from them the President understood his position, and that his (General Grant's) action would be consistent with the understanding which had been reached. To these questions General Grant replied in the affirmative.

The President asked General Grant if, at the conclusion of their interview on Saturday, it was not understood that they were to have another conference on Monday, before final action by the Senate in the case of Mr. Stanton.

General Grant replied that such was the understanding, but that he did not suppose the Senate would act so soon; that on Monday he had been engaged in a conference with General Sherman, and was occupied with "many little matters," and asked if General Sherman had not called on that day.

I take this mode of complying with the request contained in the President's letter to me, because my attention had been called to the subject before, when the conversation between the President and General Grant was under consideration.

Very respectfully, your obedient servant, Alexander W. Randall, Postmaster General. To the President.

Department of the Interior, Washington, D. C., February 6, 1868.

Sir:—I am in receipt of yours of yesterday, calling my attention to a correspondence between yourself and General Grant, published in the Chronicle newspaper, and especially to that part of said correspondence "which refers to the conversation between the President and General Grant at the Cabinet meeting on Tuesday, the 14th of January," and requesting me "to state what was said in that conversation."

In reply, I submit the following statement: At the Cabinet meeting on Tuesday, the 14th of January, 1868, General Grant appeared and took his accustomed seat at the board. When he had been reached in the order of business the President asked him, as usual, if he had anything to present?

In reply, the General, after referring to a note which he had that morning addressed to the President, inclosing a copy of the resolution of the Senate refusing to concur in the reasons for the suspension of Mr. Stanton, proceeded to say that he regarded his duties as Secretary of War ad interim terminated by that resolution, and that he could not lawfully exercise such duties for a moment after the adoption of the resolution by the Senate. That the resolution reached him last night, and that this morning he had gone to the War Department, entered the Secretary's room, bolted one door on the inside, locked the other on the outside, delivered the key to the Adjutant General, and proceeded to the headquarters of the Army, and addressed the note above mentioned to the President, informing him that he (General Grant) was no longer Secretary of War ad interim.

The President expressed great surprise at the course which General Grant had thought proper to pursue, and, addressing himself to the General, proceeded to say, in substance, that he had anticipated such action on the part of the Senate, and being very desirous to have the constitutionality of the Tenure-of-Office bill tested, and his right to suspend or remove a member of the Cabinet decided by the judicial tribunals of the country, he had some time ago, and shortly after General Grant's appointment as Secretary of War ad interim, asked the General what his action would be in the event that the Senate should refuse to concur in the suspension of Mr. Stanton, and that the General had agreed either to remain at the head of the War Department till a decision could be obtained from the court or resign the office in the hands of the President before the case was acted upon by the Senate, so as to place the President in the same situation he occupied at the time of his (Grant's) appointment.

The President further said that the conversation was renewed on the preceding Sunday, at which time he asked the General what he intended to do if the Senate should undertake to reinstate Mr. Stanton; in reply to which the General referred to their former conversation upon the same subject, and said. "You understand my position, and my conduct will be conformable to that understanding:" that he (the General) then expressed a repugnance to being made a party to a judicial proceeding, saying that he would expose himself to fine and imprisonment by doing so, as his continuing to discharge the duties of Secretary of War ad interim, after the Senate should have refused to concur in the suspension of Mr. Stanton would be a violation of the Tenure-of-Office bill. That in reply to this he (the President) informed General Grant he had not suspended Mr. Stanton under the Tenure-of-Office bill, but by virtue of the powers conferred on him by the Constitution: and that, as to the fine and imprisonment, he (the President) would pay whatever fine was imposed and submit to whatever imprisonment might be adjudged against him (the General.) That they continued the conversation for some time, discussing the law at length, and that they finally separated without having reached a definite conclusion, and with the understanding that the General would see the President again on Monday.

In reply, General Grant admitted that the conversation had occurred, and said that at the first conversation he had given it as his opinion to the President that in the event of non-concurrence by the Senate in the action of the President in respect to the Secretary of War the question would have to be decided by the court; that Mr. Stanton would have to appeal to the court to reinstate him in office; that he would remain in till they could be displaced and the outs put in by legal proceeding; and that he then thought so, and had agreed that if he should change his mind he would notify the President in time to enable him to make another appointment, but that at the time of the first conversation he had not looked very closely into the law; that it had recently been discussed by the newspapers, and that this had induced him to examine it more carefully, and that he had come to the conclusion that if the Senate should refuse to concur in the suspension Mr. Stanton would thereby be reinstated, and that he (Grant) could not continue thereafter to act as Secretary of War ad interim, without subjecting himself to fine and imprisonment; and that he came over on Saturday to inform the President of this change in his views, and did so inform him, that the President replied that he had not suspended Mr Stanton under the Tenure-of-Office bill, but under the Constitution, and appointed him (Grant) by virtue of the authority derived from the Constitution, &c.; that they continued to discuss the matter some time, and finally he left without any conclusion having been reached, expecting to see the President again on Monday. He then proceeded to explain why he had not called on the President on Monday, saying that he had had a long interview with General Sherman; that various little matters had occupied his time till it was late, and that he did not think the Senate would act so soon, and asked, "did not General Sherman call on you on Monday?"

I do not know what passed between the President and General Grant on Saturday, except as I learned it from the conversation between them at the Cabinet meeting on Tuesday, and the foregoing is substantially what then occurred. The precise words used on the occasion are not, of course, given exactly in the order in which they were spoken, but the ideas expressed and the facts stated are faithfully preserved and presented. I have the honor to be, sir, with great respect, your obedient servant.

O. H. Browning.

The President.

Department of State, Washington, February 6, 1868.

Sir: The meeting to which you refer in your letter was a regular Cabinet meeting. While the members were assembling, and before the President had entered the Council Chamber, General Grant, on coming in, said to me that he was in attendance there, not as a member of the Cabinet, but upon invitation, and I replied by the inquiry whether there was a change in the War Department. After the President had taken his seat business went on in the usual way of hearing matters submitted by the several secretaries. When the time came for the Secretary of War General Grant said that he was now there not as Secretary of War, but upon the President's invitation, that he had retired from the War Department. A Blight difference then appeared about the supposed invitation, General Grant saying that the officer who had borne his letter to the President that morning, announcing his retirement from the War Department, had told him that the President desired to see him at the Cabinet, to which the President answered, that when General Grant's communication was delivered to him the President simply replied that he supposed General Grant would be very soon at the Cabinet meeting. I regarded the conversation thus begun as an incidental one. It went on quite informally, and consisted of a statement, on your part, of your views in regard to the understanding of the tenure upon which General Grant had assented to hold the War Department ad interim, and of his replies by way of answer and explanation. It was respectful and courteous on both sides. Being in this conversational form, its details could only have been preserved by verbatim report. So far as I know, no such report was made at the time. I can give only the general effect of the conversation.

Certainly you stated that although you had reported the reasons for Mr. Stanton's suspension to the Senate, you nevertheless held that he would not be entitled to resume the office of Secretary of War, even if the Senate should disapprove of his suspension, and that you had proposed to have the question tested by judicial process, to be applied to the person who should be the incumbent of the Department, under your designation of Secretary of War ad interim in the place of Mr. Stanton. You contended that this was well understood between yourself and Gen. Grant; that when he entered the

War Department as Secretary ad interim he expressed his concurrence in a belief that the question of Mr. Stanton's restoration would be a question for the courts; that in a subsequent conversation with General Grant you had adverted to the understanding thus had, and that General Grant expressed his concurrence in it: that at some conversation which had been previously held General Grant said he still adhered to the same construction of the law, but said if he should change his opinion he would give you seasonable notice of it, so that you should in any case, be placed in the same position in regard to the War Department that you were while General Grant held it ad interim. I did not understand General Grant as denying, nor as explicitly admitting, these statements in the form and full extent to which you made them. The admission of them was rather indirect and circumstantial, though I did not understand it to be an evasive one. He said that, reasoning from what occurred in the case of the police in Maryland, which he regarded as a parallel one, he was of opinion, and so assured you, that it would be his right and duty, under your instructions, to hold the War Office after the Senate should disapprove of Mr. Stanton's suspension until the question should be decided upon by the courts; that he remained until very recently of that opinion, and that on the Saturday before the Cabinet meeting a conversation was held between yourself and him in which the subject was generally discussed.

General Grant's statement was, that in that conversation he had stated to you the legal difficulties which might arise, involving fine and imprisonment under the civil tenure bill, and that he did not care to subject himself to those penalties; that you replied to this remark, that you regarded the civil tenure bill as unconstitutional, and did not think its penalties were to be feared, or that you would voluntarily assume them; and you insisted that General Grant should either retain the office until relieved by yourself according to what you claimed was the original understanding, between yourself and him, or, by seasonable notice of change of purpose on his part, put you in the same situation which you would be if he adhered. You claimed that General Grant finally said in that Saturday's conversation that you understood his views, and his proceedings thereafter would be consistent with what had been so understood. General Grant did not controvert nor can I say that he admitted this last statement. Certainly General Grant did not at any time in the Cabinet meeting insist that he had in the Saturday's conversation either distinctly or finally advised you of his determination to retire from the charge of the War Department otherwise than under your own subsequent direction. He acquiesced in your statement that the Saturday's conversation ended with an expectation that there would be a subsequent conference on the subject, which he, as well as yourself, supposed could seasonably take place on Monday.

You then alluded to the fact that General Grant did not call upon you on Monday, as you had expected from that conversation. General Grant admitted that it was his expectation or purpose to call upon you on Monday. General Grant assigned reasons for the omission. He said he was in conference with General Sherman; that there were many little matters to be attended to. He had conversed upon the matter of the incumbency of the War Department with General Sherman, and he expected that General Sherman would call upon you on Monday. My own mind suggested a further explanation, but I do not remember whether it was mentioned or not-namely, that it was not supposed by General Grant on Monday that the Senate would decide the question so promptly as to anticipate further explanation between yourself and him if delayed beyond that day. General Grant made another explanation—that he was engaged on Sunday with General Sherman, and, I think, also on Monday, in regard to the War Department matter, with a hope, though he did not say in an effort, to procure an amicable settlement of the affair of Mr. Stanton, and he still hoped that it would be brought about.

I have the honor to be, with great respect, your obedient servant,

William H. Seward.

To the President.